The **Home**
Lawyer

The **Home Lawyer**

A Family Guide to Lawyers and the Law

Michael Mansfield QC

Edited by **Yvette Vanson**

Developed in association with
Lucy Barker

This edition published 2003
by BCA
by arrangement with Atlantic Books
an imprint of Grove Atlantic Ltd

First Reprint 2004

CN 118825

Printed and bound in Great Britain by
Mackays of Chatham Ltd, Chatham, Kent

Designed by Bryony Newhouse

Contents

Editor's note *Yvette Vanson* xiii

How to use this book xv

Acknowledgements xvi

Introduction *Michael Mansfield* xvii

PART 1 Lawyers, Funding and the Courts

1 Finding and meeting your lawyer
Martin Huseyin

Ways of finding a lawyer 3
Meeting your lawyer 4

2 Legal aid
Martin Huseyin

Criminal Defence Service 9
Public defenders 10
Duty solicitor scheme 10
Community Legal Service 11
Personal injury 11
Legal representation 13
Children 14
Statutory charge and costs 14
Contracting 15

3 Lawyers and the courts
Yvette Vanson

Lawyers 19
Solicitors 19
Barristers 20
Judges 21
Courts 22
Juries 27
Arbitration 30
Mediation 30
National Probation Service 31
Ombudsmen 31
Victims and witnesses 32

PART 2   A–Z of the Law

4   **Accidents**   Whether compensation is payable 37
    and injuries   Accidents at work 39
    Nick Armstrong   Quantifying claims 39
                       Practicalities 40

5   **Actions against**   Police Complaints Authority 45
    the police   Civil claims for damages against the police 46
    Peter Wilcock   Time limits 47
                         What are damages? 48
                         Funding and costs 48
                         Getting the best advice 49

6   **Animals**   Pet owners 51
    Sally Ann Case   Dangerous dogs 52
                        Countryside and rights of way 52
                        Cruelty to animals 53
                        Pet passports 54

7   **Consumer law**   Complaining 57
    Susan Barrett   Consumer rights 58
                        Retailer rights 59
                        Putting it in writing 60
                        Pricing and paying 60
                        Protecting your rights 61
                        Protection from harm 62
                        Pressure selling 63
                        Professional services 64
                        Estate Agents 64
                        Travel agents / Tour operators 65

8 Criminal law
Martin Huseyin

Investigation and the start of criminal proceedings 69
Police interviews and identification parades 70
Other rights of suspects held by the police 71
Charging 72
Duty solicitors 73
Legal aid 73
Solicitors and barristers 73
Public defenders – the Criminal Defence Service 74
Crown Prosecution Service 74
Summons 75
Other investigating bodies 75
Private prosecutions 76
Bail 76
Courts and sentencing 77
Appeals against conviction 81
Victims and witnesses 83
Help for the accused 84

9 Disability
Catherine Rayner

The Disability Discrimination Act 1996 87
What is disability? 88
Disability at work 88
Service providers 90
Where can I get help? 91
Benefits 92
Getting further help 95

10 Discrimination
Catherine Rayner

Direct and indirect discrimination 100
How to claim 101
Preliminary hearings 102
Continuing acts 103
Remedies 103
The right to be accompanied 104
Trade unions and trade union rights 105

11 Education
Nick Armstrong

Admissions 109
Exclusions 110
Special educational needs 111
Bullying and educational negligence 112
Universities 113
Practicalities 114

12 Employment
Catherine Rayner

Contracts of employment 117
Losing your job 120
Legal dismissal 120
Disciplinary hearings 121
Dismissal 122
Redundancy 125
Employment tribunals 127
Effective date of dismissal 128
Common problems at work 130
Finding your employment lawyer 133

13 Environment
Sandhya Drew

Do I need a lawyer? 138
When do I need a lawyer? 138
Where can I find a lawyer? 139
Who pays? 140

14 Family law
*Birinder Kang and
Patrick Roche*

Divorce 143
Judicial separation 144
Nullity 145
Ancillary relief 146
Cohabitation 148
Disputes relating to children 149
Acquiring parental responsibility 150
Child abduction 156
Local authority orders 158
Adoption 160
Domestic violence 163
Finding the right family lawyer 166

15 Housing
*Jonathan Manning
and Annette Cafferkey,
Arden Chambers*

Buying 169
Renting 175
Security of tenure 176
Eviction 181
Transfer of tenancies 182
Sub-letting and lodgers 183
Other forms of occupation 184
Termination 187
Rent and other charges 188
Anti-social behaviour 191
Repairs 192
Right to buy 194
Private sector housing standards 195
Homelessness and allocations 200

16 Human Rights Act
Navi Ahluwalia

The Human Rights Act and the European Convention
   on Human Rights 209
Remedies and just satisfaction 212
The Convention rights 213
Right to life 214
Torture 215
Slavery 216
Liberty of the person 216
Fair trial 218
Retroactive criminal offences 220
Respect for private and family life 220
Freedom of thought 221
Freedom of expression 222
Freedom of association 223
The right to marry 223
Effective remedy 224
Discrimination 224
Interpretation 225
Right to property 225
Right to education 226
Free and fair elections 227
Abolition of the death penalty 227

17 Immigration and refugees
Martin Soorjoo

Types of application 229
Sources of immigration law 230
Making an application to enter or remain 231
Appeals 231
Legal advice 231

18 Inquests
Martin Huseyin and Michael Mansfield

What is an inquest? 235
The verdict 236
Juries 237
Representation 237
Practicalities 238
Legal aid 238
Do I need a lawyer? 239

19 Intellectual property
Andrew Norris

Protecting innovation and creativity 241
Patents 243
Trademarks 244
Passing-off 245
Copyright 245
Design rights 246
Database rights 247
Confidential information 248
Further information 248

20 International issues
Yvette Vanson

Adoption from abroad 252
Abduction 252
Crimes abroad 258
Arrest/imprisonment 261
Advice for relatives 264
Prison transfers 265
Forced marriage 267
Kidnap 269
Marrying abroad 270

21 Libel
Patrick Roche

Libel 273
Slander 273
Fair comment 274
Qualified privilege 274
Malicious falsehood 275
Time limits 275
Funding 276
Representation 276
Complaints 277

22 Mental health
Anna Harding

When do you need a mental health lawyer? 279
Finding a lawyer 281
The Mental Health Act 282
Compulsory admission 282
Treatment 284
Mental Health Review Tribunal 284
Guardianship 285
Patient rights 286
Nearest relatives 287
Clinical negligence claims 288
Alternatives to legal action 290

23 Motoring
Yvette Vanson

The law and your vehicle 293
Finding the right information 294
Funding for legal representation 294
Offences and the courts 295
Sentencing and penalties 296

24 Prisoners' rights
Hugh Southey

Allocation 301
Unconvicted prisoners 302
Convicted prisoners 303
Complaints 305
Judicial review 307
Offences against prison discipline 307
Punishment 308
Appeal 308
Segregation 309
Women prisoners 309
Young Offenders' Institutions 309

25 Public inquiries
*Michael Mansfield
and Martin Soorjoo*

What is a public inquiry? 313
Benefits of public inquiries 314
The format 315
The process 316
Procedure 317

26 Public order
Tim Moloney

Riot 319
Violent disorder 320
Affray 320
Fear of violence 321
Harassment 321
Racial aggravation 322
Minor offences 322
Legal representation 323

27 Welfare benefits
Catherine Rayner

Applying for benefits 325
What are benefits? 326
Entitlement 326
Types of benefit 327
Information about benefits 329
Finding the right welfare rights lawyer 330

The contributors 333
Directory of organisations 339
Index 357

Editor's note

We have tried to make this book accessible in style and format. We have tried to condense the complexities of the law without reducing the subject matter to banalities. And we've tried to keep it affordable. The author, contributors and the publishers sincerely hope that it will benefit those struggling with legal problems, and help you find the best legal advice. Any feedback will be welcome.

WHAT THIS GUIDE WILL DO

This guide will:

- provide a basic outline of most areas of law in England and Wales
- tell you about some of the places you can go to for help and advice if you have a legal problem or query
- suggest ways to secure the right legal representation
- explain the basic procedures of some of the courts and tribunals
- give you some idea of whether you can get free or subsidised advice
- make some suggestions about solving problems without using lawyers.

WHAT THIS GUIDE WILL NOT DO

This guide does not:

- provide a detailed guide to all of the legal rules in each area
- solve your legal problem for you
- substitute for proper professional advice on your particular problem
- tell you how to run your own legal case
- describe any of the laws and legal procedures of Scotland
- suggest that legal advice is always the answer to your problem.

CONTRIBUTORS

The contributors to this book are all experts in their field but they are not liable for any errors or omissions, nor are they offering legal advice or a professional service by contributing. As the vast majority are barristers, their professional rules prohibit them from being approached directly, so they cannot enter into correspondence. They must be contacted via a solicitor first.

THE LAW

The law as outlined in this book is accurate at the time of going to press, but as the law is in constant flux some of the information contained here may be inaccurate by the time you read it. We will correct any changes and updates in future editions.

> ### Exclusion of liability
>
> The publisher, author, editor, contributors, distributors and retailers shall not be liable to any person or entity with respect to any loss or damage caused or alleged to be caused directly or indirectly by what is contained in or left out of this book, *The Home Lawyer*.

ORGANISATIONS

The lists of organisations are as accurate and relevant as we can make them. They can offer valuable advice and assistance. However, the author, editor, contributors and publishers cannot guarantee the quality of service offered by any of the organisations listed in the book.

The editor acknowledges the value of a number of websites in the writing of this book (the FOREIGN OFFICE ADVICE site, NATIONAL PROBATION SERVICE, VIVA!, ACAS, etc) and directs the reader to them in the listings at the end of each chapter.

Lawyers often have a bad press – some of it justified – but in the majority of cases they are dedicated, hard-working and committed. I trust you encounter such a lawyer in your dealings with the law.

Yvette Vanson, editor

How to use this book

This book can help you understand the basics of the area of the law that applies to your problem. It will also direct you to the right kind of legal advice and where to find it. Perhaps you should start with CHAPTER 1: FINDING AND MEETING YOUR LAWYER and follow up with CHAPTER 2: LEGAL AID, which outlines the help with costs you are likely to be awarded and the areas where financial assistance is not available.

Different typefaces correspond to:

1. *Laws and statutes*

2. **Legal terms**

3. **ORGANISATIONS AND PROFESSIONAL BODIES**

The list of organisations at the end of each chapter gives the names, addresses, telephone numbers, fax, email and websites for charities and legal bodies which may be able to offer advice or suggest the best place to find the right legal representation. These organisations are also all listed in the directory at the end of the book.

Different bullet points correspond to the following:

? denotes questions to ask

☑ denotes things to take with you

☒ denotes things not to do

> Boxed text denotes an important issue.

Acknowledgements

Thanks to Lucy Barker, for her dedication to this project despite her recent serious illness; Camilla Cameron for her invaluable help with compiling the lists of organisations; the solicitors and barristers who have given their expertise and time freely and generously to contribute to this book; Lesley Shaw at Gillon Aitken Associates for finding us Toby Mundy and his team at Atlantic Books, who have given us friendly, professional support; Alice Hunt, editor of Guardian Books, for her patience, good humour and attention to detail; good friends who shared the burden of gripes about legal jargon; and above all to Michael Mansfield, who is not only the inspirational imagination behind this book, but my personal inspiration too.

Yvette Vanson, editor

Introduction
by Michael Mansfield QC

This book is intended to help you use the law and avoid using it where there are other ways of solving problems. It is designed to give a brief guide to the main areas of law that the ordinary citizen may come across and some ideas on where and how to find the best legal advice.

The law is something that most people think only concerns someone else. You read about it in the paper or see it on TV or – usually when a disaster happens – it's followed by a blaze of publicity about a big criminal trial.

The reality for lawyers and their clients is that the law crops up in all sorts of everyday problems – the motoring case, the boundary dispute with your neighbour, the defective goods you bought from the electrical store, Grandma not getting the right state benefits or an unfair dismissal at work.

> Access to the law and the courts, combined with good quality legal advice, are essential rights of a citizen in a mature democracy.

Citizens can only assert their rights with high calibre advice behind them. People ignorant of their legal rights and responsibilities are left powerless. If decisions are being taken about you, according to rules you don't understand, without your views being taken into account, then you are not really a citizen at all. If you know or at least can find out how to identify which area of law covers the point you wish to pursue, or how the law affects you, then you are on the way to full participation in society on equal terms with everyone else.

The law is not always the answer and lawyers do not always make things better, but many problems can be solved or at least explained by lawyers and advice workers who know the rules in their field of law. You must always remember, however, that the law is by no means a perfect way of solving problems and in many cases actually going to court should be an absolute last resort. Strangely enough, avoiding litigation is often one of the best bits of advice a lawyer can give.

Mediation, arbitration and just plain polite conversation or correspondence with people can solve problems more quickly, painlessly and cheaply than an army of lawyers. We have therefore tried to mention as we go along some of the non-legal remedies available to people as well. Sometimes what is needed is a bit of both: some advice to let you know where you stand, followed by an attempt to resolve your problem without the courts if possible.

The *Human Rights Act 1998* incorporated the *European Convention on Human Rights* into the law of England and Wales. This has had some important effects on all areas of law, but more so in some areas than others. It also means that where there is a breach of a citizen's rights under the Convention and the law doesn't seem to give them a remedy, lawyers and individuals can argue for the courts to reinterpret the law to provide proper redress. We deal with some of the implications of the *Human Rights Act* under each area of law in the individual chapters, but we think it's so important we have devoted a whole chapter to it as well.

As this book goes to print, major changes are being introduced. The ancient office of Lord Chancellor has been abolished and a Minister for Constitutional Affairs has been created in its place. This is an initial step towards establishing a cleaner separation of powers and strengthening the independence of the judiciary. Presently, the **LORD CHANCELLOR'S DEPART-MENT** has only suffered a name change and remains in the same building with the same staff in Victoria Street, London. For much the same reasons, the law lords will be removed from the House of Lords and formed into a Supreme Court, probably in a separate building with increased space and resources. Meanwhile, consultation is taking place to identify a new means of appointing the judiciary (via an independent appointments commission) and to determine whether the rank of silk (QC) should be maintained amongst barristers.

The two most obvious and commonly asked questions when people are faced with a legal problem are:

❓ Who do I go to?

❓ How much will it cost?

Unfortunately, the answer to the second question may determine the answer to the first.

> The vision and concept of equal access to the law and the enforcement of individual rights is fast becoming a victim of market forces. The continuous erosion of legal aid provision has meant an increasing number of people fall through what was intended originally as a legal welfare safety net.

Some areas are not covered by **legal aid** at all, others only by lawyers prepared to act on a contingency basis (no win, no fee) or, ultimately, by lawyers willing to act **pro bono** (for free).

Discovering your financial threshold of eligibility for public funding may in some circumstances actually decide how you progress your case. This is something any solicitor you approach must clarify at an early stage. Ask for a copy of their 'terms of business', which should specify:

- their hourly rates

- whether and how much you have to pay

- whether you can pay by instalments

- whether their services could be free (either via legal aid or a pro bono arrangement).

However your case is funded, publicly or privately, you still need to establish as far as possible that you have the right lawyer for the job. You wouldn't go to a car mechanic for a haircut, so you can't necessarily assume the high street solicitor is the person for you. It is horses for courses, and this book attempts to point you in the right direction by suggesting the questions that need to be asked to get you there. Depending on the nature of the problem they will not always be the same and each chapter identifies the particular features to concentrate on.

There are now government schemes which provide benchmarks you can use as a starting point. A solicitor has to be **franchised** (approved) to undertake work which might attract state funding. The **franchise certificate** should be displayed or be available so that you can check the areas in which that solicitor specialises. If your problem is not covered, the solicitor is obliged to advise you of someone else who can help. This is called **signposting**.

Barristers – the lawyers who do the majority of advocacy in court, presenting your case having first been 'briefed' by your solicitor – are also subject to a registration scheme overseen by the LEGAL SERVICES COMMISSION. This is known as a **Quality Mark**.

> In their quest for good legal representation, the government is now advising people to call in at any COMMUNITY LEGAL SERVICE Information Point to find out about their rights and responsibilities or where to go for further advice. In time, there will be more and more Information Points in libraries and other public places. Each one will have information leaflets and a copy of the CLS Directory of Services. The CLS Directory lists all the lawyers and advice centres that have the Quality Mark, and many others. It also gives details of what, if anything, you might have to pay. At some Information Points, there will be someone you can talk to who can point out where to access the information you need. (See Organisations list at the end of this introduction for details.)

Part of the difficulty when a problem occurs is identifying into which legal slot it fits. This is why we have outlined the various areas of law so that you can understand both what it is called and a bit about how it works; avoiding as much jargon as is possible!

This book won't give you an automatic answer to your individual problem or query, but it should enable you to see where your situation fits into the legal framework and start you on the road to getting the advice you need.

Organisations $\boxed{i}$

▶ **COMMUNITY LEGAL SERVICE**
www.justask.org.uk *for the online Directory and legal information and advice.*

Tel: 0845 608 1122
(all calls charged at local rate)
minicom: 0845 609 6677
for your nearest CLS provider.

Approach a CLS General Help Point, such as a Citizens Advice Bureau, which offers advice and basic help.

▶ **DEPARTMENT FOR CONSTITUTIONAL AFFAIRS**
Selborne House
54–60 Victoria Street
London SW1E 6QW
Tel: 020 7210 8500
general.queries@dca.gsi.gov.uk
www.dca.gov.uk

▶ **LEGAL SERVICES COMMISSION**
85 Gray's Inn Road
London WC1X 8TX
Tel: 020 7759 0000
www.legalservices.gov.uk
www.justask.org.uk

PART ONE

Lawyers, Funding and the Courts

1 Finding and meeting your lawyer

This chapter will help you with finding a lawyer and what to do when you have found the right person.

Ways of finding a lawyer

- Speak to friends who have used lawyers – this is only a first step but lawyers are no different from plumbers – the only way of really knowing if they are any good is from someone who has used them.

- Ask a trade union official – they may know of lawyers the union uses – or ring the head or regional office. Many union members are surprised to find that their union offers help with legal services which is not limited to work-related matters. Unions may also pay some or all of the legal expenses for certain types of advice.

- Ask your local Citizens Advice Bureau, law centre or advice centre.

- Look in the COMMUNITY LEGAL SERVICE DIRECTORY (available in most libraries and courts) and on the website www.justask.org.uk

- Look at the LAW SOCIETY DIRECTORY OF SOLICITORS AND BARRISTERS. This lists solicitors' firms and tells you the kind of work they do. Copies of the directory are in libraries, town halls and most advice centres and Citizens Advice Bureaux.

- There are now a number of commercial law directories that list solicitors and barristers, *but* entries are often dependent on payments by the firms/chambers concerned so there may be some important omissions.

- Go to a solicitor's office to find out if they offer the service you require.

- Ask your insurance company – not only do many motor insurance policies cover legal advice on motoring matters, but also many household insurance policies cover some legal expenses.

- If you are looking for a firm or organisation that offers publicly funded legal services under a LEGAL SERVICES COMMISSION contract in your area, then you can phone 0845 608 1122 (minicom 0845 609 6677). This is a service provided by the LSC. It will only tell you who has contracts for the various areas of law and that they meet the standards under the contract.

- Consult one of the professional associations of lawyers who practise in a particular area of law – some of these are listed in the various chapters of this book – most will not give specific recommendations, but will supply lists of members' firms.

Meeting your lawyer

THINGS TO TAKE WITH YOU

> It is very important to take as many of the relevant documents as possible with you to your lawyer or adviser. Ensure you keep copies if you hand over originals. This will save a lot of time, help you get the advice you need and save costs.

Some of the things you should try to take with you are:

☑ Any letters or forms relating to the matter you want advice on – anything you have written and anything that has been written to you.

☑ Any official forms, orders or letters from a court or lawyer or the other party to a dispute.

☑ In a criminal case, the charge sheet/summons or any other papers given to you at the police station or sent to you by the court.

☑ Any statements or notes about an incident you are asking advice about.

☑ Names, addresses and telephone numbers of witnesses or other people involved in the matter you wish to discuss.

☑ Your diary. It is always advisable to keep detailed chronological records of all conversations and developments in case you end up in court, and your lawyer will often need to know your future commitments.

☑ Details of how to contact you. Always tell your lawyer if you want to be contacted in a particular way – eg, not at work – and always tell them if you are changing address.

☑ If you are likely to be asking for legal aid you should take:

- proof of your income and that of your partner – recent pay slips, for example, or your benefit books

- proof of savings (if any) – bank and building society books

- proof of essential expenses – rent books or mortgage statements, water rates and council tax bills, fares to and from work, any court orders requiring you to pay money

- information about the amount of your mortgage and the approximate equity, if any, in your home.

QUESTIONS TO ASK

? Why is the lawyer or adviser the right person to help you and what is their expertise?

? Does their firm/organisation usually advise on this area? How can you be sure of that?

? Are they members of a professional organisation for this type of work?

? What will this meeting cost? You should indicate your maximum budget.

? What will the next stage of the case cost? Lawyers should keep you updated on how costs are mounting up.

? Do they do legally aided work?

? Do they have a contract for advising on this area of law?

? Can they check your eligibility for legal help under the relevant scheme?

? Who will be dealing with your case? Will it be:

- a solicitor
- a trainee solicitor (they have passed their exams and are doing the on-the-job part of their training)
- a legal executive (these are legal workers who have passed the exams set by the **INSTITUTE OF LEGAL EXECUTIVES**)
- some other form of para-legal worker or clerk (these may have some or no legal qualifications).

? How will this affect the cost?

? Will they be dealing with all of your case or will they need to seek advice from a barrister or an expert?

? What are your choices for dealing with the matter – negotiation/ letter writing, mediation or arbitration, court proceedings – and what are the advantages and disadvantages of each?

Remember, if you are unhappy with the representation you are receiving, you can always change your lawyer (see CHAPTER 3: LAWYERS AND THE COURTS for complaints procedures).

Organisations   [i]

▶ **ADVICE UK (formerly THE FEDERATION OF INFORMATION AND ADVICE CENTRES)**

12th Floor
New London Bridge House
25 London Bridge Street
London SE1 9ST

Tel: 020 7407 4070
www.fiac.org.uk

▶ **BAR PRO BONO UNIT AND BAR IN THE COMMUNITY**

7 Gray's Inn Square
Gray's Inn
London WC1R 5AZ

Bar Pro Bono Unit: 020 7831 9711
Bar in the Community: 020 7841 1341
Fax: 020 7831 9733
enquiries@barprobono.org.uk
www.barprobono.org.uk

This organisation takes on a limited number of cases in which barristers agree to act for free.

▶ **BRITISH AND IRISH OMBUDSMAN ASSOCIATION (BIOA)**

www.bioa.org.uk

Ombudsmen are an independent and impartial means of resolving certain disputes outside the courts. They cover various public and private bodies and look into matters after a complaint has been made to the relevant body. This site lists the ombudsmen and other complaint-handling bodies.

▶ **COMMUNITY LEGAL SERVICE**

www.justask.org.uk *for the online Directory and legal information and advice.*

Tel: 0845 608 1122
(all calls charged at local rate)
minicom: 0845 609 6677
for your nearest CLS provider.

Approach a CLS General Help Point, such as a Citizens Advice Bureau, which offers advice and basic help.

▶ **FREE REPRESENTATION UNIT (FRU)**
Fourth Floor, Peer House
8–14 Verulam Street
London WC1X 8LZ
www.fru.org.uk
Please note that the FRU does NOT deal
with members of the public directly.

▶ **GENERAL COUNCIL OF THE BAR**
3 Bedford Row
London WC1R 4DB
Tel: 020 7242 0082
Records Office: 020 7242 0934
Fax: 020 7831 9217
www.barcouncil.org.uk

▶ **INSTITUTE OF LEGAL EXECUTIVES**
Kempston Manor
Kempston
Bedfordshire
MK42 7AB
DX 124780-KEMPSTON 2
Tel: 01234 841000
Fax: 01234 840373
info@ilex.org.uk
www.ilex.org.uk

▶ **LAW CENTRES FEDERATION**
Duchess House
18–19 Warren Street
London W1T 5LR
Tel: 020 7387 8570
Fax: 020 7387 8368
info@lawcentres.org.uk
www.lawcentres.org.uk

▶ **LAW SOCIETY**
113 Chancery Lane
London WC2A 1PL
Tel: 020 7242 1222
Fax: 020 7831 0344
info.services@lawsociety.org.uk
www.lawsociety.org.uk

▶ **LEGAL SERVICES COMMISSION**
85 Gray's Inn Road
London WC1X 8TX
Tel: 020 7759 0000
www.legalservices.gov.uk
www.justask.org.uk
Regional telephone helplines on various
legal subjects.

The government is now advising people
to call in at any COMMUNITY LEGAL
SERVICE Information Point to find out
about their rights and responsibilities
or where to go for further advice and
where to access the information you
need. In time, there will be more and
more Information Points in libraries and
other public places. Each one will have
information leaflets and a copy of the
CLS DIRECTORY OF SERVICES. The CLS
Directory lists all the lawyers and advice
centres that have the Quality Mark, and
many others. It also gives details of what,
if anything, you might have to pay.

▶ **NATIONAL ASSOCIATION OF**
CITIZENS ADVICE BUREAUX (NACAB)
Myddelton House
115–123 Pentonville Road
London N1 9LZ
Tel: 020 7833 2181
www.nacab.org.uk
Adviceguide: the National Association
of Citizens Advice Bureaux offers
fact sheets covering issues such as
employment, housing and taxation
www.adviceguide.org.uk

▶ **OFFICE FOR THE SUPERVISION**
OF SOLICITORS
Victoria Court
8 Dormer Place
Royal Leamington Spa
Warwickshire CV32 5AE
Public advice line: 0845 608 6565
enquiries@lawsociety.org.uk
www.oss.lawsociety.org.uk
Deals with complaints and regulation.

2 **Legal aid**

This chapter outlines the who, how and what of legal aid funding. Please note that some of the figures given for eligibility and amounts of available funding may change in the near future.

LEGAL SERVICES COMMISSION (LSC)

This is the government body responsible for publicly funded legal services. It runs two organisations that provide help to members of the public:

- **CRIMINAL DEFENCE SERVICE**
- **COMMUNITY LEGAL SERVICE**

Criminal Defence Service (CDS)

The CDS provides help in criminal cases. It funds solicitors to attend police stations and give free advice to suspects. This covers advice from a solicitor of the suspect's choice so long as that person's firm has a CDS contract.

For those who do not already have a solicitor, they may wish to use the **duty solicitor scheme**, which is also funded (see below and CHAPTER 8: CRIMINAL LAW). There is no contribution required for this service.

Advice and assistance is a system which covers getting advice on criminal or related matters, but does not cover representation in court. This is means-tested and you can find out from a solicitor whether you fall below the income and capital limits for this service. Most people on benefits and low incomes will qualify, and if you do, the service is free. Some initial advice to prisoners can be given under this scheme.

The CDS also pays for non-means-tested representation at the magistrates' court for all defendants whose cases are deemed serious enough to require a lawyer. The test that is applied is whether it is in the interests of justice to grant representation. It will normally be granted if the:

- accused is a child or young person
- consequences of conviction are serious (eg, loss of job)
- accused person cannot be expected to represent themselves – because of the legal complexity of the case or language or other difficulties
- there is any risk of imprisonment if convicted.

In cases where legal representation is granted the defendant is allowed to choose a solicitors' firm which they wish to represent them. There is a facility for changing solicitor if the firm instructed is not satisfactory, but the court is often reluctant to allow this if there would be any waste of money caused by work being repeated. If representation is refused then you can appeal to the court.

Public defenders

In some areas there is an experimental scheme where the CRIMINAL DEFENCE SERVICE directly employs its own lawyers and defendants can choose to have one of these to defend them instead of using a solicitor from a private firm. These lawyers are called **public defenders** after a similar system in the USA. It is not known how far this system will be extended, but early reports show that clients have found it less satisfactory than having a legally aided solicitor from private practice.

Duty solicitor scheme

The CDS also funds a **duty solicitor scheme** at magistrates' courts. Solicitors acting under this scheme will represent a defendant who has no lawyer in cases that can be resolved on the first hearing at court, or give some advice and assistance to enable the accused person to get legal representation by the next hearing. They can also deal with applying to the court for bail and with people who have been brought to court for not paying fines.

> If you are facing a criminal charge, seek advice before the first hearing at the magistrates' court.

For cases that go to the crown court there is no means-testing prior to the grant of representation. This usually includes the services of a solicitor and a barrister (or solicitor with higher court qualification). However, a means form does have to be filled in and the costs of representation or a contribution towards those costs can be recovered from convicted defendants. You will need to provide information about you and your partner's income, savings and outgoings.

If a legally aided case is serious or complicated enough to require more than one barrister or a Queen's Counsel (QC) then a written application is made to the crown court, which is decided by the senior judge at that court.

Community Legal Service (CLS)

The CLS runs what used to be called **civil legal aid** and also puts money into other legal help services jointly with organisations such as local authorities and advice centres – these are called **partnership projects**.

The CLS still funds a great deal of its legal service work through private solicitors' firms. All of this is done under CLS contracts and in some areas such as family cases, immigration law and clinical negligence, contracts are only supposed to be awarded to firms that qualify as having specialist expertise.

Personal injury

Injuries from car accidents and accidents at work are no longer covered by public funding. This work is now done under **conditional fee agreements** by solicitors. These agreements usually mean no costs have to be paid by the client if the case is lost, in return for increased **success fees** for the lawyers if they win.

The only exception is that the LEGAL SERVICES COMMISSION may pay for investigative help in very complicated cases – for example, where there are a lot of potential claimants against a drug company or manufacturer. To get the case to the point where a conditional fee agreement can be considered with a solicitors' firm, and if the case is very costly to run, the LSC may pay a contribution to the costs under a system of **litigation support** (see CHAPTER 4: ACCIDENTS AND INJURIES).

The Services funded by CLS are split into a lot of categories, which can be difficult for people to understand. Your adviser may be able to tell you whether you can get the appropriate help or they may need to apply to the LSC on your behalf to get funding. The main categories are:

LEGAL HELP – which covers:

- short initial advice on any legal problem
- further steps such as preliminary advice from a barrister
- writing letters and negotiating on your behalf.

HELP AT COURT – which covers:

- the funding of a lawyer to speak for you at court at a specific hearing without dealing with your case as a whole.

Legal help and **help at court** are currently subject to a limit of £500 worth of legal work after which the solicitor has to apply to the LSC for more funding. They are means-tested according to the income and capital (savings and other property) of the person seeking advice. If you qualify under the means test then there is no contribution to the costs.

FAMILY HELP – provides funding for:

- attending family mediation
- general help with other aspects of family cases
- negotiating agreements in family cases on such matters as children and finances
- applications to a court to incorporate a negotiated agreement in a court order.

Help with mediation is means-tested, but if you qualify then it is free and the LSC also pays the mediator's costs. The work is limited to relatively small amounts. **General family help** currently covers up to £1500 of work but it is means-tested. If you qualify, there is no contribution. If more work is required, further funding can be applied for, but if the matter becomes a dispute that has to go to court, full representation will be required.

Legal representation

This is either **investigative help** to see if you have a good case, or **full representation** to take your case to court – although this may be subject to limits on how much can be spent and how far the case can be taken before the funding is reconsidered.

Your solicitor has to apply to the regional LSC office for legal representation and various means tests apply. If you qualify you may have to pay a contribution depending on your level of income and capital (savings and other property).

The decision on financial eligibility is made by the LSC, except in:

- certain family cases before the **magistrates' court**
- cases before the **immigration adjudicators**
- cases in the **immigration appeal tribunal** (where contracted firms can decide themselves because of the urgent nature of the work).

> If you succeed in an application for representation, you are made an offer by the LSC which includes, where appropriate, the contribution you will be expected to make. If you accept the offer then the solicitor can start work and you will become liable to pay the contribution.

The decision whether to grant legal representation or whether to continue it at each stage of the case is subject to a complex series of tests set out in the LSC's funding code. In applying these tests the LSC will consider questions such as:

- the likely prospect of success of the case

- the cost of funding it compared with the value of winning
- matters of public interest such as the benefit to others of having a legal issue decided.

Cases in most courts are covered, but there are some exceptions such as:

- **employment tribunal** cases – however, appeals from these may be funded (see CHAPTER 12: EMPLOYMENT)
- **coroner's courts** – although deaths in custody or involving state agencies will in future be more likely to be funded (see CHAPTER 18: INQUESTS)
- **public inquiries** (see CHAPTER 25: PUBLIC INQUIRIES).

Even if your case is in one of the excluded areas you may be able to show that there is a wider public interest involved, in which case **exceptional funding** can be applied for.

Children

Children can be advised under all of the above forms of help. Where there is means-testing, their parents' or guardians' income and capital will usually be considered unless it is a case in which there is a conflict of interest between them and the child.

> A solicitor dealing with your case can check whether you qualify under the various means tests or you can even check your eligibility online at the LEGAL SERVICES COMMISSION website which also has lots of free information and downloadable leaflets.

Statutory charge and costs

If you win a legally aided case the other side will usually be ordered to pay your costs. This will include paying the value of your contribution, which you should get back. In that situation, the LSC-funded work will be paid for by the other side.

STATUTORY CHARGE If you win but do not win all of your costs, then the LSC can deduct the unpaid part of its costs out of your damages or from any property recovered or preserved in the case. Sometimes the court may decide that the losing side should not pay part of the costs because they were not reasonable (eg, they did work that was unnecessary) or because you won on one part of the case but not on another. In those situations the **statutory charge** will reduce the amount you end up with. Maintenance and (currently) the first £3000 of any property are excluded from this system.

> The **statutory charge** may be postponed – in the case of a house it can be registered as a charge like a mortgage and only collected when the property is sold. If the charge is postponed, it is usually subject to interest when it is eventually paid.

If you lose a case in which you had LSC-funded representation then the court will usually not make an order for you to pay any costs. That means that the cost to you will be limited to any contribution that was ordered when funding was granted. Sometimes the court will order costs against you, but 'not to be enforced without leave of the court'. This means that the other side cannot get their costs unless they come back to court and show that your financial situation has substantially changed or that you were concealing your true income or capital.

In exceptional cases costs can be ordered against legally aided litigants, but these are subject to strict limitations on recovery to protect such things as the value of personal clothes, household furniture, tools of trade and the first £100,000 of the value of a home.

Contracting

Private firms that provide legal work funded with public money do so under contracts and are regularly audited on some aspects of the way they operate.

Some lawyers feel that the auditing process concentrates more on administrative efficiency than on the quality of the legal work they do.

> Legal aid is under-resourced and limited. The rules are complicated. It is best to ask for advice so that you are sure what contributions (if any) you will have to make.

Organisations [i]

▶ **ADVICE UK (formerly THE FEDERATION OF INFORMATION AND ADVICE CENTRES)**
12th Floor
New London Bridge House
25 London Bridge Street
London SE1 9ST
Tel: 020 7407 4070
www.fiac.org.uk

▶ **BAR PRO BONO UNIT AND BAR IN THE COMMUNITY**
7 Gray's Inn Square
Gray's Inn
London WC1R 5AZ
Bar Pro Bono Unit: 020 7831 9711
Bar in the Community: 020 7841 1341
Fax: 020 7831 9733
enquiries@barprobono.org.uk
www.barprobono.org.uk

▶ **CHILDREN'S LEGAL CENTRE**
University of Essex
Wivenhoe Park
Colchester
Essex CO4 3SQ
Advice line: 01206 873820
www.essex.ac.uk

▶ **COMMUNITY LEGAL SERVICE**
www.justask.org.uk *for the online Directory and legal information and advice.*
Tel: 0845 608 1122
(all calls charged at local rate)
Minicom: 0845 609 6677
for your nearest CLS provider.
Approach a CLS General Help Point, such as a Citizens Advice Bureau, which offers advice and basic help.

▶ **CRIMINAL DEFENCE SERVICE**
www.legalservices.gov.uk/cds/index.htm

▶ **DISABILITY LAW SERVICE**
39–45 Cavell Street
London E1 2BP
Tel: 020 7791 9800
Fax: 020 7791 9802
advice@dls.org.uk
Offers free advice and representation.

▶ **FREE REPRESENTATION UNIT (FRU)**
Fourth Floor, Peer House
8–14 Verulam Street
London WC1X 8LZ
www.fru.org.uk
Please note that the FRU does NOT deal with members of the public directly.

▶ **JUSTICE**

59 Carter Lane
London EC4V 5AQ

Tel: 020 7329 5100
Fax: 020 7329 5055
admin@justice.org.uk
www.justice.org.uk

▶ **LAW CENTRES FEDERATION**

Duchess House
18–19 Warren Street
London W1T 5LR

Tel: 020 7387 8570
Fax: 020 7387 8368
info@lawcentres.org.uk
www.lawcentres.org.uk

▶ **THE LAW SOCIETY**

113 Chancery Lane
London WC2A 1PL

Tel: 020 7242 1222
Fax: 020 7831 0344
info.services@lawsociety.org.uk
www.lawsoc.org.uk

▶ **LEGAL SERVICES COMMISSION**

85 Gray's Inn Road
London WC1X 8TX

Tel: 020 7759 0000
www.legalservices.gov.uk
www.justask.org.uk

Regional telephone helplines on various legal subjects.

The government is now advising people to call in at any COMMUNITY LEGAL SERVICE Information Point to find out about your rights and responsibilities or where to go for further advice and where to access the information you need. In time, there will be more and more Information Points in libraries and other public places. Each one will have information leaflets and a copy of the CLS DIRECTORY OF SERVICES. The CLS Directory lists all the lawyers and advice centres that have the Quality Mark, and many others. It also gives details of what, if anything, you might have to pay.

▶ **NATIONAL ASSOCIATION OF CITIZENS ADVICE BUREAUX (NACAB)**

Myddelton House
115–123 Pentonville Road
London N1 9LZ

Tel: 020 7833 2181
www.nacab.org.uk

Adviceguide: the National Association of Citizens Advice Bureaux offers fact sheets covering issues such as employment, housing and taxation
www.adviceguide.org.uk

▶ **RELEASE**

388 Old Street
London EC1V 9LT

Tel: 020 7749 4034
info@release.org.uk
www.release.org.uk

▶ **SOLICITOR'S PRO BONO GROUP MEDIATION SERVICE**

Tel: 0870 777 5601 (extension 25)
mediate@probonogroup.org.uk
www.probonogroup.org.uk

3 Lawyers and the courts

This chapter is designed to help you through the complexity of the legal system in England and Wales (Scotland is different). It is a brief run-down of all personnel (lawyers, judges, etc), organisations (ACAS, NATIONAL PROBATION SERVICE, etc) and courts and tribunals you are likely to encounter if you are involved with a legal case. It tells you where to go for help if you are a victim or what you can expect if you are called to be a witness in court. It gives a brief description of how to use the small claims court, when arbitration and mediation are appropriate, and tells you what will be required if you are selected for jury service.

Lawyers

Lawyer is the general term for a legal representative. In England and Wales there are two kinds of lawyer: solicitors and barristers.

Solicitors

There are thousands of solicitors and they mostly operate in partnership firms from an office on the local high street. They are all members of the LAW SOCIETY and are listed in regional directories.

Most work is **non-contentious** – it doesn't require a contest – and involves correspondence, conveyancing, wills and negotiation between parties. The

contentious side of their work involves **litigation** (legal action). Solicitors are the people who prepare a case before it goes to court – taking instructions from a client and advising on a course of action. Typically they **brief** a barrister who will appear in court, although nowadays some solicitors are trained to represent their clients in court themselves, and some barristers are permitted in limited circumstances to act without a solicitor. This is called **direct access**.

You are entitled to know from the start:

- whether the solicitor has particular expertise relevant to the problem you are facing
- if the same solicitor will handle your case throughout
- how much your solicitor will charge – per hour usually
- the name of the person dealing with your affairs
- how long (and therefore how much) it will take to resolve the issues
- who to complain to if things go wrong.

If things go *really* wrong you can complain to the OFFICE FOR THE SUPERVISION OF SOLICITORS, which operates with a panel of lay members.

Barristers

Barristers are briefed by solicitors and appear in the courts (in a wig and gown). They are known as **counsel**, or **QC** (**Queen's Counsel**) if they are senior in the profession, and advocate on behalf of their client. They are self-employed and operate from their offices or **chambers**.

> It is important to remember that in most cases you cannot go straight to a barrister. They can only be consulted through a solicitor. But you can stipulate the barrister of your choice, if you know of one.

In the case of professional misconduct you should approach the BAR COUNCIL – although you should be aware that barristers have a legal immunity that protects them from claims of negligence in their presentation of a case in court.

COMPLAINTS

Always bear in mind that you are the client and if you are dissatisfied with the service you are receiving, whether from a solicitor or a barrister, you should make this known. If there is no improvement and no justification, do not be afraid to consider changing your representation.

The **LEGAL SERVICES OMBUDSMAN** is the place of last resort for complaints. It is a free service. You have three months after the professional body's decision in which to apply. Their decision will be final, but can be subject to judicial review.

> If you have no faith in lawyers, you can always represent yourself in court, and be a **litigant in person** (LIP).

Judges

MAGISTRATE

Magistrates were chosen by the **Lord Chancellor** from people who applied out of the local community. They are often called **JPs** (**Justices of the Peace**). Three magistrates sit in the local magistrates' court, hearing a range of minor issues including motoring offences, criminal and family cases. They can take advice from the magistrates' clerk, who is legally trained.

MAGISTRATES' COURT DISTRICT JUDGE (previously called stipendiary magistrate)

These are professional magistrates, drawn from the legal profession, who usually sit in the magistrates' courts of big cities on a full-time basis.

COUNTY COURT DISTRICT JUDGE

District judges sit in the county court and hear minor cases such as small claims, or they can decide on preliminary questions before a case is heard by a circuit judge.

CIRCUIT JUDGE

Circuit judges are drawn from the legal profession and sit in the six circuits (legal areas) of England and Wales, in both county and crown courts.

RECORDER

Recorders are experienced barristers or solicitors appointed to sit as part-time judges in the county and crown courts for a few weeks each year.

HIGH COURT JUDGE

High court judges sit in the **high court**, in the Strand in London and in each of the main metropolitan cities, and hear serious cases. They can also hear appeals on points of law in the **appeal court**. Judges are appointed by the Lord Chancellor. Their posts are advertised but they always come from the legal profession. There are two divisions of work: criminal and civil.

The **Lord Chief Justice** is the most senior judge in the high court.

LAW LORDS

The law lords are the ten most senior appeal judges who sit in the House of Lords. Five at a time hear appeals and they also declare on some constitutional matters.

LORD CHANCELLOR

In June 2003 the post of Lord Chancellor was abolished and a new Department for Constitutional Affairs created. This will oversee the administration of jusice in the future. The Lord Chancellor was the head of the judiciary and a member of the cabinet. He appointed judges and oversaw the administration of justice and law reform through parliament and the COMMUNITY LEGAL SERVICES funding system (see CHAPTER 2: LEGAL AID).

Courts

Courts can be inhospitable places, but they are there to dispense justice and protect your rights, and you are entitled to be helped and treated civilly by the court staff, whether you are a claimant, defendant or witness.

SMALL CLAIMS COURT

Small claims (up to £5000; personal injury up to £1000) are heard in a private room in front of a district judge.

- Fill in the appropriate form. If you need help go to your local law centre or Citizens Advice Bureau. You are known as the **claimant**.

- Send the forms to the county court with a filing fee.

- Within about two weeks the court will send a summons to the person against whom you are claiming (the **defendant**). They must reply to the court within 14 days. If they do not, the court may just rule in your favour.

- If the defendant does reply, the court may order you to exchange documents with the defendant.

- Within about three months the case will be hear in front of the judge. Both sides will have a chance to put their case. The judge will usually rule on the spot.

- If you win, you may be able to claim some expenses.

You can use the **fast track** system for claims between £5000 and £15,000. Your case is guaranteed to:

- be heard within six months

- only take a maximum of five hours in court

- be limited on costs

- only allow written expert evidence.

ENFORCEMENT

> Often the most difficult part of a small claim, even if you win, is enforcing the judgement. People often refuse to pay and then the bailiffs may need to be called in – at extra cost.

If the court judgement confirms in writing that you are owed the money by the debtor, but the debtor does not pay up, you will need to go back to court and try to collect the judgement debt by one or more methods. There will be a court fee to pay in each case. You will need to know where the debtor is living, in order to serve the necessary court papers. Enquiry agents can help with tracing debtors, but this can be expensive, and not worth it if you are chasing a small amount of money.

> It is a criminal offence to harass a debtor. It is not a criminal offence to owe money, even if the court has entered judgement. You cannot coerce a debtor into paying.

Leaflets are available from the DEPARTMENT FOR CONSITUTIONAL AFFAIRS on how to bring a small claim.

TRIBUNALS

These are informal courts with a lawyer as chairperson along with two lay members. They hear cases in such areas as:

- unfair dismissal
- discrimination
- immigration
- rent
- social security
- mental health.

There are also special tribunals such as the **Employment Appeals Tribunal** (see details in CHAPTER 12: EMPLOYMENT), the **Child Support Appeal Tribunal**, or the **Medical Appeal Tribunal**, which hears appeals against refusal of claims for:

- mobility allowance
- injury-related benefits.

> There is no public funding for legal representation at tribunals, so it is essential to try to secure free advice from your trade union or local advice centre. Some lawyers operate on a 'no win, no fee' basis, but this may end up costing more than you think. Be sure to ask in advance.

MAGISTRATES' COURT There are either three magistrates, who are not legally qualified but have a qualified clerk to help them with the law, or in some urban areas district judges, who are qualified lawyers, sit on their own.

CROWN COURT This is the court that many people think of when they imagine a criminal court. It has a judge with a wig and robes, barristers wearing wigs and gowns, and trials are conducted with a jury of 12 citizens deciding on guilt or innocence.

> Only a tiny minority of cases (about 5 per cent) are tried in the crown court, and most of those never involve a jury because the defendant pleads guilty.

COUNTY COURT This is the court that hears civil matters in front of a circuit judge, such as bankruptcy, divorce, repossession or disputes over wills.

CORONER'S COURT This is where an inquest will take place into a death by unnatural causes, in front of a **coroner** and sometimes a jury. There is usually no legal aid available for this court (see CHAPTER 18: INQUESTS).

HIGH COURT This is situated at the **Royal Courts of Justice** in the Strand, London, and in some of the large metropolitan centres. The work of the high court is allocated to three **divisions**:

Queen's Bench division – which deals with claims for damages and breach of contract, and includes:

- Commercial court
- Admiralty court
- Administrative court (formerly the divisional court), which deals with judicial reviews and appeals on points of law from the magistrates' courts.

> **JUDICIAL REVIEW** is currently one of the most significant jurisdictions, dealing with potential abuses of power and human rights by institutions, government departments and companies.

Chancery division – which deals with tax, property and trusts disputes, and includes:

- Companies court
- Patents court

Family Division – which deals with disputes in divorce cases, adoption and wards of court.

COURT OF APPEAL This is where both civil and criminal appeals are heard from county, crown and high courts in front of lord justices (see CHAPTER 8: CRIMINAL LAW).

HOUSE OF LORDS This is the final stage and the highest court in the land, where five law lords hear appeals on points of law of significant public importance. The new **DEPARTMENT FOR CONSTITUTIONAL AFFAIRS** is intending to create a supreme court where the law lords will sit instead of the House of Lords.

PRIVY COUNCIL This hears appeals from the remaining colonies and former British territories, such as New Zealand, Trinidad and Singapore, in front of a judicial committee made up of the law lords and senior Commonwealth judges.

EUROPEAN COURT OF JUSTICE This sits in Luxembourg and interprets *European Community* law, which applies to the 15 member states (soon to be 25), each of which is represented by a single judge.

EUROPEAN COURT OF HUMAN RIGHTS This sits in Strasbourg and is the court of last resort if breaches of the *European Human Rights Convention* are not satisfactorily dealt with in the national courts. Since the *Human Rights Act*, human rights arguments can be used in all courts in England and Wales (see CHAPTER 16: HUMAN RIGHTS ACT).

Juries

JURY SERVICE

The jury's main duty is to reach a verdict in criminal cases, and it usually consists of 12 people but can be as few as nine. Occasionally, juries are used in coroner's courts, where the jury must consist of no fewer than seven and no more than 11 people (see CHAPTER 18: INQUESTS). A county court jury must consist of eight people. Very few civil cases involve juries, the most usual type being libel trials.

WHO SERVES AS A JUROR?

You are normally qualified to serve as a juror if you are:

- between the ages of 18 and 65
- on the electoral register for parliamentary or local government elections
- usually resident in the UK for any period of at least five years since the age of 13.

The Lord Chancellor, using electoral registers, was responsible for issuing summonses to potential jurors. This role will now be taken by the Minister for Constitutional Affairs. The summonses are administered by a jury summoning officer for each court. You have to attend if you are summoned unless you have very good reasons (see below).

A summons is sent either by post or hand delivery. When you attend, you may be asked some questions to establish whether you are qualified for jury service.

PAYMENT OF JURORS

A juror is entitled to receive payments for:

- travelling and subsistence
- financial loss incurred because of jury service, up to a limited amount.

*WHEN YOU DO **NOT** HAVE TO SERVE*

Some people are not eligible, or may be disqualified or excused.

Ineligible people are:

- the clergy
- the mentally ill
- judges, barristers and solicitors
- police officers, probation officers and prison officers.

Disqualified people are those who have served a prison sentence, youth custody term, community service order, have a suspended sentence, or are on probation or on bail.

Excused people, as of right, are:

- those over 65 years of age
- doctors, nurses, midwives, chemists, dentists
- veterinary surgeons
- full-time serving officers of any of the armed forces
- active members of religious societies or orders
- MPs and officers of the House of Commons and House of Lords
- MEPs
- members of the NATIONAL ASSEMBLY FOR WALES.

> You *may* be excused from jury service if you have good reason, such as if you run your business alone. If your reason is not accepted, you do have a right of appeal to the court to which you have been summoned. You must give written notice of your appeal. The same applies if you wish to delay (or defer) jury service – for example, if you are pregnant or have already booked a holiday abroad. You may also make representations to the judge not to be made to sit on a lengthy case if you have a good reason.

DISCHARGE OF THE JURY

After the jury has given its verdict, the judge will discharge it. If it was a short case you may be asked to sit on another case, especially if you are still within the first two weeks of your jury service. When you have completed your jury service, you won't have to serve again within two years. If the case has been exceptionally long or difficult you may be let off (exempted) further jury service for a longer period.

OFFENCES AGAINST JURORS

It is an offence to corrupt or influence a juror by bribery or threats.
It is contempt of court to:

- use or threaten violence to a juror

- use threatening or abusive language in or near the courts.

Intimidation of jurors is becoming more frequent, and any threat should be reported as soon as possible to a court official or to the usher who is in charge of you and your fellow jurors.

MISCONDUCT OF JURORS

It is an offence for a juror to:

- allow themselves to be bribed

- agree to split the difference in reaching a verdict

- answer questions as to whether the verdict was supported by the evidence in the trial.

> You will be guilty of contempt of court if as a juror you obtain, disclose or solicit any details of statements, opinions, arguments or votes cast by members of a jury in the course of their deliberations in any legal proceedings.

There must be a new trial if the court considers that an injustice has been done and you and your fellow jurors cannot be recalled to change your verdict.

Arbitration

ACAS, THE ARBITRATION AND CONCILIATION SERVICE, will help to negotiate a settlement in employment disputes. ACAS is independent and can act as a go-between.

ACAS's telephone helplines answer over 760,000 calls a year from employers, employees and representatives. The main concerns of callers are:

- contractual issues
- discrimination
- discipline, dismissal and grievances
- family-friendly policies
- health and employment
- hours of work
- legal advice/sources of help
- pay
- redundancy and lay-offs
- trade unions.

Mediation

> Mediation is a way of resolving disputes which helps people to reach an agreement via an impartial third party – the mediator. The parties in dispute (not the mediator) decide the terms of any settlement. It is a problem-solving procedure which treats both parties equally, and they must want mutually to find a solution.

Mediators do not take sides, make judgements or give guidance. They develop interaction and build consensus between the parties. Mediations can be undertaken face to face or via a go-between (shuttle mediation). At the end of the process the parties very often agree on a settlement, which is not legally binding but can be made so if they wish.

COMMUNITY MEDIATION can involve anything from resolving conflicts between neighbours or among schoolchildren, to mediating between victims of crime and their offenders. It is used in workplace disputes and grievances against public sector service providers such as the health or education services.

There is both a voluntary and a professional mediation service, which operate to resolve disputes in many areas of the law before it becomes necessary to go to court. MEDIATION UK (a national charity) offers information on the nearest available service in your area. Many of the services are staffed by trained volunteers and are free.

National Probation Service (NPS)

THE NATIONAL PROBATION SERVICE FOR ENGLAND AND WALES was established by the *Criminal Justice and Court Services Act* in 2001 and comprises 42 probation services.

The NPS's role is to:

- administer punishment and rehabilitation of offenders in the community

- assess and manage risk and dangerousness

- prepare community supervision plan proposals

- intervene early to take young people away from crime

- enforce community orders and release licences

- provide courts with pre-trial services

- provide controlled environments for offenders on bail, community sentences and post-custody licences in approved probation hostels.

Ombudsmen

Ombudsmen exist to deal with complaints from ordinary citizens about certain public bodies or private-sector services. The service is provided free of charge. Each ombudsman scheme varies in the type of complaint it handles, the powers it has and the procedures that it uses.

These are some:

- Legal Services Ombudsman
- Health Service Ombudsman
- Police Complaints Authority
- Building Societies Ombudsman
- Pensions Ombudsman
- Broadcasting Standards Commission.

Victims and Witnesses

VICTIM SUPPORT

This is a nationwide scheme which provides advice and assistance to victims of crime. Anyone who reports a crime to the police should be contacted. Victim Support gives details of organisations such as self-help groups and counselling services, and will help victims deal with other agencies such as local council housing departments.

WITNESS SUPPORT

This is a scheme usually based at court. They arrange:

- to meet witnesses and take them to waiting areas separate from the general public where possible
- pre-trial visits to the court room so that witnesses can familiarise themselves with the surroundings
- help and support for witnesses during trials.

They cannot discuss the evidence or details of the case with witnesses.

CHILD WITNESSES

There is a **child witness officer** and special facilities for child witnesses in many crown courts. These include allowing them to give evidence from a private room via a video link with the court room.

Today's courts are trying to be much more user-friendly, but they can still be intimidating places and many of the organisations listed below can help you to navigate your way around the criminal justice system.

Organisations [i]

▶ **ARBITRATION AND CONCILIATION SERVICE (ACAS)**
Brandon House
180 Borough High Street
London SE1 1LW
National ACAS helpline: 08457 47 47 47
www.acas.org.uk

▶ **BROADCASTING STANDARDS COMMISSION**
7 The Sanctuary
London SW1P 3JS
Tel: 020 7808 1000
Fax: 020 7233 0397
bsc@bsc.org.uk
www.bsc.org.uk

▶ **COMMUNITY LEGAL SERVICE**
www.justask.org.uk *for the online Directory and legal information and advice.*
Tel: 0845 608 1122
(all calls charged at local rate)
minicom: 0845 609 6677
for your nearest CLS provider.
Approach a CLS General Help Point, such as a Citizens Advice Bureau, which offers advice and basic help.

▶ **COURT SERVICE CUSTOMER UNIT**
Southside
105 Victoria Street
London SW1 6QT
Tel: 020 7210 2269
Court Service disability helpline:
0800 358 3506
www.courtservice.gov.uk

▶ **DEPARTMENT FOR CONSTITUTIONAL AFFAIRS**
Selborne House
54–60 Victoria Street
London SW1E 6QW
Tel: 020 7210 8500
general.queries@dca.gsi.gov.uk
www.dca.gov.uk

▶ **FINANCIAL OMBUDSMAN SERVICE (formerly BANKING OMBUDSMAN)**
South Quay Plaza
183 Marsh Wall
London E14 9SR
Helpline: 0845 080 1800
www.financial-ombudsman.org.uk

▶ **GENERAL COUNCIL OF THE BAR**
3 Bedford Row
London WC1R 4DB
Tel: 020 7242 0082
Records Office: 020 7242 0934
Fax: 020 7831 9217
www.barcouncil.org.uk

▶ **HEALTH SERVICE OMBUDSMAN**
Millbank Tower
Millbank
London SW1P 4QP
Tel: 020 7217 4051
Fax: 020 7217 4000
ohsc.enquiries@ombudsman.gsi.gov.uk
www.ombudsman.org.uk

▶ **LAW SOCIETY**
113 Chancery Lane
London WC2A 1PL
Tel: 020 7242 1222
Fax: 020 7831 0344
info.services@lawsociety.org.uk
www.lawsoc.org.uk

▶ **LEGAL SERVICES OMBUDSMAN**

Office of the Legal Services Ombudsman
3rd Floor
Sunlight House
Quay Street
Manchester M3 3JZ

Lo Call No: 0845 601 0794
(Charged at local rates – available nationally)
Tel: 0161 839 7262
Fax: 0161 832 5446

DX 18569 Manchester 7
lso@olso.gsi.gov.uk
www.olso.org

▶ **MAGISTRATES' ASSOCIATION**

28 Fitzroy Square
London W1T 6DD

Tel: 020 7387 2353
Fax: 020 7383 4020
www.magistrates-association.org.uk

▶ **MEDIATION UK**

Alexander House
Telephone Avenue
Bristol BS1 4BS

Tel: 0117 904 6661
Fax: 0117 904 3331
enquiry@mediationuk.org.uk
www.mediationuk.org.uk

▶ **NATIONAL PROBATION SERVICE**

Home Office
Horseferry House
Dean Ryle Street
London SW1P 2AW

Tel: 020 7217 0659
Fax: 020 7217 0660
NPD.PublicEnquiry@
   homeoffice.gsi.gov.uk
www.probation.homeoffice.gov.uk

▶ **OFFICE FOR THE SUPERVISION
OF SOLICITORS**

Victoria Court
8 Dormer Place
Royal Leamington Spa
Warwickshire CV32 5AE

Public advice line: 0845 608 6565
enquiries@lawsociety.org.uk
www.oss.lawsociety.org.uk

Deals with complaints and regulation.

▶ **PENSIONS OMBUDSMAN**

11 Belgrave Road
London SW1V 1RB

Tel: 020 7834 9144
enquiries@pensions-ombudsman.org.uk
www.pensions-ombudsman.org.uk

▶ **POLICE COMPLAINTS AUTHORITY**

10 Great George Street
London SW1P 3AE

Tel: 020 7273 6450
info@pca.gov.uk
www.pca.gov.uk

PART TWO

A–Z of the Law

4 Accidents and injuries

Accidents and injuries can occur in a wide variety of ways and due to a wide variety of causes. The law and legal practice divide along a number of lines to cater for these, often within the general category of personal injury law. There are actions arising out of:

- road traffic accidents
- accidents at work
- highway trips.

Usually treated separately are:

- clinical negligence disputes which arise out of medical accidents
- injuries arising out of crimes, which are dealt with by the CRIMINAL INJURIES COMPENSATION AUTHORITY (see below).

This chapter is concerned with obtaining compensation for injuries. There are also a number of formal complaints processes that may be used – for example, the health services complaints system, together with the office of the HEALTH SERVICE OMBUDSMAN.

Whether compensation is payable

All injury cases tend to be dealt with in two stages:

- **liability** (whether the proposed defendant is at fault, or an amount is payable)
- **quantum** (how much compensation should be awarded).

So far as liability is concerned, the vast majority of personal injury cases are dealt with under what is known as the **tort (law) of negligence**. This holds that someone will be liable in damages (money) where:

- a duty of care is owed
- that duty has been breached
- that breach has caused loss.

It is for the claimant (the person claiming negligence) to prove each of these three elements.

DUTY OF CARE

In most cases, the question of whether **a duty of care is owed** is straight-forward. Road users owe a duty to other road users, employers owe a duty to employees, local authorities owe a duty to pedestrians and doctors owe a duty to patients.

BREACH OF DUTY

To decide whether the **duty has been breached** it is necessary to investigate whether the defendant behaved reasonably, judged in terms of other road users, authorities, employers or members of that profession. In clinical negligence cases, for example, other doctors or other experts in the field may have to be called to state whether a responsible body of professionals, holding the same qualifications, would have acted in the same way.

BREACH OF DUTY AS CAUSE OF INJURY

So far as **causation as loss** is concerned, this may often be straightforward. Did the breach of duty cause the injury? It is not difficult to show this in road traffic cases where it is clear how the injury occurred. In clinical negligence cases, however, and in other situations where there are two or more possible explanations or contributing causes to an injury (including the claimant), it can be difficult separating out who is responsible for what. This is usually a matter for expert advice.

Accidents at work

As well as liability under the **tort of negligence**, there may also be liability under specific acts of parliament in certain situations. Accidents at work are particularly ripe for this kind of claim, with liability arising under:

- *European Directives* (which are incorporated into English law)
- acts such as the *Factories Act 1961*
- the *Health and Safety at Work Act 1974.*

It is often easier to succeed in claims under these provisions than it is under the general law of tort because it is not always necessary to prove negligence; the simple failure to do something may be enough.

Slightly separate areas of liability include actions brought under:

- the *Fatal Accidents Act 1976*, which allows a dependant of the deceased to claim for a death caused by another's negligence
- the **Criminal Injuries Compensation Scheme**. This compensates injuries caused by:
  - crimes of violence
  - trespass on the railways
  - injuries sustained in the prevention or attempted prevention of crime.

Applications of this kind are made to the CRIMINAL INJURIES COMPENSATION AUTHORITY rather than to the courts.

Quantifying claims

Once liability is established, the question of **quantum** (quantifying a claim for damages) arises.

In cases where minor injuries are sustained and a full recovery is made this will be straightforward. In such cases it will usually be a question of obtaining medical advice as to the extent of the injury and the projected time to recover, and translating that into an amount of money using tables, guides and previously decided cases. All solicitors specialising in personal injury should have access to these guides and case law in their offices.

In cases where the injuries are more severe, quantifying a claim may be extremely difficult. It may require detailed medical evidence as to the extent of the injury, followed by advice on the impact such injuries may have on the victim's earning potential, and advice about levels of care as the victim gets older.

> Sometimes cases will be delayed because it is not clear exactly how someone is going to be affected by an injury and the extent to which they might recover.

Quantifying claims will also require detailed costing of equipment and other expenses that will be incurred over the time (sometimes years) that someone takes to recover. In some cases, of course, where a full recovery may never be made, this means the remainder of the claimant's lifetime. Any contributions from third parties, including welfare benefits and local authorities, may have to be taken into account. There are also **actuarial tables** designed to calculate the effect of obtaining the money early, in a lump sum that can be invested, as opposed to receiving it bit by bit over the years. The final figure awarded will reflect a combination of these detailed calculations versus the defendant's criticisms of those calculations, and the view taken by the judge or in negotiations between the paying and receiving parties.

Practicalities

TIME LIMITS

Personal injury cases, including clinical negligence cases, must be brought within:

- three years of the negligent act or omission
- or the date the claimant became aware they had sustained a significant injury due to the negligence of a third party (whichever is the later).

Detailed rules govern the calculation of the **date of knowledge**. There is a discretion to extend the time limit in certain cases, and where the claimant lacks mental capacity then the three-year clock does not start until they regain that capacity. Since children are automatically considered to lack capacity, this means that time does not begin to run until they reach 18 years old.

LEGAL AID

Legal aid is now largely unavailable in this area, with the exception of clinical negligence cases, where it is available via solicitors who have been approved by the LEGAL SERVICES COMMISSION.

> Most personal injury cases will now be funded by conditional fee agreements, more commonly known as **no win, no fee** agreements. The term is slightly misleading because depending on the precise nature of the agreement, some fee may well be payable.

BEFORE YOU SEE A SOLICITOR

There are a number of things that a solicitor or other legal adviser will need to see before being able to advise on any claim, and which they will ask a potential claiment to do. These include:

- ☑ retaining records of expenses incurred as a result of the accident (travelling to hospital, clothing or equipment purchased, lost wages, etc)
- ☑ obtaining a copy of medical records including GP notes
- ☑ finding out whether there has been any kind of criminal prosecution – for example, actions for dangerous driving in road traffic cases.

It is obvious from the above that this is a complex area of the law and specialist help is almost always required (see CHAPTER 1: FINDING AND MEETING YOUR LAWYER).

Organisations   **i**

▶ **ACTION FOR THE PROPER REGULATION OF PRIVATE HOSPITALS (APROP)**
Tel: 01932 849403

▶ **ACTION FOR VICTIMS OF MEDICAL ACCIDENTS**
44 High Street
Croydon CRO 1YB
Tel: 020 8686 8333
www.avma.co.uk

▶ **ACTION ON ELDER ABUSE**
Helpline: 0808 808 8141
aea@ace.org.uk
www.elderabuse.org
Provides information, advice, support and guidance on the prevention of abuse of older people.

▶ **ASSOCIATION OF PERSONAL INJURY LAWYERS (APIL)**
11 Castle Quay
Castle Boulevard
Nottingham NG7 1FW
Tel: 0115 958 0585
Fax: 0115 958 0885
mail@apil.com
www.apil.com

▶ **CHILD BRAIN INJURY TRUST**
The Radcliffe Infirmary
Woodstock Road
Oxford OX2 6HE
Tel: 01865 552467
info@cbituk.org
www.cbituk.org

▶ **COMPASSIONATE FRIENDS**
Helpline: 01179 539 639
www.compassionatefriends.org
www.tcf.org.uk
National self-help organisation offering support to bereaved parents and their families.

▶ **CRIMINAL INJURIES COMPENSATION AUTHORITY (CICA)**
Tay House
300 Bath Street
Glasgow G2 4LN
Tel: 0141 331 2726
Fax: 0141 331 2287
Advice line: 0800 358 3601
www.cica.gov.uk

▶ **CRUSE – BEREAVEMENT CARE**
126 Sheen Road
Richmond
Surrey TW9 1UR
Helpline: 0808 808 1677
www.crusebereavementcare.org.uk
Bereavement support, offers counselling, advice, information.

▶ **DEPRESSION ALLIANCE**
Tel: 020 7633 0557
www.depressionalliance.org
Provides support, advice, information and self-help groups for people suffering from depression.

▶ **GENERAL DENTAL COUNCIL**
37 Wimpole Street
London W1G 8DQ
Tel: 020 7887 3800
Fax: 020 7224 3294
www.gdc-uk.org

▶ **GENERAL MEDICAL COUNCIL**
178 Great Portland Street
London W1W 5JE
Tel: 020 7580 7642
www.gmc-uk.org

▶ **HEAD INJURY RE-EDUCATION (HIRE)**
Manor Farm House
Wendlebury
Bicester
Oxfordshire OX25 2PW
Tel: 01869 324 339
Fax: 01869 234 683
www.headinjuryreeducation.org.uk

▶ **HEADWAY**
4 King Edward Court
King Edward Street
Nottingham NG1 1EW
Tel: 0115 924 0800
Fax: 0115 958 4446
enquiries@headway.org.uk
www.headway.org.uk

▶ **LAW SOCIETY**
113 Chancery Lane
London WC2A 1PL
Tel: 020 7242 1222
Fax: 020 7831 0344
info.services@lawsociety.org.uk
www.lawsoc.org.uk

► **LEGAL SERVICES COMMISSION**
85 Gray's Inn Road
London WC1X 8TX
Tel: 020 7759 0000
www.legalservices.gov.uk
www.justask.org.uk

► **MOTOR ACCIDENT SOLICITORS
SOCIETY**
54 Baldwin Street
Bristol BS1 1QW
Tel: 0117 929 2560
Fax: 0117 904 7220
office@mass.org.uk
www.mass.org.uk

► **NURSING AND MIDWIFERY
COUNCIL (NMC)**
23 Portland Place
London W1B 1PZ
Tel: 020 7637 7181
www.nmc-uk.org

► **PREVENTION OF PROFESSIONAL
ABUSE NETWORK (POPAN)**
Wyvil Court
Wyvil Road
London SW8 2T6
Tel: 020 7622 6334
info@popan.org.uk
www.popan.org.uk
Provides advice, information and
support for people who have
experienced abuse from health-related
practitioners.

► **THE SAMARITANS**
Helpline: 08457 90 90 90
jo@samaritans.org
www.samaritans.org.uk
Crisis support

► **SPINAL INJURIES ASSOCIATION**
76 St James Lane
London N10 3DF
Tel: 0800 980 0501
www.spinal.co.uk

► **STILLBIRTH AND NEONATAL DEATH
(SANDS)**
28 Portland Place
London W1B 1LY
Helpline: 020 7436 5881
support@uk-sands.org
www.uk-sands.org
Telephone support, information,
befriending.

► **TRAUMA AFTERCARE TRUST (TACT)**
Buttfields
The Farthings
Withington
Gloucestershire GL54 5DF
Helpline: 01242 89 03 06
tact@tacthq.demon.co.uk
www.tacthq.demon.co.uk
Provides support, counselling and
referrals for treatment of those suffering
from post-traumatic stress disorder.

► **TUC**
Congress House
Great Russell Street
London WC1B 3LS
Tel: 020 7636 4030
info@tuc.org.uk
www.tuc.org.uk

**Specialist mediation services
for personal injury and clinical
negligence cases**

► **CENTRE FOR DISPUTE RESOLUTION**
1 Harbour Exchange Square
London E14 9GB
Tel: 020 7536 6000
Fax: 020 7536 6001
info@cedr.co.uk
www.cedr.co.uk

► **WORKITOUT**
63 Lincoln's Inn Fields
London WC2A 3LW
Tel: 020 7692 5502
www.workitout.co.uk

Further reading

Conditional fees leaflet (available from the
LAW SOCIETY)

5 Actions against the police

This chapter sets out to explain the course open to you if you have a complaint against the police and where to find the best advice.

Police Complaints Authority

The normal route for complaints against the police is via the POLICE COMPLAINTS system, but this has come in for much criticism over the past years. Although it is relatively simple and easy to use and has power to deal with a wider range of police misbehaviour than the courts, the investigation into the complaint is primarily carried out by the police themselves.

The purpose of the complaints procedure is to establish whether criminal or disciplinary charges should be brought against specific police officers. There is no power to award compensation. Serious cases will be investigated or supervised by the POLICE COMPLAINTS AUTHORITY but only a very small percentage of complaints have been upheld under the present system.

Although there are likely to be substantial changes to this system in the near future, these inadequacies often mean that the only avenue for ensuring that a complaint about police behaviour is transparently and independently investigated is by bringing a **civil claim for damages** against the police.

Civil claims for damages against the police

This area of the law is a mixture between civil and criminal proceedings. Often it will only be possible to assess the prospects of a civil case after the conclusion of the related criminal trial.

There are a number of different regional police forces in England and Wales. The chief officer of these areas is liable for any **civil wrongs** (see below) committed by police officers **in performance or purported performance** of their duties. Consequently any damages claim can be brought against the chief officer of police as well as any individual officer who has committed a civil wrong.

WHAT ARE CIVIL WRONGS?

If a person is:

- assaulted

- wrongly arrested

- maliciously prosecuted

then a civil wrong has been committed.

The law has always recognised that people are entitled to compensation if personal freedom is unjustifiably interfered with – for example, physical well-being or freedom of movement. In some circumstances police officers can be liable for negligence if they carry out any unjustified interference with property or other abuse of their power which harms a member of the public.

Some of these civil wrongs are obvious. A person is wrongly arrested if the police have no lawful power to detain them. But some are more restrictive in practice. For example, not everyone who is acquitted of a criminal prosecution is entitled to sue for malicious prosecution. On the contrary, such a claim will only be won if a claimant can prove, among other things, that the prosecution against them was started for a purpose other than to bring a suspected offender to justice.

WHICH COURT?

Claims against the police can be started in either the county court or the high court. This involves letting the defence (the police) know what allegations are being made against them and indicating the awards sought from the court as a result. However, if the damages claim is in excess of £50,000, or is complicated, it will be heard in the high court.

Time limits

Civil claims must be brought within strict time limits. This is generally six years from the time the act complained of was committed. Claims for personal injuries resulting from negligence or breach of duty by the police are subject to a three-year limitation period, although the court can extend this period.

> It is important that proceedings are started as soon as possible because it can take some years for a case to come to trial. The burden of proving the case is on the claimant, so delay, with its inevitable effects on memory and accuracy, is to be avoided if at all possible.

The **civil procedure rules** set out timetables and detailed procedures to be followed before a case will be listed for trial. These include the mutual exchange of any witness statements to be relied on at trial and the disclosure of relevant material from the police.

- Make sure every attempt has been made to obtain as much evidence as possible to support your case at a very early stage.

- Evidence can only be called at trial if the person making it has signed a statement outlining the evidence to be given and stating that they believe the facts are true.

- It is vital that all proper disclosure is obtained from the defence. Look out for officers' notebooks, crime report entries, records of police radio messages (CAD print-outs) and other documentation where the police might have recorded a version of the incident in question.

What are damages?

> Damages are awards of money designed to compensate for the wrongs done.

Where a jury is involved in deciding a claim they will assess the appropriate award of damages. The trial judge will give some guidance as to the levels of damages usually awarded in cases of this kind. Where no jury is involved the judge will decide the damages.

CIVIL JURIES

A civil jury consists of eight members of the public. They are usually drawn from the local crown court panel. Unlike a criminal jury, however, it does not bring in a simple verdict of guilty or not guilty. In cases of false imprisonment and malicious prosecution a jury can be called upon to decide any issues of disputed fact. To help them, the court will draft a series of factual questions for the jury to answer before the judge rules on who has legally won the case. Usually, the claimant has to prove that they have been wronged for their claim to succeed.

Funding and costs

Public funding (**legal aid**) is available for actions against the police. The granting of such funding is subject to strict financial and merit tests. Public funding will often be limited initially to obtaining a written advice from a lawyer to find:

- the likely prospects of the claim succeeding
- the likely damages that would be awarded compared to the costs of taking the case to trial.

Some lawyers will be prepared to take on cases on a **no win, no fee** basis. In other words, their legal fees would be paid out of any damages in the event of success. Obviously they will be choosy about which cases they are prepared to take on this basis.

Costs will be awarded against the party who loses the case.

Publicly funded parties have some protection against the extent to which such orders for costs can be made against them. Other litigants may have to pay not only the costs of their own lawyers but also those of the other side, should their claim not succeed. Those funding their claims on a **no win, no fee** basis will need insurance against having to pay defence costs.

Getting the best advice

Whatever the case, make sure that any lawyers you consult about proceedings of this sort have experience of the issues they raise. Because of the various areas of knowledge required in proceedings against the police, make sure they are competent to give you the best possible advice at all stages up to and including trial.

Ask them:

- whether they have a LEGAL SERVICES COMMISSION FRANCHISE for actions against the police? Although there are very competent solicitors in this field who do not hold such a franchise, this will give you some indication of the volume of cases handled.
- how many cases of this nature they have brought before?
- how many of these have gone to trial?
- are they members of the POLICE ACTIONS LAWYERS PRACTITIONERS GROUP?

Organisations

▶ **ADVICE UK (formerly THE FEDERATION OF INFORMATION AND ADVICE CENTRES)**
12th Floor
New London Bridge House
25 London Bridge Street
London SE1 9ST
Tel: 020 7407 4070
www.fiac.org.uk

▶ **LAW CENTRES FEDERATION**
Duchess House
18–19 Warren Street
London W1T 5LR
Tel: 020 7387 8570
Fax: 020 7387 8368
info@lawcentres.org.uk
www.lawcentres.org.uk

► **LAW SOCIETY**

113 Chancery Lane
London WC2A 1PL

Tel: 020 7242 1222
Fax: 020 7831 0344
info.services@lawsociety.org.uk
www.lawsoc.org.uk

► **LEGAL SERVICES COMMISSION**

85 Gray's Inn Road
London WC1X 8TX

Tel: 020 7759 0000
www.legalservices.gov.uk
www.justask.org.uk

► **NATIONAL ASSOCIATION OF CITIZENS ADVICE BUREAUX (NACAB)**

Myddelton House
115–123 Pentonville Road
London N1 9LZ

Tel: 020 7833 2181
www.nacab.org.uk

Adviceguide: the National Association of Citizens Advice Bureaux offers fact sheets covering issues such as employment, housing and taxation

www.adviceguide.org.uk

► **POLICE COMPLAINTS AUTHORITY**

10 Great George Street
London SW1P 3AE

Tel: 020 7273 6450
info@pca.gov.uk
www.pca.gov.uk

► **STATEWATCH**

PO Box 1516
London N16 OEW

Tel: 020 8802 1882
Fax: 020 8880 1727
info@statewatch.org
www.statewatch.org

6 Animals

This chapter aims to outline the law concerning:

- owners of dangerous wild animals and dogs
- the *Dangerous Dogs Act*
- the countryside and rights of way
- cruelty to animals
- pet passports.

Pet owners

Keepers of **dangerous wild animals** (as defined in the *Dangerous Wild Animals Act 1976*, such as many types of snake and lizards) must acquire a licence from their local authority. They must be over 18 years old. It is likely that the local authority will require a vet to inspect the premises and a fee will have to be paid.

Dog owners must ensure under the:

- *Control of Dogs Order 1992*, that their dog has a collar with identification (name and address) when in public places and on the roads
- *Dog (Fouling of Land) Act 1996*, that they clean up after their dog on designated land or face a fixed penalty fine or prosecution
- *Environmental Protection Act 1990*, that their pet does not cause unnecessary nuisance to neighbours by excessive barking or whining.

Dangerous dogs

Under the *Dangerous Dogs Act 1991* there are breeds such as pit-bull terriers and Japanese Tosa which may not be kept unless a certification of exemption has been granted for that particular animal. To be eligible for an exemption, adult dogs must be neutered, permanently identified, insured, kept secure, muzzled and on a lead when in a public place. There must be third party insurance in place in respect of death or injury to a person caused by a dog. The dogs cannot be bred or sold to others.

> Even if your dog is not one of these breeds but causes an accident or injures someone, you may be liable to pay compensation if you knew, or should have known, that your particular dog could be dangerous. To cover yourself, and others, you can obtain third-party insurance for your dog.

The police have the power to:

- prosecute the owner of any dog that is dangerously out of control in a public place.

Upon conviction, the court may make an order for the dog to be destroyed, or an order for the dog to be kept under control.

Dangerous does not mean only dangerous to humans. If the dog chases and injures farm animals or a family pet, that can also be dangerous under the law.

Countryside and rights of way

The *Countryside and Rights of Way Act 2000* covers areas of the law such as:

- access to the countryside
- public rights of way and road traffic
- nature conservation and wildlife protection.

PROTECTION OF WILD ANIMALS

It is an offence to:

- intentionally kill, injure or take any wild animal under protection

- have in your possession any live or dead wild animal specified in the *Wildlife and Countryside Act 1981*

- damage, destroy or obstruct access to any structure or place which any protected wild animal uses for shelter or protection

- intentionally cause unnecessary suffering to wild mammals by stabbing, burning, kicking, stoning, drowning or mutilation under the *Wild Mammals (Protection) Act 1996*.

These prohibited acts are criminal offences punishable by a maximum of six months imprisonment.

> Lawful shooting, hunting, coursing and pest control activity are exceptions to these offences in the 1996 Act, provided that the killing is carried out in a reasonably swift and humane manner. The government is presently addressing this issue.

If you kill a fatally disabled animal this is unlikely to be illegal, because if it is an act of mercy it is unlikely to cause unnecessary suffering.

Cruelty to animals

A prosecution can be brought against anyone who causes unnecessary suffering to an animal under the *Protection of Animals Act 1911*. It is an offence to:

- beat, kick or ill-treat an animal

- cause it terror or tease it to a point that infuriates it

- convey or carry any animal in such a manner as to cause it unnecessary suffering.

A person who abandons an animal, whether permanently or temporarily, in circumstances likely to cause the animal suffering is guilty of an offence of cruelty under the *Abandonment of Animals Act 1960*. For example, if you leave a dog in a locked car on a hot day, even for a short period, it may cause the dog unnecessary suffering through heat stress or even prove fatal. Most cruelty convictions involve dogs as victims.

If you suspect an animal is being abused, you should:

- inform the police or the RSPCA
- give them your name and address, in confidence, in case a prosecution may result and you can be a witness
- complain to your local police station. The police investigate formal complaints and may request the intervention of a vet or local RSPCA officer.

> If you try to rescue a neglected animal you may be breaking the law yourself. There is no automatic right to seize an animal. Only when an animal is in such a poor condition that it is actually 'suffering' can it be taken away from its owner, by the police, without permission.

Pet passports

It is now possible to take certain pets abroad to some countries and return with them to the UK without the need for quarantine for six months. Your pet will need the following, in this order:

- ☑ an electronic microchip inserted under the skin for identification purposes
- ☑ vaccination against rabies, with boosters if necessary
- ☑ blood tests at a recognised laboratory to show that no rabies is present.

It is best to ring your vet for all the details about time scales. Many animals may still have to be quarantined in order to prevent the spread of rabies to mainland Britain.

Organisations

▶ **ANIMAL DEFENDERS**
261 Goldhawk Road
London W12 9PE
Tel: 020 8846 9777
Fax: 020 8846 9712
info@animaldefenders.org.uk
www.animaldefenders.org.uk

▶ **BLUE CROSS HQ**
Shilton Road
Burford
Oxfordshire OX18 4PF
Tel: 01993 825500
Fax: 01993 823083
www.thebluecross.org.uk

▶ **BRITISH VETERINARY ASSOCIATION (BVA)**
7 Mansfield Street
London W1G 9NQ
Tel: 020 76366541
Fax: 020 74362970
bvahq@bva.co.uk
www.bva.co.uk

▶ **COMPASSION IN WORLD FARMING**
Charles House
5A Charles Street
Petersfield
Hampshire GU32 3EH
Tel: 01730 264208 / 268863
Fax: 01730 260791
compassion@ciwf.co.uk

▶ **EUROGROUP**
www.eurogroupanimalwelfare.org
Works towards the introduction, implementation and enforcement of legislation on the protection of animals in the European Union.

▶ **FRIENDS OF THE EARTH**
26–28 Underwood Street
London N1 7JQ
Tel: 020 7490 1555
Fax: 020 7490 0881
www.foe.co.uk

▶ **NATIONAL ANIMAL WELFARE TRUST**
Tyler's Way
Watford Bypass
Watford
Hertfordshire WD2 8HQ
Tel: 020 8950 8215 / 0177
Fax: 020 8420 4454
watford@nawt.org.uk
www.nawt.org.uk

▶ **NATIONAL CANINE DEFENCE LEAGUE (NCDL)**
17 Wakley Street
London EC1V 7RQ
Tel: 020 7837 0006
info@ncdl.org.uk
www.ncdl.org.uk

▶ **PETA EUROPE LTD**
PO Box 36668
London SE1 1WA
Tel: 020 7357 9229
Fax: 020 7357 0901
info@petauk.org
www.petauk.org

▶ **ROYAL SOCIETY FOR THE PROTECTION OF BIRDS (RSPB)**
UK Headquarters
The Lodge
Sandy
Bedfordshire SG19 2DL
Tel: 01767 680551
www.rspb.org.uk

▶ **RSPCA**
To report an act of cruelty, neglect or concern for the welfare of an animal, call the RSPCA's 24-hour national cruelty and advice line:
0870 55 55 999

▶ **VIVA!**
Vegetarians International Voice for Animals
8 York Court
Wilder Street
Bristol BS2 8QH
Tel: 0117 944 1000
Fax: 0845 456 8230
info@viva.org.uk
www.viva.org.uk

7 **Consumer law**

Consumers are protected by law from being cheated, harmed, misled or charged unreasonably by suppliers. However, as well as having rights, you also have obligations. Avoid pitfalls by reading contracts and small print carefully, shopping around, and complaining clearly and promptly when things go wrong. This chapter sets out the main areas of dispute and routes to take.

Complaining

Reporting a trader can be your best route for stopping illegal behaviour and/or getting compensation. Complain about the faulty goods or services to:

- the shop or person who gave you the service
- the trading standards department of your local authority
- the relevant trade association (if there is one)
- the ombudsman or industry regulator (if there is one).

Suing, through the small claims court, is another option (see CHAPTER 3: LAWYERS AND THE COURTS).

You can get legal advice from a solicitor, a Citizens Advice Bureau or a law centre (see CHAPTER 1: FINDING AND MEETING YOUR LAWYER).

Consumer rights

The main things that you can expect as a legal right when you are buying something from a shop, a market, on the internet, by phone or mail order is that it:

- accurately fits any description used to sell or package it
- corresponds to promotional samples
- is in good condition, works well and is safe to use
- is fit for the normal purpose for which it will be used.

> The product should be of **satisfactory quality**. Retailers may not use unfair or unreasonable terms to disadvantage you in written contracts – even lost in the small print – or in signs or notices displayed in shops.

What you can expect when you are getting a service from someone, is that:

- they will use reasonable skill and care – whether they are professionally qualified or not.

If you aren't satisfied with goods or services, check to see if a guarantee is included. This will usually, over a fixed time, cover replacement, parts or labour, and will tell you how to contact the manufacturer or the servicing firm. The guarantee cannot replace your normal, legal rights.

However, you don't have to complain to the manufacturer. Your contract (even if it wasn't in writing) when you agreed to buy was with the retailer or supplier, so first promptly complain to them. You should get:

- a full refund
- money compensation (usually to cover repairs)
- or a free repair or replacement.

> You don't have to accept a credit note, free repair or replacement item, unless you agree to them.

Retailer rights

When you enter into a contract with a retailer it is legally binding – even if you have not fully understood it, you *may not* be protected. Always read written contracts before you sign and never sign a blank or half-completed form.

If you have had a reasonable length of time to discover problems and did not complain, then you can lose your right to a full refund. However, defining what is a **reasonable** length of time to discover faults is decided in each case by the courts.

> Once a fault emerges which existed when the item was bought, you have a time limit of six years in which to complain. If the fault develops within six months of buying then it is automatically accepted that the defect was already there.

If a defect appears within two years (one year, if what you bought was second-hand) you can expect the seller to replace or repair the article or, if this is impossible, you have the right to compensation or a refund.

Of course, the fault must not have been caused by you or your inappropriate use of the item. So if you don't follow safety instructions or try to use something in a way or for a purpose for which it wasn't designed, you may not have a case – nor do you if you simply change your mind.

Even if you consider goods or services to be unsatisfactory, once you have accepted them (eg, eaten a meal or taken something away from a shop) you shouldn't refuse to pay or cancel payment – you may be sued yourself, or the supplier may hold on to any of your property in their possession. You should make your dissatisfaction clear at the time and put into writing that you are only agreeing to pay under protest.

If you haven't agreed a final price for a service beforehand and think the final charge is exorbitant, you are still obliged to pay a reasonable charge for the work.

Putting it in writing

A trader cannot and does not take away your legal rights when he displays a disclaimer in writing. For example, your basic right to return something if it is faulty is not limited by a notice saying that there is a time limit for refunds.

Even though a written contract does not have to be standardised, it is illegal to include terms that might mislead you – for example, by falsifying details about the seller or what is being sold. It is also illegal (and un-enforceable) to deny liability for causing death or injury.

When the contract is a standard, non-negotiable one (such as a car-hire form) it must be fair and clear. Even if you sign without having understood, you are still protected if you have been put at a disadvantage by the contract – for example, if the wording is baffling or misleading. Also, the seller must not give you too little or inadequate information about a product so that it cannot be used safely or satisfactorily.

Pricing and paying

NEW GOODS

The seller must display the full retail price. Packaged goods should show the unit price as well as the sale price, so that you can compare prices.

SALE OR SECOND-HAND GOODS

If an item is in a sale, unless it is clearly marked as substandard (eg, as a second or imperfect), you can expect what you buy to be of the same quality as an equal, non-sale item. And you have the same rights to return and compensation if it is of **unsatisfactory quality**. The same applies to second-hand goods – any faults should be pointed out to you.

SHODDY WORKMANSHIP

You have the right to expect that a supplier's work will be done with care and skill, even if they are not a professional. If something is badly done, you may expect compensation or to reduce the amount you pay for the job. If the work has not been finished within a reasonable/agreed time, or done so badly that it must be put right, then you can get outside quotations and charge the original contractor. However, you can only do this if they refuse to, or are unable to, finish or put right their original work and any damage caused by them. If the job is so badly done that it is unusable, then you can refuse to pay at all.

Protecting your rights

CREDIT CARDS

If you pay between £100 and £30,000 by credit card (not debit card) and you have a problem with what you bought, you may get compensation directly from the credit card company. This can help when normal consumer law can be inadequate – for example, when a firm goes bankrupt before you receive your goods, the credit card company can compensate you whereas the supplier may no longer have the funds to do so. However, credit card transactions abroad (or when buying over the internet) may not be covered.

COVERING YOURSELF

When you are getting a service without a standard contract you should still put things in writing, detailing:

☑ what you expect them to do

☑ for what (agreed) price

☑ over what, reasonable, time scale

☑ the quality and type of materials to be used.

> Even if – as in building work – it may be impossible to establish the final cost of the work at the outset, you are still entitled to an estimated bill and to be charged only what is reasonable for the actual service you receive.

SIGHT UNSEEN

For goods bought through a catalogue, by phone or over the internet you should get, and keep, as much information as you can about the name and address of the retailer, the description or picture of the item you're buying and your method of payment. And, if you are paying by credit card, you should make sure that the retailer has an encryption facility, which will keep your card details secure. If the things that you order do not arrive within 30 days then you have the right to cancel the order and receive your money back.

There is new protection in most cases when buying sight unseen, over the internet, or by mail order or phone. Where payment is made before delivery, the contract is unenforceable unless the seller gives you full details about themselves and the transaction: name, address and delivery charges. You also have a seven-day cooling-off period to withdraw from the contract in writing.

Protection from harm

SAFETY

Since 1994 it has been law that all suppliers of new or second-hand consumer goods must make sure that they are safe, with relevant safety instructions. Furniture and toys are covered by specific laws about the materials used in their manufacture – all upholstered furniture must be fire retardant and all toys sold in the EU are covered by the **CE mark**, which guarantees that they will conform to agreed safety regulations.

If you or your possessions (eg, clothes burned by a faulty iron) have been harmed by something you bought, then you have a claim against the manufacturer. You will have to prove that a defect in the product (or inadequate instructions) made it unsafe. Of course, if the defect occurred within six months of purchase, it is accepted to be the manufacturer's responsibility. To get compensation from the manufacturer, the damage caused must be over £275.

> If the faulty goods caused personal injury then you may be able to claim for time off work, pain and suffering, or specialist medical care. In personal injury cases it is important to get specialist legal advice (see CHAPTER 4: ACCIDENTS AND INJURIES).

FOOD

As with all other consumer items, food must be honestly labelled and of a quality you would reasonably expect for the price paid. It must also be fit to eat and should not make you ill – if it does, the supplier should be reported to the local environmental health officer.

> By law, all genetically modified ingredients in food must be disclosed.

Pressure selling

HOLIDAY TIMESHARES

You have a 14-day **cooling-off period** during which you can back out of the agreement, with no penalties attached and any money paid up-front to be returned. It is a criminal offence not to inform you of this right to cancel and to include a cancellation form with the contract. To be protected, the agreement must be signed in the UK, or the contract should be subject to the laws of the UK. Check first.

CREDIT AGREEMENTS AND OTHER CONTRACTS

Time to reflect and change your mind is also your right when you sign a credit agreement *off* the business premises of a creditor or trader. In this case, you will have five days to think again. If you sign at home, provided you haven't specifically invited the salesperson to call, the cooling-off period increases to seven days.

> If you sign a credit agreement *on* the retailer's/creditor's business premises and they sign at the same time then you are immediately bound by the contract.

Professional services

You can expect doctors, dentists, solicitors, architects, accountants, survey-ors, etc to provide a service using their expertise and training with reason-able care and skill. If they haven't given you a professional service then you can claim compensation. Professionals will be personally insured against liability. However, if you are not satisfied using this route, you can complain to their supervising professional body.

For example, if you want to complain about treatment by the NHS, and have not received satisfaction at local level, you can go to:

- a COMMUNITY HEALTH COUNCIL (independent patient watchdog)

- the OMBUDSMAN (also independent and free).

Private medicine is regulated, at national level, by the GENERAL MEDICAL COUNCIL. But you may have to consult a specialist solicitor (see CHAPTER 3: LAWYERS AND THE COURTS and CHAPTER 4: ACCIDENTS AND INJURIES).

Estate agents

Estate agents are employed by the seller of a property and therefore must act on their behalf. For example, they must always pass on the highest offer and they must disclose any interest they have themselves (eg, as mortgage arrangers). You should read and understand the contract you sign with an estate agent, and make clear any special services you expect and the time scale involved. Check:

- **?** if they are offering sole, joint or multiple agency

- **?** the commission percentage

- **?** what is included in this price

- **?** that commission isn't just dependent upon the introduction of a ready, willing and able purchaser but upon finalising the sale.

> If an estate agent has not acted with care on your behalf, or has knowingly misled you or failed to disclose important information which might have influenced a sale then you can complain to their association, the NATIONAL ASSOCIATION OF ESTATE AGENTS.

The OFFICE OF FAIR TRADING can ban an estate agent if they do not:

- keep customer's money in a separate deposit account

- insure customer's money

- make clear to the seller their charges before they agree to a contract

- disclose any financial interest they have in a property, to both buyers and sellers.

Travel agents/tour operators

When booking your holiday or on arrival:

- you should not be misled by the description or photographs in the brochure

- anything you agreed in writing on the confirmation form must be provided

- if your holiday package is swapped for another package, even if it is equivalent, they must inform you beforehand and let you cancel, with a full refund

- the facilities specifically described must be provided to a standard you can reasonably expect for the price and type of holiday you have booked.

COMPLAINTS

If your holiday goes wrong, your claim is against the tour operator. If you have problems with your holiday:

- quickly and clearly complain to the local representative

- you don't have to accept what the local representative offers and if it isn't an acceptable alternative you can find your own accommodation – as long as it is of around the same standard as the holiday you bought

- take photographs and written statements from other holidaymakers to support your case if you intend to ask for compensation when you get home

- get compensation by using the small claims court (see CHAPTER 3:

LAWYERS AND THE COURTS) or **ASSOCIATION OF BRITISH TRAVEL AGENTS (ABTA)** arbitration (for ABTA member firms).

If the brochure is at fault you can also approach your local **TRADING STANDARDS** officer.

STRANDED

All tour organisers must cover themselves so they will be able to get you home.

If the holiday company goes bust and it is a member of ABTA, you should get back any money you paid in advance (see also CHAPTER 20: INTERNATIONAL ISSUES).

Consumer law is one area where you have significant rights and you may be able to act for yourself. If in doubt, contact an advice agency, listed opposite.

Organisations   ⓘ

▶ **ASSOCIATION OF BRITISH TRAVEL AGENTS (ABTA)**
68–71 Newman Street
London W1T 3AH
Tel: 020 7637 2444
Fax: 020 7637 0713
www.abtanet.com

▶ **BRITISH AND IRISH OMBUDSMAN ASSOCIATION (BIOA)**
www.bioa.org.uk
Ombudsmen are an independent and impartial means of resolving certain disputes outside the courts. They cover various public and private bodies and look into matters after a complaint has been made to the relevant body. This site lists the ombudsmen and other complaint-handling bodies.

▶ **CHARTERED INSTITUTE OF ARBITRATORS**
International Arbitration Centre
12 Bloomsbury Square
London WC1A 2LP
Tel: 020 7421 7444
Fax: 020 7404 4023
info@arbitrators.org
www.arbitrators.org

▶ **CONSUMERS' ASSOCIATION**
2 Marylebone Road
London NW1 4DF
Tel: 020 7770 7062 / 7373

▶ **GENERAL MEDICAL COUNCIL**
178 Great Portland Street
London W1W 5JE
Tel: 020 7580 7642
www.gmc-uk.org

▶ **NATIONAL ASSOCIATION OF CITIZENS ADVICE BUREAUX (NACAB)**
Myddelton House
115–123 Pentonville Road
London N1 9LZ
www.nacab.org.uk
Adviceguide: the National Association of Citizens Advice Bureaux offers fact sheets covering issues such as employment, housing and taxation
www.adviceguide.org.uk

▶ **NATIONAL ASSOCIATION OF ESTATE AGENTS (NAEA)**
Arbon House
21 Jury Street
Warwick CV34 4EH
Tel: 01926 496800
Fax: 01926 400953
info@naea.co.uk
www.naea.co.uk

▶ **NATIONAL CONSUMER COUNCIL**
20 Grosvenor Gardens
London SW1W 0DH
Tel: 020 7730 3469
Fax: 020 7730 0191
info@ncc.org.uk
www.ncc.org.uk

▶ **OFFICE OF FAIR TRADING**
Fleetbank House
2–6 Salisbury Square
London EC4Y 8JX
www.oft.gov.uk
For general enquiries and guidance on who to contact for consumer complaints:
Public Liaison Unit: 08457 22 44 99
enquiries@oft.gsi.gov.uk

▶ **TRADING STANDARDS**
www.tradingstandards.gov.uk

8 Criminal law

The criminal law is a huge area with thousands of offences from murder to drunk and disorderly – far too many to list here. There are also hundreds of summary only offences including such things as not having a television licence, common assault, careless driving or criminal damage up to a value of £5000.

This chapter sets out what happens when a crime is investigated, where cases are tried and how to get help if you are:

- accused of a crime
- a victim of crime
- a witness to a crime.

Investigation and the start of criminal proceedings

Most crimes are investigated by the local police force in the area where the crime occurs. Usually uniformed police officers will turn up when a member of the public alleges a crime has happened – for example, in a 999 call – and they may arrest people there and then. If the matter requires further investigation they will hand it over to the local branch of the CRIMINAL INVESTIGATION DEPARTMENT (CID).

For serious and organised crime there are specialist squads, like the VICE SQUAD, which operate across larger areas, gathering intelligence and evidence against people believed to be committing crime, and then making arrests.

A police officer does not have to have enough evidence to get a conviction in order to make an arrest – they can arrest and then carry on looking for more evidence – but they must have at least a **reasonable suspicion** before they arrest, more than just a hunch.

Police interviews and identification parades

In most cases someone accused of a crime will be interviewed by police officers. This may not be done for simple offences such as being drunk and disorderly or minor public order offences such as causing harassment, alarm or distress, especially if the evidence just consists of what the arresting police officer saw. Interviews are now required to be tape-recorded and suspects and their lawyers can demand a copy of the tape afterwards.

Everyone is entitled to free legal advice (in private) at the police station and before a police interview. The police are obliged to call a solicitor – either selected by the suspect or from a rota of local solicitors who act under a **duty solicitors scheme.**

Unless the case is very simple and you can get the advice you need in a private telephone call with the solicitor, your solicitor should attend in person or send a member of staff who has been trained in dealing with interviews (an accredited representative).

You are entitled to have the solicitor sit in on the police interview and you can get further advice in private during the interview if you want. The officers will temporarily stop the interview to allow this.

If you are asked to attend an **identification parade** (a line-up) you are entitled to take legal advice and to have your solicitor present to check that the correct procedures are followed. In future, most identification parades will use video footage of the person suspected of the crime and some people of similar appearance, instead of the traditional line-up.

Other rights of suspects held by the police

PHONE CALLS

As well as the right to call a lawyer there is a right to have someone informed of your arrest. It doesn't have to be by phone and you are entitled to have them informed at public expense, which might involve a uniformed officer knocking on their door. If the first person cannot be contacted you can give two alternative names, and the custody officer has discretion to allow yet further names to be tried if necessary.

SERIOUS ARRESTABLE OFFENCES

The right to have someone informed of your arrest can only be denied, for up to 36 hours, if you have been arrested for a **serious arrestable offence**, such as murder, manslaughter, rape or serious drugs offences. The right can only be delayed if there is a danger of:

- injury to someone
- interference with witnesses
- alerting other people involved in the offence
- hindrance to recovering property involved in the offence.

TIME LIMITS ON DETENTION

Once the first six hours of police detention are up, further detention has to be authorised by a police inspector who is not directly involved in the investigation, and after that reviewed at least every nine hours. At each review a person can only be kept in custody if:

- the officer is satisfied that it is necessary to get evidence by questioning in an interview
- or to secure or preserve other evidence by keeping the person in custody while the investigation continues.

If that is not the case then the suspect has to be charged or released.

Once the overall time limit of 24 hours is up, an officer of superintendent rank or above can authorise an extra 12 hours for the same reasons, but only if the investigation has been proceeding efficiently and if the offence being investigated is a **serious arrestable offence**. Otherwise a suspect has to be released or charged, unless an application is made to the magistrates' court for further detention – up to 96 hours. This can only be done if the investigation is so complicated that the court can be persuaded that extra time is justified.

The rules in terrorist cases allow for longer periods of detention and a longer delay in allowing access to a lawyer and notification of the arrest.

OTHER RIGHTS OF POLICE DETAINEES

These are set out in a **code of practice** under the *Police and Criminal Evidence Act* and cover, amongst others:

- a right to have a consular official notified if you are a non-citizen
- a right to an interpreter free of charge
- a right to at least two light meals and one main meal in every 24 hours, and adequate drinks at mealtimes and in between – as far as practicable, meals should meet special dietary and religious needs
- access to toilet and washing facilities
- replacement clothing of reasonable standard and cleanliness if a suspect's clothing has had to be taken away
- medical attention
- special protections for juveniles and those with mental illness or handicap – this includes having an appropriate adult, family, friend or approved social worker, present at interviews.

Charging

If the police decide that someone ought to be prosecuted they will usually charge the person at the police station sometime after interviewing them. When a person is charged a police officer completes a **charge sheet**. This document lists the offence or offences of which they are accused. The person is charged by the officer formally reading out the offence to the accused person and asking them if they have any reply. After charge the suspect is referred to as a **defendant** and will be given a date for the first court appearance in the case. They may be bailed or remanded in custody.

Duty solicitors

If you do not have a solicitor in mind and choose a duty solicitor to advise you in the police station, or if at the first court hearing you use the **court duty solicitor**, you do not have to stick with that lawyer for the whole of your case. You may find that the duty solicitor is very good and decide to stay with them. Many fine solicitors from high-quality firms are on the duty rotas, but so are solicitors who may not do the best possible job. You can instruct a different solicitor of your own choice to advise and represent you. If you wish to do this, and you are applying for legal aid, then *you should name the solicitor you wish to take the case on the legal aid application form,* and not the duty solicitor if you no longer want them. (See CHAPTER 1: FINDING AND MEETING YOUR LAWYER.)

Legal aid

Legal aid is available for most criminal cases but in some minor matters – for example, motoring – where the case is very simple and there is no risk of imprisonment, it may not be granted.

Legal aid is no longer means-tested before being granted, but if a case is sent up to the crown court for trial then the court will require a statement of means. Subject to your means, if you are convicted you may be required to pay a contribution to the costs (see CHAPTER 2: LEGAL AID).

If you can afford it, you are perfectly entitled to pay a lawyer privately to represent you in a criminal case. Remember to check how much they charge and get an indication of how much work they propose to do. Ask for regular updates on what costs they have run up.

Solicitors and barristers

The distinction between these two types of lawyer is gradually changing. Most solicitors in criminal law give initial advice – at the police station, at the magistrates' court or when the client comes to their office – they prepare cases, collect evidence and represent clients in the magistrates' courts. Some now practise as **higher court advocates**, but usually when a case is sent to the crown court they send a **brief** – a file with details of the case – to a barrister, who will defend the client at the trial or present the mitigating circumstances in a plea of guilty.

The prosecution in the crown court and court of appeal will usually instruct a barrister to present their side of the case too.

> The essential thing is to be represented by a lawyer who specialises in crime and is experienced enough to deal with your case.

Public defenders – the Criminal Defence Service

In some areas there are lawyers directly employed by the CRIMINAL DEFENCE SERVICE – the crime part of the LEGAL SERVICES COMMISSION which handles legal aid. Currently these are experimental schemes similar to the American idea of a public defender. You do not have to take one of these lawyers, but can choose a solicitor from a private firm instead. The first surveys have shown less satisfied customers than those using ordinary solicitors.

Crown Prosecution Service

After charging, the police send a case file to the CROWN PROSECUTION SERVICE (CPS), which acts as **prosecuting solicitor**. The CPS decides whether a prosecution should go ahead and takes the case through the courts. They may decide to alter the charge(s) from the one(s) initially decided on by the police. If the case goes to the crown court they will instruct a barrister (counsel) to present the case for the crown. If the case is dealt with only in the magistrates' court a CPS lawyer will usually act as prosecutor.

If the police are not sure whether someone ought to be charged they may consult the CPS, who assess if the case has a reasonable chance of success and if the prosecution is in the public interest. Meanwhile the suspect will be bailed to return to the police station at a future date.

If the CPS advise *not* to proceed, the police write to the suspect telling them they do not need to attend. If the case is to go ahead then the suspect will be charged when they return to the police station.

Summons

This is an alternative way to charging to start a criminal case. The police submit a request to the magistrates' court, which then issues a summons requiring the defendant to attend court on a particular day. This is called **laying an information**. This procedure is often used in road traffic cases. Private individuals can also start cases by attending the magistrates' court and **swearing an information** (see **private prosecutions** below).

Other investigating bodies

CUSTOMS AND EXCISE investigates and prosecutes crimes of smuggling, money laundering and VAT fraud.

INLAND REVENUE prosecutes tax offences and frauds.

LOCAL TRADING STANDARDS DEPARTMENTS prosecute trading offences such as weights and measures, selling in breach of regulations, defective or dangerous goods, fake and pirated goods.

LOCAL ENVIRONMENTAL HEALTH DEPARTMENTS prosecute noise nuisance, food hygiene offences and similar matters.

LOCAL HOUSING DEPARTMENTS prosecute landlords for criminal offences such as unlawful eviction of tenants.

HEALTH AND SAFETY EXECUTIVE investigates and prosecutes crimes arising out accidents in the workplace.

FEDERATION AGAINST COPYRIGHT THEFT prosecutes offences in relation to fake and pirated goods.

Private prosecutions

> Private individuals can start prosecutions themselves, but the CPS has the power to take over such cases and may decide not to pursue the prosecution – either for lack of evidence or because it is not thought to be in the public interest.

There are very few private prosecutions, but the power has sometimes been used where victims or their families believe that the authorities have wrongly failed to prosecute. A notable example was the case taken by the parents of Stephen Lawrence; another concerned a rape victim who successfully prosecuted her assailant. Some private prosecutions take place for minor criminal offences such as a neighbour causing noise nuisance, or minor assaults where the police have declined to intervene.

Bail

In most cases there is a right to **bail** both after charge and after each court hearing. Most defendants in criminal cases are granted bail, except in rape and homicide (murder or manslaughter) cases if the person concerned has a previous conviction for such an offence.

Bail in all cases can be refused if the court decides there are substantial grounds for believing that the defendant will:

- not turn up at court

- commit further offences if given bail

- interfere with witnesses if given bail.

Bail may be unconditional – just a promise to turn up – or may be granted with conditions. Conditions may include:

- promising to sleep each night at a named address

- reporting to a police station at regular intervals

- handing passports to the police

- staying out of a particular area

- not contacting named people (eg, victims or witnesses).

In cases where the court fears that the accused may not turn up, then bail will sometimes only be given on condition that the court has:

- a **surety** – a promise from a reputable person to pay a set sum of money to the court if the accused does not turn up; no money is actually paid into court when bail is granted

- or a **security** – a fixed sum of money actually paid into court before a person is released.

> Not turning up to court if on bail is a separate offence for which the accused can be sent to prison or fined. If a person does not stick to their bail conditions they can be arrested and brought back to court where the court can take away their bail and put them in custody.

Courts and sentencing

MAGISTRATES' COURTS

Magistrates' courts sit with either three magistrates who are not legally qualified but have a qualified clerk to help them with the law, or in some urban areas with a district judge who sits alone and is a qualified lawyer.

SENTENCING IN THE MAGISTRATES' COURT

Magistrates can impose up to six months imprisonment, or 12 months where the offence concerned allows it. If they feel their powers of sentence are not enough (if they are told after conviction that someone has a lot of previous convictions) then they can send the case to the crown court for sentence. This is called a **committal for sentence**. They can also impose community punishments such as a **community rehabilitation order**. The court can order that compensation to victims, fines and court costs be awarded and paid in fixed instalments. Failure to pay can be punished by prison sentences.

SUMMARY OFFENCES

These are offences that can only be heard in the magistrates' court. They usually start and finish there, unless there is an appeal. The highest penalties for these are usually fines or short prison sentences.

TRIABLE-EITHER-WAY OFFENCES

These can be dealt with either in the magistrates' court or the crown court, and include a lot of common offences such as:

- theft

- obtaining property by deception

- assault occasioning actual bodily harm.

The defendant is asked whether or not they intend to plead guilty, then the magistrates, after a summary of the prosecution case, will decide if it is too serious a matter for their court. If so, they will send it to the crown court for trial. If not, they will offer to try it in the magistrates' court. In that situation, the defendant can still choose to go to the crown court – this is called **electing jury trial**.

A **committal hearing** is where the defence can argue that there is insufficient evidence to send the case for trial.

Racial hatred is a criminal offence. Either:

- using threatening, abusive or insulting words or behaviour or displays or

- possessing, publishing, distributing or performing racially inflammatory material

with the intention of stirring up racial hatred is an offence under the law. It cannot be prosecuted if the offences occur in a dwelling but it can be if they can be heard or seen from that dwelling.

INDICTABLE OFFENCES

These are the more serious offences – murder, manslaughter, rape, robbery, causing grievous bodily harm with intent. The magistrates just send these cases straight to the crown court and merely deal with the question of bail. The crown court then has a hearing to set a timetable for the evidence to be served (in the form of statements from witnesses) and for preparation for trial.

YOUTH COURT

This is a special form of magistrates' court. It often sits in a different building with a separate entrance. The hearing and language are less formal. Defendants usually sit next to their lawyer (with their parents, who are encouraged to attend) and are called by their first name.

After a finding of guilt, this court has the power to make a wide range of orders for:

- a fine
- detention in a YOUNG OFFENDERS' INSTITUTION
- supervision by the local social services department
- attendance at a special centre for a fixed number of days
- referral to a YOUTH OFFENDER PANEL, which will decide on a programme of rehabilitation.

CROWN COURT

This is the typical TV criminal court, with wigs and gowns, judge, barristers and a jury of 12 citizens deciding on guilt or innocence.

Only about 5 per cent of cases are tried in the crown court and most never involve a jury because the defendant pleads guilty.

At trials the evidence is given in the form of live witnesses and read-out statements, which are used where there is no disagreement about a witness's evidence. The judge summarises the evidence and tells the jury the legal framework for their decision. They then go to a private area to decide on a verdict.

PRE-SENTENCE REPORT

After someone pleads guilty or is found guilty, the case will often be adjourned for the probation service to compile a report about the offender – looking at their history and personal circumstances, and assessing the risk of further offences. At the sentencing hearing the defence lawyer will make a speech in **mitigation** – making points to try to reduce the sentence – and the judge then decides the sentence to be imposed.

PLEA-BARGAINING

Sometimes the prosecution will offer a **deal** whereby a defendant pleads guilty to some charges in return for others being dropped. Judges are not supposed to get involved by letting people know in advance what this will mean for the sentence.

> If you are a defendant you should think very carefully before getting involved in a deal – *if you plead guilty to something it is almost impossible to withdraw that plea afterwards.* If you are innocent you should not plead guilty as part of a deal just because you are told that it is 'a good deal' and if you fight the case you may be found guilty of a more serious charge. If you are innocent it is almost always better to plead not guilty.

SENTENCING IN THE CROWN COURT

The crown court can pass a wide variety of sentences up to and including life imprisonment – the maximum sentence for each offence is mainly set by statute. Orders may also be made for mentally ill offenders to be sent to hospital. Drug users may be supervised by the probation service while attending rehabilitation projects, or put on a drug-testing and treatment order. However, if they are found to be still taking drugs they can be brought back to court and resentenced.

CONFISCATION

In addition to sentencing, the crown court has wide powers to confiscate items used in crime and to confiscate the profits of serious crime such as drug trafficking. The prosecuting authorities can get orders from the court against a suspect freezing assets such as bank accounts and preventing property being sold pending trial, so as to make money available for confiscation if there is a conviction.

Appeals against conviction

Convictions and sentences from the magistrates' court can be appealed to:

- the crown court, where the whole case is heard again by a judge and two magistrates, instead of a jury
- to the high court, where there is a point of law to be clarified rather than an argument purely about who is telling the truth.

There is a time limit of 21 days for filing the forms applying for an appeal.

APPEALS FROM CROWN COURT CASES

These are taken to the **court of appeal (criminal division)**. Both conviction and sentence can be appealed. There is a time limit of 28 days. For appeals against conviction time runs from the date of the conviction, *not* from the date of the sentencing hearing if that is later.

Grounds of appeal The lawyer who has conducted the trial will usually be able to give advice on whether there are good grounds for an appeal and draft the necessary documents. If not, then obtain a second opinion from a solicitor or the **registrar of criminal appeal** at the **criminal appeals office**.

All such appeals go first to a high court judge (the **single judge** stage) whose task is to sift out weak cases. If that judge does not grant permission (**leave**) to appeal then the application will fail unless an application to renew is sent to the court of appeal. This will then result in a short hearing before the court of appeal itself to look again at whether the case should go forward or not.

> Legal aid is not generally available once permission to appeal has
> been refused by the single judge, but many barristers will act for free
> (**pro bono**) at this stage if they think that the arguments are good
> enough to get permission to appeal from the court of appeal itself.
> The court can then grant legal aid for the full appeal.

Most appeals from the crown court do not succeed and the court of appeal
is generally felt to be reluctant to interfere unless there is some strong
reason to do so. The current legal test is that they have to conclude that the
conviction was **unsafe**. This usually means that there was some serious legal
error in the proceedings, such as:

- a mistake by the judge in his explanation of the law to the jury

- some evidence was wrongly introduced or has come to light since the
  conviction and may well have affected the result.

Merely saying the jury got it wrong does not provide a winnable appeal.

If new evidence comes to light or some serious fault in the original conviction is found then there can be an application for an appeal even outside
the time limits, but again it is difficult to persuade the court of appeal to
grant such applications.

CRIMINAL CASES REVIEW COMMISSION (CCRC)

This body reviews convictions on application from convicted people and
has the power to refer cases to the court of appeal (or the crown court if the
conviction was by magistrates). It will only do so if its members find that
there is a real prospect of a successful appeal. Usually it will not act until
after there has been an unsuccessful application to appeal in the normal
way. It has the power to investigate cases but does not have very large
resources to do so, and although it has some staff it generally has to ask
police forces to conduct enquiries for it. There is some legal aid provision for
getting help from a solicitor in making an application to the commission.

Victims and witnesses

(See CHAPTER 3: LAWYERS AND THE COURTS.)

VICTIM SUPPORT

This is a nationwide scheme which provides advice and assistance to victims of crime.

WITNESS SUPPORT

This is a scheme usually based at a court. They provide help and support for witnesses during trials but cannot discuss the evidence itself with witnesses.

SPECIAL MEASURES

If witnesses have difficulty giving evidence for any reason (fear, physical disability, age), courts have the power to implement a wide range of special measures, including signing, interpreters, screens to hide frightened witnesses, induction loops and physical rearrangement of the court room. Young or vulnerable witnesses may be allowed to give their evidence via a video link instead of coming into court.

> ### WITNESS INTIMIDATION
>
> Any attempts to stop witnesses giving evidence should be reported to the police who can arrest anyone involved in such activities for crimes such as **witness intimidation** or **acts tending to pervert the course of justice**.

CRIMINAL INJURIES COMPENSATION

This is a government-funded scheme to provide compensation to victims of crime who have suffered personal injury. Victims can make an application regardless of whether there has been a conviction of the person who caused the injury. A report to and co-operation with the police is usually required. The amounts awarded are usually lower than the amounts that are awarded in damages for similar injuries in personal injury cases in the civil courts (see CHAPTER 4: ACCIDENTS AND INJURIES), but it provides a valuable way of getting compensation in most cases where it is not practical to sue the offender. Application forms are available from the police or directly from the CRIMINAL INJURIES COMPENSATION AUTHORITY (CICA).

Help for the accused

If you are accused of a crime and you require legal advice, you should always use a solicitor who is a specialist in crime. Before engaging someone to represent you, consider if the lawyer:

- ❓ is familiar with the magistrates and district judges at the local courts – this may prove useful

- ❓ is prepared to act under the **legal aid scheme** – this is important because occasionally people pay out quite sizeable sums of money before realising that the same service can be obtained without this burden (see CHAPTER 2: LEGAL AID)

- ❓ will be available – one of the most common complaints is a last-minute change of representation by a barrister.

Ensure an early **conference** (meeting) with your barrister to assess their competence and grasp of detail and to give them a clear picture of your case (see CHAPTER 1: FINDING AND MEETING YOUR LAWYER).

Organisations   ⓘ

▶ **CRIMINAL CASES
REVIEW COMMISSION**
Alpha Tower
Suffolk Street
Queensway
Birmingham B1 1TT
Tel: 0121 633 1800
Fax: 0121 633 1804 / 1823
info@ccrc.gov.uk
www.ccrc.gov.uk

▶ **CRIMINAL DEFENCE SERVICE**
www.legalservices.gov.uk/cds/index.htm

▶ **CRIMINAL INJURIES
COMPENSATION AUTHORITY (CICA)**
Tay House
300 Bath Street
Glasgow G2 4LN
Tel: 0141 331 2726
Fax: 0141 331 2287
Advice line: 0800 358 3601
www.cica.gov.uk

▶ **CROWN PROSECUTION SERVICE
(CPS)**
www.cps.gov.uk

▶ **HM CUSTOMS AND EXCISE**
National Advice Line: 0845 010 9000
+44 208 929 0152 *for international callers*
www.hmce.gov.uk

▶ **FREE REPRESENTATION UNIT (FRU)**
Fourth Floor, Peer House
8–14 Verulam Street
London WC1X 8LZ
www.fru.org.uk
Please note that the FRU does NOT deal
with members of the public directly.

▶ **GENERAL COUNCIL OF THE BAR**
3 Bedford Row
London WC1R 4DB
Tel: 020 7242 0082
Records Office: 020 7242 0934
Fax: 020 7831 9217
www.barcouncil.org.uk

▶ **HEALTH AND SAFETY EXECUTIVE**
Postal enquiries:
HSE Infoline
Caerphilly Business Park
Caerphilly CF83 3GG
Infoline (Monday to Friday, 8.30am to 5.00pm):
08701 545 500
Fax: 02920 859260
hseinformationservices@natbrit.com
www.hse.gov.uk

▶ **INLAND REVENUE**
www.inlandrevenue.gov.uk

▶ **JUSTICE**
59 Carter Lane
London EC4V 5AQ
Tel: 020 7329 5100
Fax: 020 739 5055
admin@justice.org.uk
www.justice.org.uk

▶ **LAW CENTRES FEDERATION**
Duchess House
18–19 Warren Street
London W1T 5LR
Tel: 020 7387 8570
Fax: 020 7387 8368
info@lawcentres.org.uk
www.lawcentres.org.uk

▶ **LAW SOCIETY**
113 Chancery Lane
London WC2A 1PL
Tel: 020 7242 1222
Fax: 020 7831 0344
info.services@lawsociety.org.uk
www.lawsociety.org.uk

▶ **LIBERTY**
21 Tabard Street
London SE1 4LA
Tel: 020 7403 3888
Fax: 020 7407 5354
info@liberty-human-rights.org.uk
www.liberty-human-rights.org.uk

► **NATIONAL ASSOCIATION FOR THE CARE AND RESETTLEMENT OF OFFENDERS (NACRO)**

169 Clapham Road
London SW9 0PU

Tel: 020 7582 6500
Fax: 020 7735 4666
communications@nacro.org.uk
www.nacro.org.uk

► **NATIONAL CIVIL RIGHTS MOVEMENT (NCRM)**

14 Featherstone Road
Southall
Middlesex UB2 5AA

Tel: 020 8574 0818 or 020 8843 2333
Fax: 020 8813 9734
info@ncrm.org
www.ncrm.org.uk

► **OFFICE FOR THE SUPERVISION OF SOLICITORS**

Victoria Court
8 Dormer Place
Royal Leamington Spa
Warwickshire CV32 5AE

Public advice line: 0845 608 6565
enquiries@lawsociety.org.uk
www.oss.lawsociety.org.uk

Deals with complaints and regulation.

► **RAPE CRISIS FEDERATION WALES AND ENGLAND**

Unit 7, Provident Works
Newdigate Street
Nottingham NG7 4FD

Tel: 0115 900 3560
Fax: 0115 900 3562
info@rapecrisis.co.uk
www.rapecrisis.co.uk

Rape Crisis: There are many local rape crisis services, usually providing telephone advice lines. They will give direct counselling and support, such as providing a person to be present when dealing with the police.

Incest crisis: Available in some areas as a telephone service, sometimes combined with Rape Crisis lines, which will always try to help incest victims in any event.

► **VICTIM SUPPORT**

National Office
Cranmer House
39 Brixton Road
London SW9 6DZ

Tel: 020 7735 9166
Fax: 020 7582 5712
contact@victimsupport.org.uk
www.victimsupport.org.uk

► **WOMEN'S AID FEDERATION**

PO Box 391
Bristol BS99 7WS

National Domestic Violence helpline (24 hour): 08457 023468

Fax: 0117 924 1703
info@womensaid.org.uk
www.womensaid.org.uk

Helps women and their dependants who are suffering from domestic violence and abuse of all sorts; provides refuges for victims of domestic violence.

9 **Disability**

This chapter gives you information about three aspects of being a disabled person:

- some of the specific state benefits that may be available
- what to do if you are discriminated against, either at work or by someone providing a service
- what you need to know about how to engage a lawyer who has the right expertise in the field.

Disability Discrimination Act 1996

If you have a disability the *Disability Discrimination Act* gives you the right not to be discriminated against, by:

- your present employer
- someone to whom you are applying for a job
- an organisation that you want to provide you with a service.

The Act places duties and responsibilities on employers and service providers – for example, to make reasonable adjustments to the workplace or ensure that facilities, such as libraries, are accessible.

What is disability?

The Act only protects you if your illness, condition or impairment is within the definition of disability in the Act. That is, if:

- you suffer from an impairment or condition that is recognised by the medical world
- *and* the condition or impairment has already lasted, or is expected to last for at least 12 months
- *and* the impairment or condition affects your ability to carry out normal day-to-day activities in a substantial way.

Whether you have a disability or not within the meaning of the Act can be a complicated question, and you should take further advice about this. A disability can be physical or mental and can cover disfigurement, but not if the disfigurement is self-inflicted (eg, tattoos).

Disability at work

WHO IS COVERED?

The Act applies to all employers with 15 or more employees. So, if your employer only has five people working as employees, then the Act will not cover you at work.

WHAT DOES THE ACT SAY?

The Act makes it unlawful for an employer, or someone that you have applied to work for, to discriminate against you because you have a disability, in:

- the way they select staff for jobs
- the employment they provide
- the way you are treated at work.

This means that you cannot be discriminated against in promotion, or selection for redundancy, or pay just because you have a disability, unless the employer can show that the discrimination is justified.

Similarly, it will be unlawful discrimination to dismiss you from your job just because you have a disability, unless there are no reasonable adjustments that the employer can make to your job and the dismissal is justified.

> You are discriminated against if the employer treats you less favourably than they treat another employee, or than they would treat another employee in your position who does not have a disability.

An example might be an internal promotion for which you are competing with another employee. If you have a disability but do not get the post, you can say you have been treated less favourably because you did not get the promotion. The question is why did you not get the promotion? If it is because the other person has better qualifications, or more experience, and your disability has nothing to do with the decision, then you have not been discriminated against because of your disability.

However, if your qualifications and experience are the same and the real reason that you were not promoted is because you are a wheelchair user, and the directors think it would be difficult to get the chair into the boardroom, or there is no lift access, this is discrimination, and unless the reason for the refusal to appoint you can be justified the employer will have acted unlawfully.

JUSTIFICATION

An employer may be able to show that in the particular circumstances the discrimination is justified. They will only be able to do this if the reason for the treatment is **objectively justifiable**. This will usually mean that:

- there are no adjustments that can be made to the workplace
- it is too expensive to make the changes necessary for you to work in the organisation
- it is simply not practical to do so.

You can get more guidance and information on what your employer ought to do from the DISABILITY RIGHTS COMMISSION.

REASONABLE ADJUSTMENTS

Your employer must consider making **reasonable adjustments** to the workplace to enable you to do the job, if adjustments would help and if they are not too expensive. A number of changes should be considered, from changing the hours of work to providing special equipment. However, the employer only has to do what is reasonable.

Service providers

As well as giving protection to employees, the Act makes it unlawful for any person or organisation that provides services to the public to treat you less favourably because of your disability. For example, this means that pubs and clubs cannot refuse you entry, ask you to sit in designated areas, or refuse to serve you. However, this is subject to the same rules about justification.

WHICH PROVIDERS ARE COVERED?

Any organisations providing services, goods or facilities are covered by the Act, with the following exceptions:

- education services
- transport, although stations and airports are covered
- private clubs.

In addition, there are special rules for insurance, deposits and guarantees. Otherwise, all types of service and goods providers are covered, including:

- shops, restaurants and hotels
- pubs and clubs
- accommodation agencies
- courts and law firms
- mail order firms
- local and central government
- libraries, cinemas and museums.

WHAT IS COVERED?

If you are disabled, organisations cannot:

- refuse you service

- give you worse service

- only give you service on less favourable terms than other people.

An example would be a restaurant saying they could serve you and your friends but you would have to sit in a separate room, and they would make an extra charge for the inconvenience.

Access to buildings is often a problem, but from 2004 all organisations offering a service will have to ensure that they make reasonable adjustments to their buildings to overcome physical boundaries.

This will include ramped and lift access in many cases, but may also include fitting induction loops in places where you need to talk to someone, such as banks, building societies and post offices.

Where can I get help?

The government has established a statutory body, called the DISABILITY RIGHTS COMMISSION (DRC), whose purpose is to help secure civil rights for disabled people. The DRC:

- advises government on issues that affect people with disabilities

- offers advice and assistance to organisations to improve their practices

- produces leaflets and booklets, on audio cassette and in Braille as well as ordinary text, on a number of areas.

In addition, the DRC has a telephone helpline. All the details are at the end of this chapter.

Benefits

A general overview of the benefits system, and the way benefits are calculated, can be found in CHAPTER 27: WELFARE BENEFITS. This section explains the basics of some of the particular benefits that are specifically targeted at people who have a disability. There is no single definition of disability for the purposes of claiming these benefits, since each one is designed for a different level of ability. You should take care to check the criteria for eligibility before making a claim.

INDUSTRIAL INJURIES BENEFITS

If you have been working in a job and being paid and you suffer an industrial injury at work, or develop an industrial injury, which leads to a loss of faculty and a disability, you may be eligible for this benefit. You will not be eligible for the benefit if you are self-employed – you must be an employed earner. The accident must arise in the course of your employment and not be something incidental.

To be able to claim the benefit the loss of faculty must usually lead to at least 14 per cent disability. Some assessment of the degree of your disability is set out in legislation, giving usual percentages for loss of sight, loss of a limb or a finger and so on. However, your own particular experience of the disability, and how severely it affects you, will also be considered.

Once you satisfy the criteria you could be eligible for one of three benefits:

- disablement benefit
- reduced earnings allowance
- retirement allowances

> **Disablement benefit** is the main benefit paid to people who suffer disablement at work. It is paid if your disablement results from an industrial injury or disease and your disablement is at least 14 per cent. There is also a delay in the benefit, and 90 days must have elapsed since the accident or onset of the illness.

REDUCED EARNINGS ALLOWANCE

This is only available if your accident or the date you started to suffer from your disease was before 1 October 1990. If you think you may qualify for this, you should talk to a benefits adviser.

RETIREMENT ALLOWANCE

This is payable to people who were entitled to the reduced earnings allowance (above) and are over pensionable age. This benefit will also be phased out.

DISABILITY LIVING ALLOWANCE

Disability living allowance (DLA) can be claimed for two different aspects of life:

- mobility
- care.

DLA mobility benefit is paid at a higher rate for some people and a lower rate for others. Whether you qualify for the benefit at all, and if so whether for the higher or the lower rate, will depend upon how seriously your mobility is affected.

For example, if you are both deaf and blind, or if you have a physical disability that means you are unable or virtually unable to walk, you will usually qualify for the higher rate, provided you satisfy other criteria as well.

The lower rate is paid if, although you are able to walk, you are seriously disabled to the extent that you cannot go for a walk without assistance other than by familiar routes.

DLA care benefit is payable to you if you are disabled and need care or supervision. There are three levels at which the benefit can be paid – low, middle and high – and the criteria for each are different.

Because the benefit is about care, the criteria look at whether you:

- can cook for yourself
- can wash yourself
- need constant supervision in order to avoid danger to yourself.

For both the mobility and the care element of DLA, you must be:

- under 65
- satisfy residence conditions
- not subject to immigration controls.

> If you are over 65 and have mobility or care needs, you may be eligible for an **attendance allowance**. This is a comparable benefit, with varying rates and criteria.

SEVERE DISABLEMENT ALLOWANCE

This benefit was abolished for new claimants on 6 April 2001. You will only be able to claim it after that date if you were entitled to it for at least one day before 1 April 2001 in your present period of incapacity for work. If you think you may fall within this category, you should talk to a CITIZENS ADVICE BUREAU or other advice agency.

DISABLED PERSONS TAX CREDIT

This is paid to employees who normally work for 16 hours a week or more for a period of 26 weeks. The credit will be paid by your employer if your claim is successful. To be eligible for the credit, you must:

- be over 16 years of age
- normally work for 16 hours or more
- have a physical or mental disability which puts you at a disadvantage in getting a job or, if you have recently developed a disability, means that your earnings are reduced because of your disability
- have a sufficiently low income, and savings and capital of not more than £16,000
- either be receiving, or have recently been receiving, incapacity or disability benefit
- not be receiving **working families tax credit** – and neither must your partner.

Getting further help

If you need further help or information about employment rights, discrimination or in-service provision, or help finding a specialist lawyer, the first step is to contact one of the organisations listed below. Many of them have free telephone helplines and some give advice on various problems or send out information sheets.

HOW DO I FIND A LAWYER TO HELP?

If you think that you need a lawyer to help you, have a look at CHAPTER 1: FINDING AND MEETING YOUR LAWYER.

Citizens Advice Bureaux, charities and voluntary organisations dealing with your disability and local law centres may have lists of solicitors' firms which they know have relevant experience, so ask for a referral.

If your concern is a benefit problem, the Citizens Advice Bureau will probably be able to help, and this is the best place to start.

If your problem is employment-related and you cannot get a referral, then you may have to research local solicitors. Ideally you want a solicitor who:

☑ has some recent experience of disability discrimination casework – this is most likely to be in the employment field

☑ has recent experience of other types of discrimination work, such as race or sex discrimination – although there are some significant differences, the areas are similar

☑ is a member of the DISCRIMINATION LAW ASSOCIATION, a specialist organisation for lawyers who work in this area of law

☑ has experience of representing applicants in employment tribunals or claimants in the county court.

Organisations   [i]

▶ **BRITISH HEART FOUNDATION**
14 Fitzhardinge Street
London W1H 6DH
Tel: 020 7935 0185
Fax: 020 7486 5820
www.bhf.org.uk

▶ **CHARITIES AID FOUNDATION**
Kings Hill
West Malling
Kent ME19 4TA
Tel: 01732 520 000
Fax: 01732 520 001
enquiries@cafonline.org
www.cafonline.org

▶ **DIAL UK**
www.dialuk.org.uk
Online information on disability advice
centres run by and for people with
disabilities.

▶ **DISABILITY LAW SERVICE**
39–45 Cavell Street
London E1 2BP
Tel: 020 7791 9800
Fax: 020 7791 9802
advice@dls.org.uk
Offers free advice and representation.

▶ **DISABILITY RIGHTS COMMISSION**
Freepost MID02164
Stratford-upon-Avon CV37 9BR
Helpline: 08457 622 633
enquiry@drc-gb.org
www.drc-gb.org
Factsheets are available by post, or you
can order or download them from the
Disability Rights Commission website:
http://www.drc-gb.org/drc/default.asp
In addition, there are many charities
and voluntary organisations working
for specific disabilities. The organisations
vary, but many of them have
information helplines, websites and
publications. Some of the best known
are listed below, but if you want to
know whether there is a charity dealing
specifically with your disability or
condition, try contacting the NATIONAL
COUNCIL FOR VOLUNTARY ORGANISATIONS
or the CHARITIES AID FOUNDATION.

▶ **DISABILITY WALES**
Wernddu Court
Caerphilly Business Park
Van Road
Caerphilly CF83 3ED
Wales
Tel: 029 2088 7325
Fax: 029 2088 8702
www.dwac.demon.co.uk

▶ **DISCRIMINATION LAW
ASSOCIATION**
PO Box 6715
Rushden
Northamptonshire NN10 9WL
Tel/Fax: 01933 412 337
info@discrimination-law.org.uk
www.discrimination-law.org.uk

▶ **DOWN'S SYNDROME EDUCATIONAL
TRUST / SARAH DUFFEN CENTRE**
The Sarah Duffen Centre
Belmont Street
Southsea PO5 1NA
Tel: 023 9282 4261
Fax: 023 9282 4265
www.downsyndrome.info

▶ **MENCAP**
123 Golden Lane
London EC1Y ORT
Tel: 020 7454 0454
Fax: 020 7696 5540
Free helpline: 0808 808 1111
Helpline Wales: 0808 8000 300
Helpline Northern Ireland: 0845 763 6227
Minicom: 0808808 8181
information@mencap.org.uk
www.mencap.org.uk

▶ **MIND**
15–19 Broadway
London E15 4BQ
Tel: 08457 660 163
contact@mind.org.uk
www.mind.org.uk

▶ **NATIONAL ASSOCIATION OF CITIZENS ADVICE BUREAUX (NACAB)**

Myddelton House
115–123 Pentonville Road
London N1 9LZ

Tel: 020 7833 2181
www.nacab.org.uk

Adviceguide: the National Association of Citizens Advice Bureaux offers fact sheets covering issues such as employment, housing and taxation
www.adviceguide.org.uk

▶ **NATIONAL COUNCIL FOR VOLUNTARY ORGANISATIONS (NCVO)**

Regent's Wharf
8 All Saints Street
London N1 9RL

Tel: 020 7713 6161
Helpdesk: 0800 2 798 798
ncvo@ncvo-vol.org.uk
www.ncvo-vol.org.uk

▶ **NATIONAL DISABLED PERSONS HOUSING SERVICE (HoDIS)**

17 Priory Street
York YO1 6ET

Tel: 01904 653888
Fax: 01904 653999
info@hodis.org.uk
www.hodis.org.uk

▶ **RADAR**

12 City Forum
250 City Road
London EC1V 8AF

Tel: 020 7250 3222
Fax: 020 7250 0212
Minicom: 020 7250 4119
radar@radar.org.uk
www.radar.org.uk

▶ **ROYAL NATIONAL INSTITUTE FOR THE BLIND (RNIB)**

Helpline: 0845 766 9999 *(UK callers)*
Textphone:
add 18001 before the above number
www.rnib.org.uk

▶ **ROYAL NATIONAL INSTITUTE FOR THE DEAF (RNID)**

19–23 Featherstone Street
London EC1Y 8SL

Tel: 0808 808 0123
Fax: 0207296 8199
Textphone: 0808 808 9000
information@rnid.org.uk
www.rnid.org.uk

▶ **SCOPE**

Helpline: 0808 800 3333
cphelpline@scope.org.uk
www.scope.org.uk

Services for people with cerebral palsy, their families and carers.

10 **Discrimination**

It is against the law for your employer to discriminate against you because:

- of your race or ethnic origin

- you are a woman

- you are pregnant

- you have a disability

- of your marital status

- you are having gender reassignment

- of your religion or sexuality, from December 2003.

This chapter sets out what to do and how to seek advice if you feel you have suffered discrimination.

Discrimination at work can happen in many ways, and these are just a few examples:

- name-calling or constant offensive jokes, called **racial** or **sexual harassment**

- giving all the good or clean work to white staff, and all the bad or dirty jobs to black staff

- not promoting a woman, Asian person or disabled person, but promoting a white man instead

- not giving everyone the same chances to attend training courses

- giving pay rises to only some staff

- insisting that everyone work on Saturdays, which for Jewish people is a religious day

- not giving holidays to Muslim staff at religious festivals such as Eid but letting everyone take the Christian festival of Easter.

> In law, discrimination means to treat someone less favourably than another person. For legal purposes, discrimination is divided into two types: **direct discrimination** and **indirect discrimination**.

Direct and indirect discrimination

Direct discrimination happens when a person does something that means they treat you less well than they treat someone else or other employees.

Indirect discrimination is the sort of discrimination that happens because an organisation has a rule or policy that is unfair to one group of employees but not to others. For example:

- a rule that requires all employees to be available from 8.30am until 6.00pm may discriminate against women with children, if they have to collect them from school

- a policy that requires all staff over a certain grade to be over 6 feet tall will discriminate against most women and many Asian people.

Indirect discrimination will not always be unlawful, but if you can show that there is a rule or policy and that it does have a worse effect on one group than another – for example, on black or ethnic minority people, or women, than on white men – then the employer or organisation will have to provide a proper justification for it.

An employer will usually try to justify the policy – for example, on hours of work, by arguing that customers are still contacting the business, or the shop is still open, or that the busiest times of the working day are morning and evening. In some cases they will be able to show this, and the business objectives will win out. In other cases, the reasons will not be convincing or serious enough. Employers are expected to take equality seriously, and to consider flexible working hours, including alternatives to working on Saturdays, and other solutions to business considerations.

If you would like more information, contact the EQUAL OPPORTUNITIES COMMISSION for details about all aspects of sex discrimination, or the COMMISSION FOR RACIAL EQUALITY with any questions about race equality at work.

How to claim

If you think you have been discriminated against at work, you can complain to an **employment tribunal**. Unlike **unfair dismissal** and some other claims, you can claim at any time in your employment. There is no qualifying period.

So if you start work and during the first week of your job you are insulted and abused because you are black, you can complain to a tribunal immediately. You do not have to have been dismissed.

Many people claim discrimination when they are sacked because they believe it has happened merely because they are black or a woman. However, many claims are about harassment at work, lack of promotion or general bad treatment over many months or years.

There is a time limit of only three months for bringing all discrimination claims to a tribunal.

However, tribunals do have discretion to extend the three-month time limit, and still hear a claim if they think that it is **just and equitable** to do so. This will usually be dealt with at a preliminary hearing.

Preliminary hearings

These are hearings that are held before the full case is heard, to decide any matters that may mean that the case cannot continue. If you are late filing your claim, the employer will usually argue that the tribunal should not hear the claim and that it should be struck out. A tribunal will want to know why your claim is late. The sorts of things that they will consider are:

- your health – for example, if you have been very ill, perhaps as a result of the dismissal, or if you have been having a baby; you should bring medical certificates and, if possible, a note from your doctor explaining why you could not make your claim earlier

- whether you have been wrongly advised by someone about the time limit – a very long delay will need a much better explanation than a short one, although any delay must be explained

- if the employer did not tell you that you had been dismissed

- if you are trying to resolve the matter through an **internal complaints procedure** which is ongoing (but see below).

Taking a claim to an **employment tribunal** can be complicated, distressing for everyone involved, and a long process. Before you start, it is sensible to try to resolve your dispute using an internal grievance or complaints procedure. Some organisations will have a specific policy which deals with complaints about discrimination.

> Remember, if you do use an internal complaints procedure, you are still bound by the three-month time limit, starting from the time of the event you complained about.

If you have made a complaint, and the internal investigation is still ongoing, you should make a claim to the tribunal anyway, explaining that you are trying to resolve the matter. The tribunal will usually delay the hearing of your case until the internal procedures have been completed. Then, if you are not happy with the outcome, you will be able to continue with your claim, without worrying about being out of time.

Continuing acts

In real life, people are discriminated against in different ways, at different times, often by more than one person in an organisation. If you have suffered discrimination over several months, or even years, and the place where you work has taken no action even though you have complained about it, you may be able to claim that all the treatment is part of a continuous act of discrimination. This will mean that you can claim for all the different discriminatory acts.

For example, if over several months or a year you have been called names by other workers, been passed over for promotion, not allowed training or privileges that other staff have got, or if you have seen many staff being asked to act up and you never have, you may claim that these are all part of a policy or practice of discrimination.

The advantage of arguing in this way is that you can claim for all the bad treatment, because the three-month time limit starts at the *end of the last act*, whether it is a racist insult, a refusal to promote you, or even your dismissal. This is not an easy argument to make on your own, and you should get help from a trade union, the **COMMISSION FOR RACIAL EQUALITY (CRE)**, the **EQUAL OPPORTUNITIES COMMISSION (EOC)** or an employment solicitor.

Remedies

If you win your case of discrimination, the tribunal can award you damages for any or all of the following:

- any wages which you have lost because you have been sacked. You must show the tribunal that you have looked for another job.

- injury to your feelings. This is only awarded in discrimination cases and is paid to compensate you for the feelings of anger, hurt and outrage that you feel because of the discrimination. Discrimination at work can have really appalling effects on people, but everyone is different so you must tell the tribunal how the discrimination has affected you.

> Many people lose sleep, feel very ill, worthless, disillusioned and bitter as a result of discrimination. Others have their reputation in their local community damaged, or find their family life is broken because they lose all confidence and their personality changes.

The amount of damages awarded varies enormously, but most people who are successful will receive between £3000 and £8000 for this part of the claim.

- damages for **personal injury** (see CHAPTER 4: ACCIDENTS AND INJURIES).
  If the discrimination you have suffered has made you ill (some people have nervous breakdowns, or suffer post-traumatic stress which can last years), you can be awarded damages. This is complicated and you should get help, probably from a solicitor. Because **personal injury awards** can be worth a lot of money, many solicitors will act on a conditional fee basis or **no win, no fee.**

The tribunal can also make recommendations about how the employer should behave in the future. This can include things like monitoring staff recruitment, revising an equal opportunities policy or putting in place training for managers.

The right to be accompanied

If you have trouble at work and are told that you must attend a disciplinary or grievance hearing, the employer cannot force you to have a particular person accompany you. You have a right to choose the person who accompanies you, but they must:

- be a trade union official or another worker employed by the same employer
- be given time off to attend the hearing, and must not be penalised by losing pay or having to work extra hours.

They may speak and confer with you during the hearing, but may not answer questions on your behalf.

Trade unions and trade union rights

Trade unions are independent workplace organisations which are set up to represent the interests of the employees both to the management and at a national level. Many trade unions are big national organisations representing workers from similar industries all over the country. In addition, the union will have local officials, a branch committee in the workplace and shop stewards, who will be other workers like yourself and the first point of contact with the union if you have a problem or a query.

Unions are funded by each employee paying a small subscription each week or month. Most employers will deduct this at source, if you ask them to, and send it to the union directly.

Trade union membership has many advantages, including:

- negotiation, collective bargaining and representation on pay and terms and conditions of employment

- help at disciplinary and grievance hearings

- advice about general workplace problems

- legal advice

- benefits such as cheap insurance and travel.

THE RIGHT TO JOIN A TRADE UNION

All employees have the right to join a trade union, but employers do not have to recognise trade unions. If you belong to a union that is not recognised, or if you want to set up a union and there is not one at your workplace, you should talk to the trade union itself, or the TRADES UNION CONGRESS, the membership body which supports trade unions nationally.

RECOGNITION

Not all employers want to recognise a trade union, but if there are over 21 employees and enough support in your workplace or section then you may be able to force the employer to accept the union. Apply to the CENTRAL ARBITRATION COMMITTEE, who will go through a procedure to see whether the employer must recognise the union.

DISCRIMINATION ON TRADE UNION GROUNDS

If you are treated less favourably than others because of your trade union membership or activity, this is unlawful and you can take your employer to an **employment tribunal** and claim damages. This is particularly important if you are selected for redundancy or dismissed because of your union work. Your trade union will be able to give you further advice about this.

Discrimination as described above is a civil matter but racial hatred is a criminal offence. Either

- using threatening, abusive or insulting words or behaviour or displays

- or possessing, publishing, distributing or performing racially inflammatory material

with the intention of stirring up racial hatred is an offence under the law. It cannot be prosecuted if the offences occur in a dwelling but it can be if they can be heard or seen from that dwelling. You should report such instances of racial hatred to the police. See CHAPTER 8: CRIMINAL LAW.

Organisations   ℹ️

▶ **ADVICE UK (formerly THE FEDERATION OF INFORMATION AND ADVICE CENTRES)**
12th Floor, New London Bridge House
25 London Bridge Street
London SE1 9ST
Tel: 020 7407 4070
www.fiac.org.uk

▶ **CAMPAIGN AGAINST RACISM AND FASCISM (CARF)**
BM Box 8784
London WC1N 3XX
Tel: 020 7837 1450
info@carf.demon.co.uk
www.carf.demon.co.uk

▶ **CENTRAL ARBITRATION COMMITTEE (CAC)**
Third Floor, Discovery House
28–42 Banner Street
London EC1Y 8QE
Tel: 020 7251 9747
Fax: 020 7251 3114
enquiries@cac.gov.uk
www.cac.gov.uk

► **COMMISSION FOR RACIAL EQUALITY (CRE)**

St Dunstan's House
201–211 Borough High Street
London SE1 1GZ

Tel: 020 7939 0000
Fax: 020 7939 0001
info@cre.gov.uk
www.cre.gov.uk

The CRE has regional offices and race equality councils which give advice and fund legal representation. A leaflet *Advice and Assistance from the CRE* is available from the website or by post.

► **DISCRIMINATION LAW ASSOCIATION**

PO Box 6715
Rushden
Northamptonshire NN10 9WL

Tel/Fax: 01933 412 337
info@discrimination-law.org.uk
www.discrimination-law.org.uk

► **EQUAL OPPORTUNITIES COMMISSION (EOC)**

Arndale House
Arndale Centre
Manchester M4 3EQ

Tel: 0845 601 5901
Fax: 0161 838 1733
info@eoc.org.uk
www.eoc.org.uk

► **LAW CENTRES FEDERATION**

Duchess House
18–19 Warren Street
London W1T 5LR

Tel: 020 7387 8570
Fax: 020 7387 8368
info@lawcentres.org.uk
www.lawcentres.org.uk

► **MATERNITY ALLIANCE**

3rd Floor West
2–6 Northburgh Street
London EC1V 0AY

Tel: 020 7588 8583
Information line: 020 7490 7638
Fax: 020 7014 1350
info@maternityalliance.org.uk
www.maternityalliance.org.uk

► **NATIONAL ASSOCIATION OF CITIZENS ADVICE BUREAUX (NACAB)**

Myddelton House
115–123 Pentonville Road
London N1 9LZ

Tel: 020 7833 2181
www.nacab.org.uk

Adviceguide: the National Association of Citizens Advice Bureaux offers fact sheets covering issues such as employment, housing and taxation

www.adviceguide.org.uk

► **TRADES UNION CONGRESS (TUC)**

Congress House
Great Russell Street
London WC1B 3LS

Tel: 020 7636 4030
info@tuc.org.uk
www.tuc.org.uk

Further reading

Employment Law: An Advisor's Handbook published by the LEGAL ACTION GROUP

Advice and Assistance from the CRE

11 Education

Education law covers a wide range of subjects from schools to further education colleges to universities. The majority of it, however, concerns just five areas, concentrating on state education. The particular problems that can arise with private schools and colleges are mentioned separately where relevant.

Admissions

The process of getting children into schools is often very contentious, with too many parents chasing too few places. The law requires local education authorities to have regard to parental choice and admissions policies must reflect that. What parents want for their children must inevitably be weighed against what is available.

Parents will fill in a form showing where they want their child to go to school. The local education authority will then decide whether or not they agree. However, it is becoming more common for schools to introduce a selection process – even into state schools. This may entail your child taking one or more entrance exams, depending on the school or the policy of the local authority. If the school of choice is not available, parents then have a right of appeal to a panel set up by the authority.

Admissions appeals panels look at whether:

- admissions polices have been followed

- admitting a child would prejudice efficient education or use of resources

- that prejudice is outweighed by the reasons for the parents wanting the school.

This means that parents need to prove either that admitting their child would make very little difference to the running of the school or that, if it would, it is justified in the circumstances. Parents are well advised to prepare thoroughly for these appeals by going to the school and looking at classroom size and numbers of pupils attending. If parents are still dissatisfied after the appeal, the only remedy is by **judicial review**.

> **Judicial review** is a process by which the high court in London checks that public bodies have complied with the law. It is very expensive and is only available in a small number of cases. Formal legal advice and representation will usually be required.

Exclusions

Exclusion is what used to be called 'expelling' children from school. The government has been very concerned about the number of children excluded from schools every year, and the law makes it clear that it should rarely be used. Following a number of high-profile cases concerning very disruptive and sometimes violent pupils, the government has backed down slightly with the result that exclusions are still quite common. The main things to note are that:

- headteachers must ensure that an appropriate investigation has been carried out and be satisfied that the child did what she/he is accused of
- only a headteacher or someone senior acting with the head's authority can exclude a pupil
- exclusion should generally only be used after alternatives have been tried
- exclusion is a last resort and should only be used for serious breaches of school discipline and where the education/welfare of other pupils is at stake
- particular caution should be exercised over children with **special educational needs**.

Parents have a right of appeal against all exclusions to the school governors, and in the case of permanent exclusions to the local education authority.

Like admissions (see above), judicial review is available in some cases. In preparing for appeals, parents should look at the evidence, the consequences for their child of exclusion, and what might be done instead.

Special educational needs

The law concerning **special educational needs** (SEN) ensures that children whose access to learning is impaired still receive appropriate education, whether by the provision of additional equipment, an assistant in class or a special school. In the most serious cases, SEN provision will be made with a **statement of special educational needs**, which is a legal document setting out a child's entitlement and is enforceable by proceedings in the high court. Children who require education in a special school will always have a formal statement. In less serious cases, provision may be made by schools without one.

The law sets out a detailed procedure for the assessment of children who are thought to have special educational needs and for the provision of statements, and provides parents with a right of appeal to an **independent tribunal** when they disagree with what the local education authority does. In outline, the steps and the rights of appeal are as follows.

ASSESSMENT

Parents and schools both have the right to request what is known as a **statutory assessment** of a child's special educational needs. Local education authorities must comply with that request where steps already taken by the school are not working and alternative provision may be required.

STATEMENTING

Once an assessment has been carried out, the authority must decide whether or not a statement is necessary. The test is very similar to that for an assessment: does the child require provision outside that which is normally available in mainstream schools in the area? If so, a statement should be issued.

The statement will then be drafted, setting out what exactly the child in question requires. There are rules about the contents of statements, such as the level of detail required, the difference between educational and other kinds of provision, and when parents can choose the school their child attends.

> The basic rule is that local education authorities must provide an appropriate education. If the school chosen by the parents is the only appropriate option then it will be provided. If there are two appropriate alternatives then the one chosen by the parents must be provided so long as it is not too expensive or incompatible with the efficient education of other children.

APPEALS

Parents can appeal to the SPECIAL EDUCATIONAL NEEDS AND DISABILITY TRIBUNAL (SENDIST) against:

■ refusal to assess

■ refusal to issue a statement

■ the contents of the statement

■ a decision to withdraw a statement

■ and, in some cases, refusal to comply with a request to change school.

The tribunal consists of three people, only one of whom will be a lawyer, and operates nationally. It is currently taking about four months to hear appeals.

Bullying and educational negligence

An increase in awareness of the consequences of bullying and the failure to identify special educational needs, together with the recent agreement from the country's highest court, the House of Lords, that such cases could be brought, has led to an increase in **litigation** (legal action) in this area. In essence, these cases are very similar to **personal injury cases** (see CHAPTER 4: ACCIDENTS AND INJURIES) in that they require claimants (usually children acting through their parents) to prove that the school or local education authority acted negligently towards them, and that they suffered as a result.

These cases are not easy to bring and deciding whether or not a school or authority acted negligently, and what the consequences were, will usually require detailed expert evidence. Educational experts will need to consider what was done and what should have been done. After that, other experts in fields such as employment will consider what impact the bullying or the failure to identify special educational needs has had on the child's life. These cases are **claims for damages** (money) and turning these judgements into precise figures is an involved process.

So far as private schools are concerned, in addition to children claiming negligence parents may be able to claim that the school has **breached a contract** with them by failing to comply with an (often implied) agreement that the standard of teaching or protection against bullying would be of a reasonable level.

Universities

Litigation concerning universities is also growing, with students suing their universities over inadequate teaching, supervision of research theses and so on. These disputes are generally **contract disputes** which depend on what was agreed between the student and the university before the student started the course. That in turn depends upon what the university prospectus and other course documentation promised (implicitly or otherwise) in terms of quality of teaching, availability of equipment and other provision.

A smaller number of disputes arise out of university disciplinary or academic procedures, including examination boards. Here, students may be disputing their grades or decisions to suspend them from a course. Some of these disputes can be dealt with as above – the student leaves and sues for money afterwards – but others will require direct challenges to the decision in question. Such challenges may be brought by judicial review in the high court (see Admissions above).

Practicalities

TIME LIMITS

Time limits are much tighter in education law than in many other areas of law, not least because educational problems need to be dealt with quickly. So far as admissions and exclusions are concerned, appeals to local education authorities must usually be brought within 14 days and 15 school days respectively. For appeals to school governors, the time limit depends on when the governors' meeting is scheduled. Judicial reviews must be brought as quickly as possible, and in any event no later than three months from the date of the decision.

As for special educational needs, both the authority and parents are subject to a strict timetable. Authorities must take only six weeks to decide on assessment, a further 12 weeks to produce a statement and so on. Parents have to lodge any appeal against an authority's decision within two months of the decision.

Bullying and other negligence claims need to be brought before the child is 21. Contract claims against universities must be brought within six years of the alleged breach.

FUNDING

Legal aid is available for some but not all education disputes. For admissions, exclusions and the tribunal stages of special educational needs, a lesser form of legal aid known as **legal help** is available, subject to parents' (note, not children's) means. For the high court stages of education law, and for bullying and education negligence claims which are brought in either the high court or county court, full legal aid is available subject to means and merit tests (see CHAPTER 2: LEGAL AID).

In many of these cases, expert advice is required from lawyers who are familiar with education law (see CHAPTER 1: FINDING AND MEETING YOUR LAWYER).

Organisations　　　　　　　　　　　　　　　　　　[i]

▶ **ADVISORY CENTRE FOR EDUCATION (ACE) LTD**
1c Aberdeen Studios
22 Highbury Grove
London N5 2DQ
General advice line: 0808 800 5793
www.ace-ed.org.uk

▶ **ALLIANCE FOR INCLUSIVE EDUCATION (formerly INTEGRATION ALLIANCE)**
Unit 2, Ground Floor
70 South Lambeth Road
London SW8 1RL
Tel: 020 7735 5277
www.allfie.org.uk

▶ **BRITISH DYSLEXIA ASSOCIATION**
98 London Road
Reading RG1 5AU
Helpline (Monday to Friday 10.00am–12.45pm and 2.00–4.45pm): 0118 966 8271
Fax: 0118 935 1927.
admin@bda-dyslexia.demon.co.uk
www.bda-dyslexia.org.uk

▶ **BRITISH EPILEPSY ASSOCIATION**
New Anstey House
Gate Way Drive
Yeadon
Leeds LS19 7XY
Free helpine: 0808 800 5050
From abroad: 0113 210 8850
helpline@epilepsy.org.uk
www.epilepsy.org.uk

▶ **CAMPAIGN FOR STATE EDUCATION (CASE)**
158 Durham Road
London SW20 0DG
Tel: 020 8844 8206
www.casenet.org.uk
Advises parents about issues concerning comprehensive education and maintaining the state sector.

▶ **CENTRE FOR STUDIES ON INCLUSIVE EDUCATION (CSIE)**
New Redland
Frenchay Campus
Coldharbour Lane
Bristol BS16 1QG
Tel: 0117 344 4007
Fax: 0117 344 4003

▶ **CONTACT A FAMILY**
209–211 City Road
London EC1V 1JN
Tel: 020 7608 8700
Fax: 020 7608 8701
www.cafamily.org.uk
Links up parents of children with learning difficulties.

▶ **COUNCIL FOR DISABLED CHILDREN**
8 Wakeley Street
London EC1V 7QE
Tel: 020 7843 6000
Fax: 020 7278 9512
www.ncb.org.uk

▶ **DEPARTMENT FOR EDUCATION AND SKILLS**
Tel: 0870 000 2288
Fax: 01928 794 248
info@dfes.gsi.gov.uk
www.dfes.gov.uk

▶ **DOWN'S SYNDROME EDUCATIONAL TRUST / SARAH DUFFEN CENTRE**
The Sarah Duffen Centre
Belmont Street
Southsea PO5 1NA
Tel: 023 9282 4261
Fax: 023 9282 4265
www.downsyndrome.info

▶ **DYSLEXIA INSTITUTE**
Broom Hall
8–10 Broom Hall Road
Sheffield S10 2DR
Tel: 0114 281 5905
www.dyslexia-inst.org.uk

▶ INDEPENDENT PANEL FOR
SPECIAL EDUCATION ADVICE
(IPSEA)

6 Carlow Mews
Woodbridge
Suffolk IP12 1DH

Tel: England and Wales: 0800 018 4016
        Scotland: 0131 454 0082
        N. Ireland: 01232 705 654
www.ipsea.org.uk

▶ LAW CENTRES FEDERATION

Duchess House
18–19 Warren Street
London W1T 5LR

Tel: 020 7387 8570
Fax: 020 7387 8368
info@lawcentres.org.uk
www.lawcentres.org.uk

▶ NATIONAL AUTISTIC SOCIETY

393 City Road
London EC1V 1NG

Tel: 020 7833 2299
Fax: 020 7833 9666
nas@nas.org.uk
www.nas.org.uk

▶ PARENTS FOR INCLUSION

Unit 2, 70 South Lambeth Road
London SW8 1RL

Tel: 020 7735 7735
Helpline: 020 7582 5008 (Tues, Wed, Thurs
10–12pm and 1–3pm)
www.parentsforinclusion.org

▶ SPECIAL EDUCATIONAL NEEDS
AND DISABILITY TRIBUNAL
(SENDIST)

7th Floor, Windsor House
50 Victoria Street
London SW1H 0NW

Tel: 020 7925 6926
tribunalenquiries@sendist.gsi.gov.uk
www.sendist.gov.uk

Further reading

On admissions see the DfES *School Admissions Code of Practice*.

On exclusions see DfES guidance *Improving Behaviour and Attendance: Guidance on Exclusion from Schools and Pupil Referral Units*.

On special educational needs see the DfES *Code of Practice on the Identification and Assessment of Special Educational Needs* and the booklet *How to Appeal*.

Many of the DfES publications are available online at www.dfes.gov.uk

12 **Employment**

This chapter deals with contracts, legal, unfair and wrongful dismissal, disciplinary hearings, redundancy, employment tribunals and more.

Contracts of employment

A contract is a legally binding agreement which sets out what each person involved in making the contract has agreed to do, and what they will get in return.

If you accept paid, rather than voluntary, work, and provided you are not self-employed, you will be an employee and will have a contract of employment. However, it might not be written down in one place but be made up of several documents which outline the terms of your employment contract.

RIGHT TO A WRITTEN STATEMENT OF TERMS

Because you do need to know what your basic rights are, such as when and how much you will be paid, every employee has the right to receive from their employer a written statement of the main terms and conditions of employment within two months of starting work. This will tell you:

- your name and your employer's name – this might be the company you work for, or the name of the owner if it is a small business

- your employer's address – if you work for a large company the company address may not be your workplace

- the date your employment started, and any continuous employment
- how much and how often you will be paid, and how the pay is calculated
- the hours you will be expected to work, including normal working hours
- what holidays, including public holidays, you are allowed to take, and what you will be paid
- how much paid time-off you are allowed if you are sick or injured, and what you must do to claim the sick pay
- what sort of pension the company offers
- the job title or a description of the work you are employed to do
- the place where you will be working, and any right the employer has to move you to another place of work
- how much notice your employer must give you, and how much notice you must give them, if either of you wants to end the contract
- if the contract is not permanent, how long it will last
- any collective agreements affecting the contract (these are agreements made by a trade union with the employer about issues affecting the whole workforce, such as pay and conditions, overtime and so on)
- if you will have to work outside the UK for longer than one month certain further details must be given
- the procedure the company will follow if it takes disciplinary action against you
- the name of the person you should talk to if you have a grievance about your work.

Some of these details might be included in a staff handbook or a set of company rules.

> All employees have some minimum employment rights as a matter of law. The contract may give better rights, but cannot take the minimum rights away. If your contract gives you less entitlement, it will not be enforceable.

The minimum rights are to:

- the minimum wage – this is set by law
- four weeks paid holiday in each year
- work no more than 48 hours a week, averaged over a period, unless you agree to do so
- join a trade union
- one week's paid notice of dismissal with an additional week's notice for each full year of employment, up to a maximum of 12 weeks, after one month's employment.
- statutory sick pay
- maternity leave – all women employees have the right to 26 weeks leave; if you are a woman who has been employed continuously for one year you may also qualify for additional maternity leave of a further 26 weeks (for **statutory maternity pay**, see CHAPTER 27: WELFARE BENEFITS)
- parental leave
- compassionate leave.

If you are not given the written statement of terms, or if you think that you are not being paid properly, or are worried about your contract and your rights, you should speak to your trade union representative, if you have one. If there is no recognised trade union at your workplace, you are still entitled to join one.

THE DEPARTMENT OF TRADE AND INDUSTRY is responsible for all employment law, and has produced a series of leaflets about employment contracts. Look on their website, ask at your library or Citizens Advice Bureau (see below).

Many larger cities have law centres, which offer free legal advice on many employment matters. You may need an appointment or to attend an advice session at a particular time. Contact **THE LAW CENTRES FEDERATION**.

If you want to know about your rights when you are pregnant, or when you are on maternity leave, the **MATERNITY ALLIANCE** gives free advice .

Losing your job

You may leave your job because you:

- get a promotion
- get another job
- are dismissed.

If you decide to leave your job, you must give your employer the notice required by contract, in writing if asked for. When you leave, you may be entitled to outstanding holiday pay.

Legal dismissal

If you have worked for your current employer for a year or more, you can only be legally dismissed for one of the following reasons:

- **Misconduct**. If you break the rules, or commit an offence, or get into a fight, or are disciplined on a number of matters, eventually being given a final warning, then dismissal will be for misconduct.

- **Redundancy**. If your company closes down all or part of the company, or reduces an area of work, or reorganises the way the work is done, any job losses that follow are likely to be redundancies. If you are being made redundant, your employer must consult with you or your trade union, and you should make sure you get advice early on.

- **Capability**. If you are not doing your job properly or do not have the qualifications needed, you may be dismissed.

- **Sickness record**. Health can affect capability either if you have had a lot of short absences (eg, for flu or colds) or if you have been off work for one long illness.

- **Illegal to continue to employ**. You may be dismissed because you no longer satisfy a legal requirement and to continue to employ you would break the law (an example would be if you are employed as a driver and are banned from driving).

- Some other reason which justifies dismissal. This is not common, and covers circumstances that could not be predicted by the legislation. An example is an employee's refusing to accept new terms and conditions of employment, and the employer dismissing them because of economic necessity.

If you are dismissed and the above circumstances do not apply, your dismissal is automatically unfair (see below). If you have worked for your employer for a year, you have the right to ask for a written statement of the reason for your dismissal. Your employer should reply, giving clear reasons within 14 days. If they do not, you can ask an **employment tribunal** for damages of two weeks pay.

Disciplinary hearings

If you are accused of a disciplinary offence at work, you have the right to:

- a hearing at which you can make representations, before any warning is given or before you are dismissed

- be accompanied to the hearing by a work colleague or a trade union representative.

For the disciplinary hearing to be fair and legal, your employer should make sure that you:

- are given notice of the hearing

- have advance notice of any meeting – you should not just be called away from your desk, or the shop floor, into a meeting. It is good practice to give a few days notice at least, and if the matter is serious then your employer should give you a letter.

- are told what is alleged.

If the employer does not do this, you can complain by using the company **grievance procedure**.

> If you are accused of doing something wrong at work, you need some time to think about what you did do, and why, or why the employer is wrong in thinking that it is your fault, or that you were involved. Your employer ought to tell you what the problem is either by talking to you or putting it in a letter.

For example, if you have been late for work several times, you may want to explain about family problems, or bus strikes, or an accident on the way to work.

If there has been a theft at work, you may want to think about who you were with, what days you worked and so on.

RIGHT TO BE SHOWN THE EVIDENCE

If your employer does have evidence, such as time sheets showing that you have been late, or perhaps a closed-circuit television film showing you looking suspicious, you must be allowed to see it. This is so that you can point out any errors and offer any explanations.

RIGHT TO BE ACCOMPANIED TO THE HEARING

Your employer cannot stop you from taking someone to the meeting to take notes, but they can restrict it to a trade union representative or someone with whom you work. In some companies, this person will be allowed to represent or speak for you. However, the employer does not have to allow this. They must let you talk to the person, perhaps to get advice or a suggestion of what to say next.

RIGHT TO ASK QUESTIONS

During the meeting, you can ask questions about any of the evidence, or question any of the witnesses whom the employer may bring along.

Dismissal

If your employer sacks you, you may have the right to complain to a court or a tribunal and to claim notice pay and unpaid holidays.

RIGHT TO NOTICE AND PAY

If you have worked for your employer for less than one month, you are not entitled to notice or notice pay unless your contract says so. After one month, you have the right to be given at least one week's notice before you are dismissed. This is a legal right. Your contract of employment might give you the right to a longer notice period.

If you are dismissed without notice, you have the right to be paid for the week instead. This is called **pay in lieu of notice**.

If you have worked for the same employer for several years, you may be entitled to a longer notice period. The statute says that you are entitled to one week for each complete year that you work, up to 12 weeks. For example, this means that if you work for six years, you are entitled to six weeks' notice, but 12 weeks maximum even if you have worked for twenty years. Your contract may give you a more generous provision, so check this.

If your employer dismisses you instantly because of **gross misconduct**, you will not be entitled to any notice or **pay in lieu of notice**. If this happens, and you believe you are innocent of gross misconduct, you should get help from your trade union or from an advice agency.

RIGHT TO A WRITTEN STATEMENT OF THE REASON FOR DISMISSAL

If you are dismissed but have been employed by the same company for one year or more, you have a right to be told why in writing.

WRONGFUL DISMISSAL

Sometimes an employer does not follow the contractual procedure for dismissal – for example, by not going through the disciplinary procedure. In other cases, employers may dismiss without notice. This may be a **wrongful dismissal**. This is different from **unfair dismissal** (see below). If you think that you may have been wrongfully dismissed, you may have a county court claim for damages for loss of wages. Your trade union or a Citizens Advice Bureau will be able to advise you.

UNFAIR DISMISSAL

Once you have been employed for one continuous year by the same employer, you have the right not to be unfairly dismissed. What this means is that the employer can only dismiss you for a reason that is approved by parliament and is in the *Employment Rights Act 1996*.

REASONABLENESS

Even if your employer can show that one of these reasons applies, it will not necessarily be fair to dismiss. The employer must show that it was reasonable to dismiss you on this occasion, taking into account the size of the business, the administrative resources they have, and the reason for the dismissal.

For example, if you have been disciplined for being late for work three times, but have worked for twenty years with a clean work record, and there was a good reason for the lateness, it will probably not be reasonable to dismiss you. You may have been unfairly dismissed.

If you have an accident and are in hospital, but your doctor tells you that you will be back to work in two weeks with no further problems, your employer should meet with you and give you the chance to say this, and it would probably be unfair to dismiss you, unless it was crucial to have the staff over the next two weeks.

QUALIFYING PERIOD

If you think you have been unfairly dismissed, you can make a claim to the **employment tribunal** for damages for the loss of your job, and in some cases can also ask to be reinstated. Apply to the **employment tribunal** within three months of the ending of your employment, or the claim will be disallowed.

Before you can claim unfair dismissal you must have worked for at least one year, continuously. However, there is no qualifying period, and you can claim unfair dismissal even if you have only been employed for one day, if you have been dismissed and think that it might be because of any of the following:

- your race, or your ethnic origin
- you are a woman
- you are pregnant or have asked to take maternity leave
- you are a parent and have asked for parental leave
- you are a trade union official
- you are a health and safety officer
- you have complained about something that you have a statutory right to – for example, the minimum wage.

Redundancy

Unfortunately, from time to time, organisations find that they cannot continue to run the business, or part of the business, effectively, and decide either to reduce the workforce or to close down a part of or the whole factory or workplace.

> A person who is made redundant lawfully is dismissed fairly, and cannot complain to a tribunal.

In order for a redundancy to be fair, the following conditions must be satisfied:

- there must be a genuine redundancy situation
- if twenty or more employees are going to be made redundant, the employer must ensure that they consult properly with the trade union or staff representatives
- any selections for redundancy must be fair and for proper reasons
- efforts must be made to find suitable alternative employment
- redundancy pay must be paid.

WHAT IS A GENUINE REDUNDANCY?

> A genuine redundancy exists if the need for the worker to do the job for which he or she was employed has reduced or diminished.

This can arise because the factory is not profitable and is going to be closed down, or because the company has decided to stop producing a certain type of goods and concentrate on another aspect of its industry, leading to closure of part of the business or a reduction in the size of the workforce.

Redundancy does not usually occur simply because one organisation buys another workplace or company and changes its name. This is a **transfer of an undertaking**, and the employees will usually keep the same contractual rights, regardless of the company owner or the change in name.

If this happens to you and you are told that you will be made redundant, you should take advice immediately.

CONSULTATION

Employers should talk to the trade unions or staff representatives as soon as they realise they are going to make redundancies, in order to try to avoid them. Trade union members often come up with ideas that can reduce the effects of redundancy, such as:

- shorter hours
- part-time working
- job-sharing
- voluntary redundancy and early retirement.

Consultation should be open and genuine, and should involve discussion of:

- the level of redundancy payments
- voluntary redundancy schemes
- how workers will be selected for redundancy
- the timescales for implementation.

The amount of notice of redundancy that an employer must give is set out in law, and will vary depending on how many employees are threatened with redundancy.

SELECTION FOR REDUNDANCY

Often a company will decide that it needs to reduce its workforce, but not close down completely. They will then have to choose who is made redundant and who stays. Different employers will use different methods to choose who stays and who goes, but the decision must be fair. They are not allowed, for example, to select you for redundancy because:

- you are pregnant or on maternity leave
- you are a trade union member
- of your race or your sex
- you have a disability

- you have made complaints about any of your statutory rights in the past
- you have taken, or asked to take, parental leave.

Many employers will, however, look at the length of service and the disciplinary records of employees, and the skills which they most need for the business. The decision-making process should be fair and open, and you should be able to find out why you have been selected, and should have a right of appeal if a mistake has been made, or you think the reasons are unfair.

REDUNDANCY PAYMENTS

All employees are entitled to a redundancy payment if they have worked for the same employer continuously for at least two years, of:

- a week's wage for each complete year of service, provided that your weekly wage does not exceed the cap, which is currently £230.00
- 1½ times your weekly wage for every year that you have worked for your employer when you are forty-one or over, subject to the same cap.

Entitlement continues until the normal retirement age for your business, or until you reach age 65.

Of course, some employers will pay much more generous redundancy payments, particularly if employees agree to take voluntary redundancy.

Employment tribunals

HOW TO CLAIM

If you have a complaint about something at work, the best way to deal with it is to use an **internal complaints** or **disciplinary procedure**, or ask your trade union or staff association to help you. However, if you have tried this and the problem still exists, you may be able to ask an **employment tribunal** to decide the case.

Employment tribunals can deal with a variety of employment disputes, but cannot deal with everything. What they can and cannot do is set out in statute and is called the tribunals' **jurisdiction**. They can hear claims relating to:

- unfair dismissal

- any type of discrimination in employment
- the minimum wage
- working-time regulations.

If you think you have a claim, you must send details of you, your employer and what you are complaining about to the central office of the employment tribunals. The easiest way to do this is to fill in a form called an ET1 (the **originating application**). If you are taking a case to an employment tribunal, there are some booklets produced by the DEPARTMENT OF TRADE AND INDUSTRY that explain the various steps. The address is at the end of this chapter.

TIME LIMITS

You should get advice as soon as possible. All cases that go to court have time limits, and if you miss the time limit you may be prevented from taking your case any further, even if it is a good claim. For most employment cases the time limit is only three months from the date of the event about which you are complaining.

> In some cases the employment tribunal can extend the time if you are late, but this is only in very limited circumstances, and in unfair dismissal cases is very rare indeed. So if you are dismissed, make sure you get a copy of the appropriate form as soon as possible, and send it off in good time.

You do not have to send a copy to the employer, the tribunal will do that, and will then write to you to tell you what will happen next.

Effective date of dismissal

Sometimes the date on which you are dismissed is not clear, perhaps because of notice pay or because of a hearing.

> In law, the date of the dismissal is the day it takes effect, which usually means the last day that you are paid for.

- So, if you are sacked but given two weeks' notice, and have to work the notice, the last day of work will be the date of the dismissal.

- If, on the other hand, you are sacked and given two weeks' pay in lieu of notice and told to leave the same day, then that will be your last day of work, and the date of your dismissal.

The three months will start to run from the following day, and it does not matter if it is a Saturday, it still counts. If you are not sure about this date, get help from an advice agency as soon as possible.

FORMALITY

Employment tribunals are not the same as the courts. They are not so formal, nobody will wear any robes or wigs, but people will dress smartly when they go to give evidence or represent someone. There are rules about who speaks first, and what sort of questions can and cannot be asked.

The tribunal will usually be made up of three people. The chairman, who sits in the middle, will be a lawyer with experience of employment law issues. The two members, who sit either side, are not legally qualified, but are appointed from industry, the trade unions, voluntary organisations and employer organisations.

If you are representing yourself, the chairman of the tribunal can explain the procedure to you, and if you do not understand anything, you should ask for help.

COSTS

There is no **legal aid** available for representation at an employment tribunal hearing, although some people may be eligible for **green form advice** (initial help) before the hearing.

The general rule is that there are no costs awarded in the tribunal. This means that you should not have to pay costs if you lose, but you will not be able to recover any costs from the employer if you win.

However, the tribunal does have discretion to award costs to either you or the employer if it thinks that either of you have behaved in a way that is unreasonable. For example, if you have been constantly asked to give the employer a copy of a letter that you say is important, or have been very rude and aggressive, or if they have sent you numerous threatening letters, or have not given you any of their documents.

However, in general, tribunals are unwilling to award costs, and before they do, they have to take account of the ability of the person to pay. So, if you have lost your job and are in receipt of benefits, this would be taken into account.

SETTLEMENT OF CASES AND ACAS

Once you have sent your claim to the tribunal, you will be sent a copy of the employer's answer, and the ARBITRATION AND CONCILIATION SERVICE (ACAS) will write to you, offering to help to negotiate a settlement. ACAS is independent and can act as a go-between (see CHAPTER 3: LAWYERS AND THE COURTS). It is always a good idea to talk to them and tell them what you want to happen. For example, if your claim is for unfair dismissal, you may be asking for notice pay, a basic award and some compensation.

Common problems at work

DEDUCTIONS FROM PAY

Employers are only allowed to make deductions from your wages if the law allows or requires them to do so, for tax and national insurance, or if you have a contractual agreement with them to do so. This will cover things like deductions made as contributions to a pension scheme, or payments for private health insurance or to a trade union for your membership.

If you think your employer is deducting money for something to which you have not agreed, you should find out what they say it is for and take some advice. If the deduction is not lawful, you can claim repayment through a tribunal, if the employer refuses to refund your money.

PAYSLIPS

All employees are entitled to receive payslips which set out what they have earned each pay period, what tax and national insurance has been deducted and any other alterations made to pay. You do not have to ask for this, it is an absolute right.

If you do not get payslips, or if the slips you get do not set out all the deductions, and your employer will not put this right, you can apply to an **employment tribunal** for a declaration of your rights. Tribunals also have a discretion to award compensation.

BULLYING AND HARASSMENT

If you are bullied or harassed at work, you should complain to your union or staff representative, or use the grievance procedure to make a complaint. This can be very difficult, especially if the person bullying you is a manager or more senior person. Try to talk to colleagues and get support.

> Bullying at work is a recognised problem, and employers have a contractual duty to take complaints seriously. If the bullying or harassment makes you ill, the employer may be breaching health and safety rules requiring them to provide a safe place of work.

If you feel so demoralised and fed up with work that you want to leave, try to take some advice from one of the agencies listed at the end of this chapter. In some cases, the employer's treatment can amount to a breach of contract, and your decision to leave may be a **constructive dismissal**, which may be an unfair dismissal.

CHANGES TO JOB DESCRIPTION

Many employers will try to change your contract while you are working for them. This may be to change the hours you work, the job you do, or even the place that you work. In general, an employer can only change your contractual terms if you agree to the changes, or if the changes are vital to ensure that the business can keep going.

Employees can agree to some changes in the contract itself – for example, by agreeing to move workplace – so you should always read your contract of employment carefully to see what it says about variations to the contract.

The second way that employees can agree to changes is if a trade union negotiates with the employer on their behalf. Often the trade union will agree to some changes, in exchange for other advantages. If your trade union is negotiating for you, ask your shop steward for more information.

If your employer tries to impose a change on you, without discussing it with you or a trade union, and it is not something you agree to, the change may not be legal and may not bind you. If this happens, take advice and do not accept the changes until you have done so.

HEALTH AND SAFETY

All employers have a duty to provide their employees with a safe system of work. This covers obvious things like:

- safe machinery
- supplying the correct tools for a job
- ensuring that people are properly trained and supervised
- fire regulations and fire exits
- safe bricks and mortar.

So a leaking roof, or dangerous cables, could mean a breach of health and safety.

However, health and safety requirements will also vary depending on the work you do. So, if you:

- work with the public, you may need to be given extra support or protection
- use computer screens, your employer needs to make sure that you take adequate breaks and have eye tests
- work in a hospital, the employer will need to make sure that all hygiene regulations are complied with
- work with dangerous substances, special masks, gloves, and disposal methods may be required.

Each workplace must have a designated health and safety representative. If you are concerned about your workplace, this is the first person to talk to, if your manager does not take any notice of your concerns.

LONG HOURS OF WORK

Many workers are protected by law from having to work more than 48 hours in any seven-day period. The rules apply to all workers, *except* those who have signed an agreement with their employer to exclude them from the legal provisions, and those who work as or in:

- air, rail, road, sea, inland waterway or lake transport

- sea fishing

- doctors in training

- the police and armed forces.

> **The working time regulations** state that no worker, unless excluded, should work longer than eleven hours in any 24-hour period, and that all workers should have at least 24 hours' continuous break in every seven-day period of work.

Finding your employment lawyer

If you think you may have a legal claim against your employer, the first place to go is to your trade union. If you are a member, you will be able to get advice and, if the union thinks you have a good claim, you can get representation from the union, or a firm of solicitors funded by the union.

If you are not a member of a trade union, you should check all your household insurance policies and your personal insurance policies if you have any. Many policies also provide free legal advice on a whole range of issues, including problems at work.

Otherwise, if you need good, free advice, contact one of the organisations listed below. The Citizens Advice Bureau should be able to advise whether you need legal help or not. They will have lists of local solicitors who specialise in particular problems, such as employment matters.

Remember, many people do represent themselves at employment tribunals. The government website has many information leaflets to help. These are also available by telephone, or from some libraries and advice centres.

If you need to find a solicitor, a local advice agency is a good first stop. Otherwise, a local library may have the LAW SOCIETY list of solicitors. You should look for a firm which:

- is reasonably local

- has recent experience of employment case work

- has a **legal aid franchise** to do employment work, even if you are not eligible for legal aid.

If you are not earning, or are on a very low wage, then a firm with a legal aid franchise to do employment work is important, otherwise you cannot be advised under the scheme.

> Although there is no legal aid available to represent employees at tribunals, you can receive legally aided advice and assistance to help you prepare a case, and maybe to negotiate a settlement.

If you cannot get free advice, and money is a problem, ask if the solicitor will advise under a **conditional fee agreement**. Under the agreement, you will only pay the solicitor if you win or settle the case and recover damages.

Organisations   i

► **ARBITRATION AND CONCILIATION SERVICE (ACAS)**
Brandon House
180 Borough High Street
London SE1 1LW
www.acas.org.uk
National ACAS helpline: 08457 47 47 47

► **BRITISH SAFETY COUNCIL**
70 Chancellors Road
London W6 9RS
Tel: 020 8741 1231
Fax: 020 8741 4555
www.britishsafetycouncil.org

► **DEPARTMENT OF TRADE AND INDUSTRY**
DTI Enquiry Unit
1 Victoria Street
London SW1H 0ET
Tel: 020 7215 5000
dti.enquiries@dti.gsi.gov.uk
www.dti.gov.uk

► **EMPLOYMENT APPEAL TRIBUNAL**
Audit House
58 Victoria Embankment
London EC4Y 0DS
Tel: 020 7273 1040
Enquiry line: 020 7273 1041
Fax: 020 7273 1045
www.employmentappeals.gov.uk

► **EMPLOYMENT SOLICITORS ONLINE**
www.employment-solicitors.co.uk

► **EQUAL OPPORTUNITIES COMMISSION**
Arndale House
Arndale Centre
Manchester M4 3EQ
Tel: 0845 601 5901
Fax: 0161 838 1733
info@eoc.org.uk
www.eoc.org.uk

▶ **HEALTH AND SAFETY EXECUTIVE**

Postal enquiries:
HSE Infoline
Caerphilly Business Park
Caerphilly CF83 3GG

Infoline (Monday to Friday, 8.30am to 5.00pm):
08701 545500

Fax: 02920 859260
hseinformationservices@natbrit.com
www.hse.gov.uk

▶ **LAW CENTRES FEDERATION**

Duchess House
18–19 Warren Street
London W1T 5LR

Tel: 020 7387 8570
Fax: 020 7387 8368
info@lawcentres.org.uk
www.lawcentres.org.uk

▶ **LAW SOCIETY**

113 Chancery Lane
London WC2A 1PL

Tel: 020 7242 1222
Fax: 020 7831 0344
info.services@lawsociety.org.uk
www.lawsoc.org.uk

▶ **MATERNITY ALLIANCE**

3rd Floor West
2–6 Northburgh Street
London EC1V 0AY

Tel: 020 7588 8583
Information line: 020 7490 7638
Fax: 020 7014 1350
info@maternityalliance.org.uk
www.maternityalliance.org.uk

▶ **NATIONAL ASSOCIATION OF CITIZENS ADVICE BUREAUX (NACAB)**

Myddelton House
115–123 Pentonville Road
London N1 9LZ

www.nacab.org.uk

Adviceguide: the National Association of Citizens Advice Bureaux offers fact sheets covering issues such as employment, housing and taxation

www.adviceguide.org.uk

▶ **TRADES UNION CONGRESS (TUC)**

Congress House
Great Russell Street
London WC1B 3LS

Tel: 020 7636 4030
info@tuc.org.uk
www.tuc.org.uk

Other useful websites

▶ **LAWRIGHTS**

www.compactlaw.co.uk
www.employmenttribunals.gov.uk

This site provides information and guidance about employment tribunals.

Further reading

Employment Law: An Advisor's Handbook, published by the LEGAL ACTION GROUP.

13 **Environment**

Environmentalists need to be sure of the legal framework in which they are operating. This chapter suggests ways of finding that information and the right legal help.

If you are reading this, it may be because you:

- are plagued by noisy neighbours or rats or damp (see CHAPTER 15: HOUSING)

- believe the health of your household is being damaged or put at risk by night flights, electricity pylons or mobile phone masts

- need to do something about a company causing water pollution or air pollution in the region

- want to investigate and expose damage to biodiversity in Papua New Guinea or icebergs in Antarctica or patenting of grains in India.

Few environmentalists would draw a rigid distinction between what occurs directly in their neighbourhood and what occurs on the other side of the world but has a global effect. The points raised by them may be in the public interest as well as their narrow personal interest.

Environmental law reflects this. It is a mixture of international treaties and European directives, national law bringing these into effect, and local law such as planning law or the *law of nuisance*. Other laws, such as those affecting trade, may have implications for the environment.

Do I need a lawyer?

> The first question to ask is whether you need a lawyer at all. Lawyers can advise you on the legal framework. They are not in the best position either to collect evidence and information or to campaign, both of which are essential to succeeding in your aim.

Many environmental concerns relate to the impact of outside events on the homes of local people – for example, the siting of a new airport, railway line, waste tip, or factory. *Article 8* of the *European Convention on Human Rights*, now part of the *Human Rights Act 1998* – the right to respect for private and family life and home and correspondence – implies a duty of the state to provide sufficient information on matters affecting the person's home (see CHAPTER 16: HUMAN RIGHTS ACT). A number of statutes set out an obligation to provide information on the environmental effect of decisions. Where there is no specific statutory provision, the *Environmental Information Regulations 1992/3240* apply (available via HER MAJESTY'S STATIONERY OFFICE (HMSO)). You may be able to become a shareholder in a corporation to obtain more information about them.

You can also approach the ENVIRONMENT AGENCY, which is the state agency with overall responsibility for safeguarding the environment.

However, one of the best sources of information is via other environmentalists. The environmental movement was one of the first to see the potential of the internet and email: in 1998, the first round of *GATT, MAI*, was aborted after a successful internet-based campaign. So do not underestimate the importance of local groups and networks.

When do I need a lawyer?

You might need a lawyer in the following situations:

- you are launching a campaign directed at corporate or individual threats to the environment that may infringe the *law of libel/slander* (see CHAPTER 21: LIBEL)

- you are planning direct action or a demonstration – you should seek advice from a specialist who has expertise in both environmental and criminal law

- representation at a planning enquiry

- judicial review or action under the *Human Rights Act* or cases relying on international law: all these require some legal expertise (see CHAPTER 16: HUMAN RIGHTS ACT)

- a legal opinion for use in a campaign

- a private action for personal injury (see CHAPTER 4: ACCIDENTS AND INJURIES)

Where can I find a lawyer?

It is important always to ask any lawyer you approach about their expertise, their commitment and their knowledge of this area of law. An obvious test is to ask how many cases in the field they have handled and how recently.

Many environmentalists rely on committed lawyers whom they know. This has the advantage that the lawyers will be specialists, with knowledge of international developments. If you do not have your own contacts, there are networks of environmental lawyers who will provide free initial advice, such as:

- ENVIRONMENTAL LAW FOUNDATION

- EARTHRIGHTS

- FIELD

- or, transnationally, E-LAW.

There is generally greater availability in London than elsewhere, which is another reason for developing your own network.

In some cases, in particular those involving housing, the local law centre or Citizens Advice Bureau may be able to help.

Three non-governmental organisations (NGOs), FRIENDS OF THE EARTH, GREENPEACE and the WORLDWIDE FUND FOR NATURE (WWF) have their own in-house legal expertise and you can try approaching one of them if your case raises public interest questions. NGOs that do not have in-house lawyers may be able to approach barristers directly under the BAR DIRECT SCHEME (contact GENERAL COUNCIL OF THE BAR).

Who pays?

In some cases, especially public interest ones, the lawyer will act for free or under a conditional fee agreement, or you may get the support of an NGO.

If you qualify (it is means-tested), the LEGAL SERVICES COMMISSION will fund cases if they are also satisfied that the merits of the claim warrant it being given public funding: the criteria are set out at on their website. In other cases the court can order that a litigant bringing a case in the public interest should not pay costs, even if they lose, although in our system dominated by the 'loser pays' principle, this is unusual.

Organisations   [i]

▶ **BRITISH SAFETY COUNCIL**
70 Chancellors Road
London W6 9RS
Tel: 020 8741 1231
Fax: 020 8741 4555
www.britishsafetycouncil.org

▶ **EARTHRIGHTS CHARITY**
Jamie Woolley
41 Rupert Road
Sheffield SR7 1RN
Tel: 01142 205575 / 020 8977 7413
www.earthrights.org.uk

▶ **EARTHRIGHTS SOLICITORS**
Little Orchard
School Lane, Molehill Green
Takeley
Essex CM22 6PJ
Tel: 01279 870391
earthrights@gn.apc.org

▶ **ENVIRONMENT AGENCY**
www.environment-agency.gov.uk

▶ **ENVIRONMENTAL LAW ALLIANCE WORLDWIDE (E-LAW)**
1877 Garden Avenue
Eugene OR 97403
USA
elawus@elaw.org
www.elaw.org

▶ **ENVIRONMENTAL LAW FOUNDATION**
Suite 309, 16 Baldwin's Gardens
Hatton Square
London EC1N 7RJ
Tel: 020 7404 1030
Fax: 020 7404 1032
info@elflaw.org
www.elflaw.org

▶ **FIELD**
52–53 Russell Square
London WC1B 4HP
Tel: 020 7637 7950
Fax: 020 72637 7951
field@field.org.uk

▶ **FRIENDS OF THE EARTH**
26–28 Underwood Street
London N1 7JQ
Tel: 020 7490 1555
Fax: 020 7490 0881
www.foe.co.uk

▶ **GENERAL COUNCIL OF THE BAR**
3 Bedford Row
London WC1R 4DB
Tel: 020 7242 0082
Records Office: 020 7242 0934
Fax: 020 7831 9217
www.barcouncil.org.uk

▶ **GREENPEACE UK**
Canonbury Villas
London N1 2PN
Tel: 0207 865 8100
Fax: 020 7865 8200
info@uk.greenpeace.org
www.greenpeace.org

▶ **HER MAJESTY'S STATIONERY OFFICE (HMSO)**
www.hmso.gov.uk

▶ **LAW CENTRES FEDERATION**
Duchess House
18–19 Warren Street
London W1T 5LR
Tel: 020 7387 8570
Fax: 020 7387 8368
info@lawcentres.org.uk
www.lawcentres.org.uk

▶ **LEGAL SERVICES COMMISSION**
85 Gray's Inn Road
London WC1X 8TX
Tel: 020 7759 0000
www.legalservices.gov.uk
www.justask.org.uk
Regional telephone helplines on various legal subjects.

▶ **NATIONAL ASSOCIATION OF CITIZENS ADVICE BUREAUX (NACAB)**
Myddelton House
115–123 Pentonville Road
London N1 9LZ
Tel: 020 7833 2181
www.nacab.org.uk
Adviceguide: the National Association of Citizens Advice Bureaux offers fact sheets covering issues such as employment, housing and taxation
www.adviceguide.org.uk

▶ **WORLD WILDLIFE FUND (WWF)**
WWF–UK
Panda House
Weyside Park
Godalming
Surrey GU7 1XR
Tel: 01483 426444
Fax: 01483 426409
www.wwf.org.uk/core/index.asp

14 **Family law**

The aim of this chapter is to try to address some of the many and varied areas of law that affect family life, and to indicate where to turn for help and advice.

Divorce

The law on divorce is currently in a state of flux. The *Family Law Act 1996* envisaged a radically reformed divorce procedure. The Lord Chancellor announced in June 1999 that there is to be an indefinite delay in the implementation of these provisions. We have therefore set out the current law on divorce, but it is unclear whether the *Family Law Act 1996* will be brought in at all.

GROUNDS

Under the current law, the court has to be satisfied that the marriage has **irretrievably broken down** before granting a divorce. The court cannot reach this conclusion unless the petitioner (the person seeking the divorce) establishes one of the following grounds:

- that the **respondent** (the other partner, whom the petitioner wishes to divorce) has committed adultery and the petitioner finds it intolerable to live with the respondent

- that the respondent has behaved in such a way that the petitioner cannot reasonably be expected to live with the respondent

- that the respondent has deserted the petitioner for a continuous period of at least two years immediately before the presentation of the petition

- that the parties to the marriage have lived apart for a continuous period of two years immediately before the presentation of the petition, and the respondent consents to a decree being granted

- that the parties to the marriage have lived apart for a continuous period of at least five years immediately before the presentation of the petition.

PETITION FOR DIVORCE

This cannot be issued until a year has passed since the marriage. In addition to contesting the five grounds set out above, there are two other potential defences:

- Where a petition is based on five years' separation, the respondent can defend the petition on the basis that the dissolution of the marriage will result in grave financial or other hardship and that it would in all the circumstances be wrong to dissolve the marriage.

- In a case based either on two years' separation plus the consent of the respondent or on five years' separation, the respondent can apply to the court for consideration of their financial position after divorce. The court is then prohibited from making the decree absolute unless it is satisfied:

  - that the petitioner should not be required to make any financial provision for the respondent

  - or that the financial provision made by the petitioner for the respondent is reasonable and fair or the best that can be made in the circumstances.

  It follows that this ground can only be used to delay a **Decree Absolute** (the final stage of the divorce) and not to prevent such a decree being granted.

Judicial separation

The law on **judicial separation** will also be changed if the *Family Law Act 1996* comes into force. Decrees of judicial separation will be replaced with **separation orders**. The one-year bar on divorce petitions does not apply to petitions for judicial separation. The grounds for judicial separation are similar to those for divorce, except that it is currently unnecessary to show that the marriage has broken down irretrievably. This requirement will be added if the *Family Law Act 1996* comes into force. It is not possible to defend the proceedings on the basis that the decree will result in grave financial or other hardship.

> The court can make orders for the sale of the matrimonial home and/or for the transfer of assets from one party to the other on judicial separation.

Nullity

> In limited circumstances a party to a marriage can obtain a **decree of nullity**. The effect of a decree of nullity is that in law there has never been an existing marriage.

Section 11 of the *Matrimonial Causes Act* states that a marriage is **void** (legally over) if:

- it is not a valid marriage under the *Marriage Act* because:
  - the parties are in a prohibited relationship (eg, parent and child, brother and sister)
  - either person is under 16
  - the marriage ceremony did not comply with the necessary legal formalities
- the husband and wife are not male and female
- either the husband or the wife was lawfully married at the time of marriage
- in the case of a polygamous marriage (more than one wife) entered into outside England or Wales, that either party was living in England or Wales at the time of the marriage.

Under Section 12 of the *Matrimonial Causes Act* a marriage is voidable if:

- it has not been consummated owing to the incapacity of either party

- it has not been consummated owing to the wilful refusal of the other party

- either party did not validly consent to the marriage

- at the time of the marriage either party was suffering from mental disorder of such a kind or to such an extent as to be unfit for marriage

- at the time of the marriage the other party was suffering from venereal disease in a communicable form (the party seeking the decree has to be ignorant of the fact at the time)

- at the time of the marriage the respondent was pregnant by someone other than their spouse (the party seeking the decree has to be ignorant of the fact at the time).

A voidable marriage is legally over once the **decree of nullity** is granted.

The Act prevents the court from granting nullity on the grounds that the marriage is voidable if:

- the party seeking a decree led their spouse reasonably to believe that she/he would not seek to do so

- it would be unjust to the other party to grant the decree.

The court has the same financial powers on granting a decree of nullity as it has in cases of divorce. Unlike divorce, an application for nullity can be brought within the first year of marriage.

Ancillary relief

Ancillary relief is the term given to the procedures of the court dealing with the financial position of the parties to a marriage on divorce.

CHILD MAINTENANCE

The court no longer deals with the majority of cases of child maintenance, where applications have to be made to the **CHILD SUPPORT AGENCY (CSA)**. The court does still retain power to make orders for child maintenance, if:

- the income of the parent who is not looking after the child is large enough to bring the assessment up to the ceiling for payments under the CSA, and the parent looking after the child seeks more maintenance

- an order to pay school fees for the child is sought

- the child has a disability and an allowance is needed to cover the extra costs of caring for the child

- a lump sum, property adjustment or transfer of property order is sought for the benefit of a child

- an application is made for an order against the person caring for the child.

The system under the *1991 plus 1995 Child Support Acts* was inflexible and unfair. The *Child Support, Pensions and Social Security Act 2000* introduced a simplified system based on three rates:

- the basic rate

- a reduced rate

- a flat rate.

Under the basic rate the non-resident parent will pay 15 per cent of his/her net income for the first child; 20 per cent for two children; 25 per cent for three or more children.

A reduced rate will apply when that parent's net income is between £100 and £200 per week.

A flat rate will apply where the non-resident parent's income is less than £100 per week or she/he is in receipt of prescribed benefits. There are also reductions in the amount payable depending on the number of nights the children stay with the contributing parent or if that parent has other relevant children.

> If a parent deliberately makes a false statement or does not provide the information requested, they are liable to a fine. Penalties for non-payment include imprisonment and disqualification from driving.

The main powers that the court has are as follows:

- **Periodic payments orders** The court can grant periodic payments to a spouse to cover maintenance, and it can grant maintenance before a final order is made. At the final hearing the court will consider what maintenance should be granted. Many orders now contain provision for a link between maintenance and the retail price index. The party who has been awarded maintenance can return to court if circumstances change or the value of the order has not kept up with inflation.

- **Lump sum** or **property adjustment orders** The court can order either party to pay to the other a lump sum, and if necessary can order assets including the matrimonial home to be sold in order to realise such a sum. Alternatively the court has wide powers to order the transfer of property from one party to the other, including transfer of the matrimonial home.

- **Earmarking pensions** Since August 1996 the court has had the power to earmark pensions or death-in-service benefits. Under this provision the court can decide what percentage of a pension should be payable to the spouse who has obtained the order. This order lapses on the death or remarriage of the beneficiary under the order.

- **Pension-sharing order** In cases where the petition for divorce or nullity is filed after 1 December 2000 the court also has the power to make a pension-sharing order. The beneficiary under the order gets a percentage of their ex-spouse's pension fund transferred to them.

Once the court has made an order at the final hearing of an application for ancillary relief it is not normally possible to reapply to the court for an order for a lump sum or transfer of property. The court does retain the power to vary a periodic payments order while it is still in effect. It can also make a lump sum payment or property adjustment order in favour of a party who has the benefit of a periodic payments order.

Cohabitation

The rights of a **cohabitee** (someone living with a partner, but who is not married) are considerably less than those of a husband or wife. It comes as an unpleasant surprise to many partners who are breaking up to find that they have contributed significantly to the family income but have few rights.

A cohabitee:

- needs the permission of the court to seek any order in relation to the child of their partner

- has no right to apply for maintenance on the break-up of a relationship

- may not have acquired an interest in a joint property.

It is important to take legal advice if buying a property with another person.

The deeds relating to the property are conclusive and can specify:

- that a property is jointly owned

- the proportions in which the parties own it.

It commonly occurs that both parties have their names on the deeds but there is no declaration of their interests. In such a case the court will first of all decide whether there was an express agreement between the parties as to their respective shares in the property. This agreement need not be in writing.

If there was no agreement, the court will have to decide what is fair. The court will look at the contributions to the purchase of the property and the mortgage, but also at other factors such as financial expenses borne by the parties, in order to determine how the property should be divided.

Where the property is registered in only one name, the onus is on the other party to satisfy the court that she/he has an interest. The court will decide whether there was an express agreement, not necessarily in writing, that the applicant should have an interest. In the absence of any such agreement the court will look at whether the applicant contributed directly to the purchase price or to the mortgage. Other contributions to the household budget such as paying for food or even towards the upkeep of the property are unlikely to be sufficient. (See CHAPTER 15: HOUSING.)

Disputes relating to children

The majority of disputes between parents in relation to their children are governed by the *Children Act 1989*.

PARENTAL RESPONSIBILITY

> The *Children Act 1989* defines parental responsibility as: 'all rights, duties, powers, responsibilities and authority which by law a parent of a child has in relation to the child and his property'.

Parental responsibility has many different aspects to it. They include:

- naming a child
- determining the child's religion
- determining the child's education
- consenting (or not) to the child's medical treatment
- consenting (or not) to the taking of blood for testing
- consenting (or not) to adoption
- arranging for the child's emigration
- protecting and maintaining the child
- administering the child's property
- allowing the child to be interviewed.

The above list is not exhaustive, as parental responsibility is continually developing to address different circumstances and situations.

Acquiring parental responsibility

MARRIED PARENTS

If the parents are married when the child is born then both mother and father acquire parental responsibility automatically.

UNMARRIED PARENTS

If the parents are not married when the child is born then currently only the mother acquires parental responsibility automatically.

An unmarried father can obtain parental responsibility in two ways:

- by agreement with the mother – by filling out the appropriate form and registering the agreement with the PRINCIPAL REGISTRY OF THE FAMILY DIVISION

- by court order – if the mother does not agree to share parental responsibility, the father may apply to the court for an order.

In considering whether to make an order for parental responsibility the court will take into account the following factors:

- the reasons for applying for the order

- the attachment between the child and the father

- the commitment the father has shown to the child.

Parental responsibility can also be acquired (to take effect after the parent's death), if a parent appoints a guardian for the child.

> The *Adoption and Children Act 2002* (to be implemented in stages during 2003 and 2004) will amend how parental responsibility can be aquired. Section 111 of the Act will amend the *Children Act 1989* so that a father not married to the mother at the time of the child's birth will acquire parental responsibility if his name is placed on the birth certificate or registered under the *Births and Deaths Registration Act 1953*. A father cannot *not* register his name on the child's birth certificate without the consent of the mother.

EXTENDED RIGHTS FOR STEP-PARENTS

Section 112 of the *Adoption and Children Act 2002* when implemented will amend the *Children Act 1989* to allow a step-parent to acquire parental responsibility for a child of his/her spouse:

- agreement between step-parent and parents who have parental responsibility for the child

- or by order of the court.

TERMINATION OF PARENTAL RESPONSIBILITY

An appointment of a **guardian** can be changed and/or **revoked** (set aside) either by the individual who has been appointed as guardian or by court order. The child can also apply to the court to revoke the order.

If parental responsibility has been acquired automatically (by married parents when the child is born and by unmarried mothers), it can only be terminated by the granting of an adoption order in favour of another party.

Where parental responsibility has been obtained by agreement or court order it can be revoked by a court order.

Parental responsibility ends automatically when a child reaches the age of 18.

CHILDREN'S ACT 1989 SECTION 8 ORDERS

Section 8 orders deal with:

- residence
- contact with a child
- disputes that may exist between individuals who share parental responsibility.

Section 8 orders currently cannot be made for a child who has reached the age of 16. However, when the *Adoption and Children Act 2002* is implemented, the court will have the power to direct that a residence order can remain in force until the child is 18.

Section 8 orders should be made at the magistrates'/county court that is local to the child, not the applicant.

RESIDENCE ORDERS

A **residence order** determines with whom a child should live, and can be made in favour of any individual. More than one person can have a residence order and it is usual for the order to set out who the child will live with either over certain specified times or indefinitely.

An order that has been made indefinitely can still be challenged and revoked either by court order or agreement.

> If a child is taken into care by a local authority then any existing residence orders are automatically superseded (invalid).

Where a residence order exists, the person whom it favours can remove the child from the jurisdiction of the court for up to 28 days. For any longer periods they must have the agreement of someone who either has parental responsibility or has a court order.

CONTACT ORDERS

A **contact order** is an order that sets out when the person with whom the child lives should make the child available to spend time with another person. The contact can be visiting or staying. Contact orders can be varied or revoked.

PROHIBITED STEPS ORDER

This is an order which specifically directs the person named in the order not to do a specified act without permission of the court.

SPECIFIC ISSUE ORDER

This is an order that deals with a specific aspect of parental responsibility, where those with parental responsibility cannot agree and so the matter must be determined by the court – for example, if parents are unable to agree on which school a child should attend.

APPLYING FOR SECTION 8 ORDERS

In the majority of cases, it is usually the parents that are in disagreement. However, other people can in certain circumstances apply:

- a parent or guardian of a child
- any individual who has a residence order in their favour.

The following individuals are also entitled to apply for residence or contact orders automatically:

- a person with whom the child has lived for three years – the period of time does not have to be continuous but must not begin more than five years, or end more than three months, before the making of the application
- a spouse or ex-spouse, where the child is a child of the family
- where the person applying has the consent of those who have parental responsibility.

> If a person is not entitled to apply automatically for a residence
> or contact order, then they must first obtain permission from the court
> to make this application. This is known as obtaining **leave to apply**.
> For example, where a grandparent is seeking an order for contact.

APPLICATION FOR LEAVE

In considering whether to grant leave the court will take into account the
following factors:

- the nature of the proposed application
- the applicant's connection to the child
- any risk there might be of the proposed application disrupting the
  child's life to such an extent that the child may be harmed by it
- if the child is being looked after by a local authority
- the authority's plans for the child's future
- the wishes and feelings of the parent.

APPLICATIONS BY CHILDREN

A child can in certain circumstances make a *Section 8 application*. As courts are
cautious of involving children in what can become a highly charged emotional situation, a child must also seek leave before an application can be
pursued. For a child seeking leave, the only factor the court is directed to
consider is:

- whether the child has sufficient understanding to make the proposed
  application.

However, the fact that the child does have sufficient understanding to make
the application does not mean the court must grant leave. The court will
consider all the general circumstances of the case, including:

- the best interests of the child
- the nature of the application and whether the child's case is the same as
  another party's
- the likelihood of success.

Applications for leave by children should be made in the High Court.

A child may also apply to become a **respondent** in a *Section 8 application*. The request must be made by filing a form C2. The court will then consider the application at a hearing where all parties are present.

For further guidance contact the CHILDREN'S LEGAL CENTRE or NATIONAL YOUTH ADVOCACY SERVICE.

APPLICATION FOR SECTION 8 ORDERS – PROCEDURE

Directions appointment
Once the application has been issued, the court will list the matter for a short hearing (the **directions appointment**), for usually not more than 30 minutes.

Conciliation appointment
If a CHILDREN AND FAMILY COURT ADVISORY SUPPORT SERVICE (CAFCASS) officer is available at the first directions appointment, the parties will be asked to speak to the officer without their lawyers. This is called a **conciliation appointment** and the purpose is to see if some agreement can be reached without further court involvement.

If an agreement is reached to each party's satisfaction then the court will consider whether that agreement needs to be set down in a court order or not. An order will only be made where it is considered necessary.

If it is not possible to resolve the matter at the conciliation appointment, the parties and the court will consider what needs to be done before the matter can be adjudicated upon. It is usual for statements to be filed and a CAFCASS officer to report on the issues in dispute. These reports can take up to four months to prepare and include the relevant child(ren) being seen by the officer.

PRINCIPLES APPLIED BY THE COURT IN DETERMINING SECTION 8 ORDERS

> The fundamental principle is that the child's welfare is the paramount consideration when the court is considering an application.

The CAFCASS officer and the courts apply the **welfare checklist** when considering the child's welfare. It is set out in the *Children Act 1989* and consists of the following:

- the wishes and feelings of the child (considered in the light of age and understanding)

- physical and emotional needs

- the likely effect of any change in circumstances

- age, sex and background, and any other characteristics that the court considers relevant

- any harm the child has suffered or is at risk of suffering

- how capable each of the parents (and any other person the court considers to be relevant) is of meeting the child's needs

- the range of powers available to the court under this Act.

All these factors must be taken into account when the court is asked to make, vary or discharge a Section 8 order. The significance and weight attached to each factor will depend on the facts of the case. For example, the court is more likely to take into account the wishes and feelings of a 14-year-old than a five-year-old child.

Child abduction

DISAPPEARANCE OF A CHILD

The *Family Law Act 1986* provides a court with the power to order any person to disclose information to the court as to the whereabouts of the child, if the child's whereabouts are not sufficiently known. This can include members of the family, schools and organisations such as the CHILD BENEFIT AGENCY. Once the information has been obtained the court can then serve any court papers on the applicant's behalf should there be legitimate reasons (eg, domestic violence) why the respondent does not want their address disclosed.

A court can authorise an officer of the court or a constable to take charge of a child and deliver the child to the relevant person who is entitled to have the child reside with them. Such an order may be appropriate where a child is being unlawfully held after contact. However, as this order authorises the use of force to take charge of a child, it is not granted unless it is in the interests of the welfare of the child.

If it is feared that an attempt may be made to remove a child from the jurisdiction of England and Wales, the child may be made a **ward of court** and orders made to prevent the removal of the child.

WARDSHIP

Where a child is made a **ward of court**, the court has the power to grant orders that are thought necessary for the protection of the child as the court is temporarily responsible for the care and control of the child.

LAWFUL REMOVAL

A parent who has a **residence order** in their favour is allowed to remove a child from the country for up to 28 days. For any longer period, or for permanent removal, the consent of all parties that have parental responsibility needs to be obtained. In the absence of such consents, the matter must be put before the court on an application to remove from the jurisdiction.

PREVENTING UNLAWFUL REMOVAL

This is covered in detail in CHAPTER 20: INTERNATIONAL ISSUES.

COMMITTAL

If an order already exists from an English court and this has been breached, the parent can apply for the **committal of the abducting parent**. If the court finds the abducting parent has breached a court order, then a punishment, including custody, can be imposed. However, if the abducting parent is out of the jurisdiction, the committal will have little practical effect and may even deter the return of the parent.

SEQUESTRATION

If the abducting parent has assets in the UK then an application may be made against those assets. Orders can be made freezing assets. If the abducted parent owns a property, the court can make orders against that property to assist the other parent to raise money to finance litigation abroad.

Local authority orders

If a local authority has concerns about the care of a child that is resident in its borough, it has a duty to investigate and the power, in certain circumstances, to intervene.

EDUCATION ORDER

If there are concerns regarding a child's education this order allows the child to be placed under the supervision of the local education authority. The court will make an order where it concludes that the child is not being properly educated.

CHILD ASSESSMENT ORDER

If a local authority considers a child may be at risk but is having difficulties obtaining access to the child, it can apply for a **child assessment order**. The local authority must satisfy the court of the following factors before an order is made:

- the applicant has reasonable cause to suspect that the child is suffering or likely to suffer significant harm
- this can only be determined by an assessment of the child's health and development
- it is not likely that an assessment can be made without an order.

The order can last for a maximum of seven days and allows the local authority to remove the child from its home, if it considers it necessary.

EMERGENCY PROTECTION ORDER

If the local authority's concerns are significant, it can apply for an **emergency protection order**. The order can be made **ex parte**, which means that the local authority does not need to inform the parents or any other person before making the application. The local authority must satisfy the court of the following before an order is made:

- that enquiries are being frustrated and that access to the child is urgently required
- there is reasonable cause to believe that the child is likely to suffer significant harm if not removed from the home.

The initial order lasts for eight days and can be extended for a further seven days. During the time the order is in force the local authority has parental responsibility for the child.

SUPERVISION AND CARE ORDERS

A **supervision order** places a child under the supervision of a local authority. The local authority does not have the power to remove the child from the home, nor does it obtain parental responsibility for the child. However, supervision orders can have conditions attached to them. A supervision order can be for any period up to two years.

> A **care order** places the child into the care of the local authority. This means that a child can be removed from the home and placed either with foster carers or in a local authority care home. In some circumstances a child may continue to reside at home even though the local authority has a care order. The local authority obtains parental responsibility for the child. A parent or guardian who has parental responsibility for a child does not lose it once a care order is obtained. However, any residence orders that are in existence are automatically terminated. A care order, unless discharged earlier, lasts until the child reaches 18.

Before a care or supervision order is granted the court must be satisfied:

- that the child has suffered or is likely to suffer significant harm
- that the harm or likelihood of harm is attributable to the care given to the child, or likely to be given if the order were not made
- the child is beyond parental control.

> ### CARE PLAN
> When the local authority applies for a care or supervision order, they must file with the court a care plan for the child. This sets out the local authority's concerns and their plans for the child's future.

The court, through CAFCASS, appoints a **children's guardian**. Once proceedings have been commenced, the guardian will represent the child in the proceedings. The guardian's role is to investigate and make representations on behalf of the child.

PARENTAL CONTACT WITH A CHILD IN CARE

When an emergency protection order is granted, the local authority is under a duty to allow reasonable contact between the child and the parents. If a child is to be removed prior to a **child assessment order**, the court order must contain directions (as the court considers appropriate) regarding contact between the child and any relevant persons.

If a care order is granted, the local authority must allow reasonable contact between the child and the parents. In certain circumstances, a local authority can refuse contact for up to seven days. If it wishes to refuse contact for any longer period, it must apply to the court.

> If a parent is not satisfied with the contact that they are receiving to a child in care then they are entitled to make an application to the court for contact.

Adoption

An **adoption order** is a court order which gives the parental responsibility for a child to the adopters. Its effect is to extinguish the parental responsibility which anyone, including a parent, has for the child prior to the order's being made.

Where the applicant is:

- a parent

- step-parent

- relative of the child

- someone with whom the child was placed by an adoption agency

- someone with whom the child was placed following a High Court order.

an **adoption order** shall not be made unless the child is at least:

- 19 weeks old and has had their home with at least one of the applicants throughout the previous 13 weeks

- 12 months old and has lived with at least one of the applicants throughout the previous 12 months.

Currently, an **adoption order** may be made on the application of one person as long as they are at least 21.

> In deciding whether to adopt, the court is bound to give first consideration to the need to safeguard and promote the welfare of the child throughout their childhood.

An **adoption order** shall not be made unless:

- the child has been the subject of a **freeing order**
- the court is satisfied that each parent or guardian has freely and unconditionally agreed to the making of an **adoption order**
- the agreement of each parent or guardian can be dispensed with on the basis that she/he:
  - cannot be found or is incapable of giving agreement
  - is withholding their agreement unreasonably
  - has persistently failed without reasonable cause to discharge parental responsibility for the child
  - has abandoned or neglected the child
  - has persistently ill-treated the child
  - has seriously ill-treated the child, and the rehabilitation of the child within the household of the parent or guardian is unlikely.

Where the court is considering dispensing with the agreement of the parent/guardian it must first decide that adoption is in the best interests of the child.

The *Adoption and Children Act 2002* (to be implemented by summer 2004) makes changes to the current adoption process.

The welfare of the child will be the paramount consideration in all decisions relating to adoption.

Placement orders will replace **freeing orders**, and will create a new legal process for placing a child for adoption through an adoption agency.

It will be the duty of the local authority to apply for a placement order where it is satisfied that the child should be adopted but the parents do not consent to the placement or have withdrawn their consent.

Parental responsibility under a placement order will be vested in the adoption agency, and while the child is placed with prospective adopters, in them also.

> The definition of a couple for the purposes of adoption includes married, unmarried and same sex couples 'living as partners in an enduring family relationship'.

ORDER FOR CONTACT

On making an **adoption order** the court has the power to attach conditions, but will generally be reluctant to do so. The court can consider whether to make an **order for contact** at the same time as making an adoption order.

Contact could consist of:

- direct face-to-face contact with the child, which will normally be with the agreement of the adopters
- or indirect contact such as the sending of letters or cards and the exchange of information.

The *Adoption and Children Act 2002*, when implemented, will introduce **special guardianship orders** which will create a 'half-way house' between a parent maintaining parental responsibility and losing parental responsibility on adoption. Special guardianship orders will be suitable in cases where, although adoption is considered to be in the best interests of the child, the child may wish to maintain contact and other ties with his/her natural parents. The natural parent will not lose parental responsibility for the child, and thus a legal relationship will remain between the child and the natural parent. However, the special guardian(s) once appointed will be able to exercise parental responsibility to the exclusion of all others who have parental responsibility.

Upon application, a court will be able to vary and or discharge special guardianship orders.

Domestic violence

NON-MOLESTATION ORDER

The *Family Law Act 1996* allows individuals to obtain protection against violence, threats, molestation and harassment.

The court takes into account all the circumstances of the case, including the need to secure the health, safety and well-being of the applicant or any relevant child (see below).

The order can prohibit the respondent from:

- using or threatening violence
- molesting
- harassing
- intimidating the applicant.

The order may refer to other particular acts that are prohibited, and can last for a specified period or until further order.

In order to apply for a non-molestation order, the applicant must be associated with the person against whom they require the order (who would be known as **the respondent**). The applicant is associated with the respondent if they are a:

- spouse
- former spouse
- cohabitant
- former cohabitant
- relative (including stepfather, stepmother, etc)
- they live in the same house
- they have lived in the same house
- they have agreed to marry each other
- they have a child together
- they are involved in family proceedings.

> Children are entitled to make their own applications for a
> **non-molestation order**. Children aged 16 or 17 may apply for
> a **non-molestation** or **occupation order** without leave of the court.
> An application by a child should be commenced in the High Court.

A child under the age of 16 must apply to the court for **leave**. Leave will only be granted where the child has sufficient understanding to make the application. As with *Section 8 applications*, the court does not have to grant leave even if the child is of sufficient understanding. The court will consider the general circumstances of the case, as well as:

- the nature of the application
- the likelihood of success.

Children can also be included in applications as a **relevant child**, defined as any child:

- who is living with, or might reasonably be expected to live with either of the parents
- in relation to whom an order under the *Adoption Act 1976* or *Children Act 1989* is being considered
- whose interests the court considers relevant.

OCCUPATION ORDERS

Where the applicant would not be safe residing in the same house as the perpetrator, she/he may apply for an **occupation order**. Occupation orders can prohibit, restrict or terminate rights of occupation to part or the whole of the family home (whether owned or rented). So a respondent could be ordered to leave the home and not return to it for a specified period of time, or could be ordered not go into certain parts of the house during specified times.

In order to apply, the applicant must be **associated with the respondent** (see above). The orders that can be obtained depend on whether the applicant is **entitled or not**. An **entitled applicant** is someone who has either a legal or a beneficial interest in the property. A **non-entitled applicant** does not.

A non-entitled applicant can only apply for an order against a former spouse, a former cohabitant or a current cohabitant.

Occupation orders are granted after consideration of all the relevant circumstances of the case, including:

- the housing needs and housing resources of the parties and of the relevant child
- the financial resources of any of the parties
- the likely effect of any order, or of a decision not to make an order, on the health, safety and well-being of either party or relevant child
- the conduct of the parties in relation to each other or otherwise.

BALANCE OF HARM TEST

The court also considers whether the applicant or any relevant child is likely to suffer any significant harm from the respondent if the order is *not* made. If this is the case, the court will make the order unless it appears that the respondent or any relevant child will suffer significant harm if the order is made. This harm must be greater than the harm that is likely to be suffered by the applicant or any relevant child anyway.

ADDITIONAL ORDERS

When making an **occupation order** a court may also make either party:

- repair and maintain the home
- pay the rent
- pay the mortgage
- be responsible for other household outgoings.

POWER OF ARREST

Where the court is satisfied that the respondent has used or threatened violence, it can attach a **power of arrest** if it concludes that the applicant (or relevant child) will not be adequately protected without it. A power of arrest can be attached to either **occupation** or **non-molestation orders**.

> If a **power of arrest** is attached to an order, and the respondent breaches the order, the police have a duty to arrest the respondent and produce them at court as soon as practicable, but within 24 hours.

Where orders are breached, the court has the power to extend orders as well as to fine or imprison the respondent.

OBTAINING AN ORDER

Non-molestation and **occupation orders** can be obtained in two ways.

Ex parte

An **ex parte order** is an order obtained without giving notice to the respondent and in their absence. It may be justified in certain circumstances (where serious violence is used or threatened, or where the applicant may be put off making the application if the respondent is given notice). An ex parte order will be made on the same day the application is submitted to the court.

On notice

Where the situation is not so serious as to merit an **ex parte application**, the applicant must apply to the court for the matter to be listed for hearing. The applicant must also file and serve on the respondent a copy of the application along with the court date. The respondent must be given two clear days' notice. Both parties then attend the court on the specified day.

Finding the right family lawyer

See also CHAPTER 1: FINDING AND MEETING YOUR LAWYER.

Your local law centre or Citizens Advice Bureau may have a lawyer who specialises in family law. They may also be able to assist in providing a list of lawyers in your local area. The organisations listed below will also be able to provide lists of specialist family lawyers.

Organisations $\boxed{i}$

▶ **CENTRAL AUTHORITY FOR ENGLAND AND WALES**

The Child Abduction Unit
Lord Chancellor's Department
81 Chancery Lane
London WC2A 1DD

Tel: 020 7911 7045 / 7047
www.offsol.demon.co.uk

▶ **CHILD SUPPORT AGENCY**

P.O. Box 55
Brierly Hill
West Midlands DY5 1YL

Tel: 08457 133 133
Minicom: 08457 138 924
csa-nel@dwp.gsi.gov.uk
www.csa.gov.uk

▶ **CHILDREN AND FAMILY COURT ADVISORY AND SUPPORT SERVICE (CAFCASS)**

2nd Floor, Newspaper House
8–16 Great New Street
London EC4A 3BN

Tel: 020 7210 4400
Fax: 020 7210 4422
webenquiries@cafcass.gov.uk
www.cafcass.gov.uk

▶ **CHILDREN'S LEGAL CENTRE**

University of Essex
Wivenhoe Park
Colchester
Essex CO4 3SQ

Advice line: 01206 873820
www.essex.ac.uk

▶ **FREE REPRESENTATION UNIT (FRU)**

Fourth Floor, Peer House
8–14 Verulam Street
London WC1X 8LZ

www.fru.org.uk

Please note that the FRU does NOT deal with members of the public directly.

▶ **LAW CENTRES FEDERATION**

Duchess House
18–19 Warren Street
London W1T 5LR

Tel: 020 7387 8570
Fax: 020 7387 8368
info@lawcentres.org.uk
www.lawcentres.org.uk

▶ **LAW SOCIETY**

113 Chancery Lane
London WC2A 1PL

Tel: 020 7242 1222
Fax: 020 7831 0344
info.services@lawsociety.org.uk
www.lawsoc.org.uk

▶ **NATIONAL ASSOCIATION OF CITIZENS ADVICE BUREAUX (NACAB)**

Myddelton House
115–123 Pentonville Road
London N1 9LZ

Tel: 020 7833 2181
www.nacab.org.uk

Adviceguide: the National Association of Citizens Advice Bureaux offers fact sheets covering issues such as employment, housing and taxation

www.adviceguide.org.uk

▶ **NATIONAL COUNCIL FOR ONE PARENT FAMILIES**

255 Kentish Town Road
London NW5 2LX

Tel: 020 7428 5400
Lone Parent Helpline: 0800 018 5026
Fax: 020 7482 4851
info@oneparentfamilies.org.uk
www.oneparentfamilies.org.uk

▶ **NATIONAL MISSING PERSONS HELPLINE**

0500 700 700

If you are calling from outside the UK:
+ 44 20 8392 4545

▶ **NATIONAL SOCIETY FOR THE PREVENTION OF CRUELTY TO CHILDREN (NSPCC)**

0800 800 500
www.nspcc.org.uk

▶ **NATIONAL YOUTH ADVOCACY SERVICE**

99–105 Argyle Street
Birkenhead
Wirral CH41 6AD

Freephone: 0800 616 101
Tel: 0151 649 8700
Young people: help@nyas.net
General enquiries: main@nyas.net

▶ **PARENTS AND ABDUCTED CHILDREN TOGETHER (PACT)**
PO Box 31389
London SW11 4WY
www.pact-online.org

▶ **PRINCIPAL REGISTRY OF THE FAMILY DIVISION**
First Avenue House
42–49 High Holborn
London WC1V 6NP
Tel: 020 7947 6980
www.courtservice.gov.uk

▶ **REUNITE INTERNATIONAL**
P.O. Box 7124
Leicester
LE1 7XX
Advice line: 0116 2256 234
reunite@dircon.co.uk
www.reunite.org

▶ **SEARCH UK**
www.missingkids.co.uk
Police database of photos and information on missing and abducted children.

▶ **SOLICITORS' FAMILY LAW ASSOCIATION**
PO Box 302
Orpington
Kent BR6 8QX
Tel: 01689 850227
Fax: 01689 855833
sfla@btinternet.com
www.sfla.co.uk

▶ **UNITED KINGDOM PASSPORT SERVICE**
United Kingdom passport advice line:
0870 521 0410
www.ukps.gov.uk

Many of the following women's organisations give advice and assistance to women suffering from domestic violence. These organisations will also have lists of solicitors who specialise in this area.

▶ **CAMPAIGN AGAINST DOMESTIC VIOLENCE (CADV)**
PO Box 2371
London E1 5NQ
Tel: 020 8520 5881
Fax: 020 8988 8767
enquiries@cadv.org.uk
www.cadv.org.uk

▶ **NATIONAL DOMESTIC VIOLENCE HELPLINE**
08457 023 468
Fax: 0117 924 1703

▶ **NEWHAM ASIAN WOMEN'S PROJECT**
661 Barking Road
Plaistow
London E13 9EX
Tel (general): 020 8472 0528
Tel (advice): 020 8552 5524
info@nawp.org
www.nawp.org

▶ **REFUGE**
Helpline (open seven days a week, 24 hours a day): 0870 599 5443

▶ **SOUTHALL BLACK SISTERS**
52 Norwood Road
Southall
Middlesex UB2 4DW
Tel: 020 8571 9595

▶ **WOMEN'S AID FEDERATION**
PO Box 391
Bristol BS99 7WS
National Domestic Violence helpline (24 hour): 08457 023468
Fax: 0117 924 1703
info@womensaid.org.uk
www.womensaid.org.uk

15 **Housing**

Where you live is one of life's central concerns. This chapter deals with the most important legal issues that can arise in relation to the occupation of your home, whether you rent it or own it.

Regrettably, housing law is very complex. Your rights depend on what sort of agreement you have, when it was entered into, and a range of other considerations that are impossible to detail here. We can do no more than outline the main provisions, which apply in most circumstances: you may be among the exceptions!

It is imperative that anyone confronting a legal dispute over the right to occupy housing, its cost, or over responsibility for its condition, takes qualified advice at the earliest possible opportunity.

Buying

INTERESTS IN LAND

There are two types of legal ownership: **freehold** and **leasehold**.

> Freehold is where you buy the property outright and forever; leasehold is where you buy the lease for a fixed period of time, commonly 99 or 125 years.

Even if you are not the legal owner, you may have the right when the property is sold to share in the proceeds of the sale. This is known as an **equitable** or **beneficial interest**. This kind of interest is likely to arise when you contribute to the purchase price of your home or to the mortgage, or sometimes if the legal owner promises you a share of the proceeds of sale. **Equitable interests** can arise in many different situations and to find out whether you have one you should see a lawyer.

FREEHOLD

In its popular sense, a **freehold interest** in a property means that the property to which it relates is owned absolutely by the freeholder. The freeholder therefore has the right to enjoy the property as they wish, including renting the property to other people (see below), although if there is a mortgage on the property these rights are highly likely to be limited by the terms of the mortgage agreement.

Generally, if you buy a house, you will be buying a freehold interest in it; if you buy a flat, you will probably be buying a leasehold interest. Sometimes, all the leaseholders of the flats in a building have joined together to buy the freehold of the building. In this case, you would have a lease of the flat together with a share of the freehold of the building.

SALE / EVICTION

The sale of a freehold interest is a **conveyance**, and you should seek the advice and assistance of a solicitor or **licensed conveyancer** about this. A freeholder can, of course, sell the property whenever they wish. Apart from this, the freeholder can only be forced to sell or be evicted in certain circumstances.

> If the freeholder has not kept up the mortgage payments then the mortgage company can take possession of the property under a court order in order to sell it and get their money back.

Where people buy a home together but subsequently want to go their separate ways, if they cannot agree between themselves how to divide up the home (eg, by sale, or one buying out the other), any one of the joint owners can apply to the court for an order that will decide what is to happen.

Other than in these situations, the circumstances in which a freeholder can be forced to give up the property are limited and unusual (eg, **compulsory purchase** by the council).

If you are a freeholder and your interest in your property is threatened, you should immediately seek professional legal advice from a solicitor.

LEASEHOLD

A leasehold interest only gives the leaseholder the right to occupy a property for a fixed period of time, which will eventually run out. If you buy a flat you will probably be buying a leasehold interest (but this may soon change). The terms **lease** and **leasehold** can refer both to long leases and to short-term lettings. A long lease grants the leaseholder the right to occupy the property for 21 years or more. A short-term letting is usually referred to as a **tenancy**.

WHO CAN GRANT A LEASE?

A leasehold interest in property is granted by someone who has a greater legal interest in the same property. This greater interest can either be the freehold interest or a longer leasehold interest. A lease created from a longer lease is generally known as a **sub-lease**. As with freehold, the leaseholder may be one person, or more than one person sharing. The price that is paid to buy a long lease is called the **premium**.

COVENANTS

The long leaseholder, or **lessee**, can occupy the property as they wish, subject to the terms of the lease. These terms will include the benefits given to and obligations imposed on the leaseholder, or **covenants** (promises). These will usually detail:

- the parts of the building that the landlord must insure, repair and decorate, and the parts that are the leaseholder's responsibility.

- the leaseholder's obligation to pay rent (usually a nominal amount, called ground rent) and charges for the services – including insurance, repairs and maintenance – provided by the landlord.

BUYING AND SELLING LEASES

As with freeholders, a leaseholder can generally buy and sell a lease whenever she/he wishes. Long leases can normally be sold on the open market: again, if there are joint leaseholders and they cannot agree between themselves as to whether the property they own should be sold, they may apply to the court for an order that will determine what should happen.

ASSIGNMENT

It is usually only when a flat is first occupied that a long lease will be acquired from the freeholder or a superior leaseholder. Normally, a lease will be transferred from one leaseholder to another. This form of purchase is called **assignment**. This saleability of a long lease is one of the things that distinguishes it from a short-term lease.

There are a limited number of long leases that cannot be assigned. The terms of the lease itself may expressly prohibit assignment, or may specify that the landlord's permission is required. Whether and how far such a provision in the lease is enforceable is complex and requires specialist knowledge.

CONVEYANCE

The sale or purchase of a long lease (whether or not by assignment) is a **conveyance of land** and you should therefore seek legal advice in relation to this.

FORFEITURE

If the leaseholder breaks a covenant of the lease, the landlord may be entitled to **forfeit the lease**. This means, in effect, to cancel the lease and take the property back. Almost all leases contain such a right.

Before forfeiting, however, the landlord must normally serve a notice or demand on the leaseholder advising which covenant has been broken and, assuming the breach can be remedied, giving the leaseholder a reasonable time to remedy the breach, make good any damage, pay compensation or pay any arrears of ground rent. If the leaseholder fails to pay the service charges due under the terms of the lease, the landlord will have to take court proceedings in order to establish exactly how much is due – the amount will be determined by the court.

The landlord will have to take court proceedings in order to obtain possession of the property. The leaseholder will only have to leave the property if the court orders possession. If the landlord tries to forfeit the lease and seeks possession of the property, the leaseholder can apply to the court for **relief from forfeiture**. Relief may be granted by the court if the leaseholder can remedy the **breach of covenant** within a certain period of time.

Where the breach of covenant is a failure to pay ground rent or charges, the leaseholder's mortgage lender will often be entitled, under the mortgage agreement, to pay the charges and add them to the amount of the mortgage loan. This is in order to prevent the landlord forfeiting the lease, which would remove the mortgage lender's security for the loan.

> If you have not paid service charges under your lease because of a genuine dispute with your landlord, and you do not wish the mortgage company to pay them for you, you should write to the mortgage company and tell them this. You should also seek legal advice.

ENFRANCHISEMENT

A long leaseholder can, in certain circumstances, compel the landlord to sell them the freehold interest in the property (called **enfranchisement**) or to grant a further 50-year, or in some cases 90-year, extension of the lease. Similarly, long leaseholders of residential flats situated in a separate building can collectively acquire the freehold title to that building (**collective enfranchisement**). This is desirable since it gives the leaseholders greater control over the management and maintenance of the building in which their home is situated.

> ### COMMONHOLD
>
> A new way of holding property – primarily relating to flats – is in the process of being introduced into the UK. Under the **commonhold system**, a purchaser will buy the freehold of a flat, rather than a long lease, and in doing so will become part of a commonhold scheme to manage the building in which the flats are contained.

Commonhold will provide a way of owning flats on a freehold basis but linked to a management scheme so that the properties are properly maintained. It is anticipated that most flats in new developments will be sold as commonhold.

MORTGAGES

Most people buying their home freehold, or by way of a long lease, will do so by borrowing money to help pay for it from a building society or bank. In return for the money, the borrower grants the lender a **charge over the property** as security for the loan. The lender will register their interest at the **land registry**. Anyone trying to buy the property after this will be able to find out about the mortgage.

TERMS

The terms of the mortgage agreement will restrict what the owner can do with her/his home (eg, renting it out with **security of tenure**). These restrictions are intended to protect, as far as possible, the value of the property so that it remains good security for the money lent by the lender.

POSSESSION

If you do not maintain your mortgage payments, or break some other term of the mortgage agreement, the lender may take proceedings against you, in effect to repossess and sell the property. They can only do this through court proceedings, and the court has power to postpone a **possession order** to give you time to remedy any breach or pay off any arrears. If the lender seeks possession against you, you should seek legal advice immediately.

CONVEYANCING

Conveyancing is the process by which the freehold or leasehold of a house or flat is transferred between owners. Normally, after the price is agreed, the purchaser will have the property surveyed by a properly qualified surveyor. This will be for the sake both of the purchaser and of any mortgage lender, so as to ensure, as far as possible, that the property is in adequate condition and worth the price that is being paid.

SEARCHES AND ENQUIRIES

Once the survey has been done, it is usual to instruct either a solicitor or a licensed conveyancer who will carry out various checks in relation to the property, to ascertain:

- no one else has rights over the property which will interfere with the purchaser's rights (e. rights of way over the property)

- there are no current problems with occupation of the property
- the council does not have or know of plans for the local area which will affect the value of the property or the rights of the purchaser (eg, a plan to redevelop the area, or an application for planning permission next door)
- what items the vendor is leaving behind (carpets, curtains, cooker etc).

> Buying a property can be a complicated process and – given the current state of the law – it is best to employ a solicitor or a licensed conveyancer. It should be possible to obtain such services at a reasonable and fixed price, which you should settle at the beginning. It is worth shopping around, as the prices charged for these services can vary.

Renting

A **tenancy** will normally be created when a landlord agrees to allow a person to occupy premises for a given period, and the person agrees to pay rent for occupying those premises. A **joint tenancy** is one granted to one or more tenants. A tenancy may be for a fixed term or may be periodic.

FIXED-TERM TENANCIES

A **fixed-term tenancy** – like a long leasehold – is granted for a specified period of time, but usually for less than 21 years. When the fixed term ends, the tenant will normally enjoy **security of tenure** which will allow them to remain in the premises.

PERIODIC TENANCIES

A **periodic tenancy** is a tenancy that:

- continues from period to period (eg, week to week or month to month, although it could be quarter to quarter or even year to year)
- carries on automatically unless and until either the landlord or the

tenant gives the other a written **notice to quit** – at least 28 days' written notice must be given

- will generally have **security of tenure**, so that a landlord's notice to quit may not actually mean the tenant has to leave.

> If you are given a **notice to quit**, you should seek legal advice immediately.
>
> The landlord will usually have to take possession proceedings in court before the tenant can be evicted – this is when it will be established whether or not you have to leave, or whether you enjoy security of tenure allowing you to stay.

Security of tenure

Most residential tenants will have **security of tenure**, whether they were granted a **fixed-term** or a **periodic tenancy**. This means that, so long as the tenant occupies the property as their only or main home, they are entitled to remain in their homes, whatever their tenancy agreement may say, until such time as a court orders them to be evicted.

The requirement to use property as an only or main home does not mean that the tenant can never go away from the property, but it does stop a tenancy from being secure if, for example, the tenant only uses the property as a holiday home or sub-lets it to someone else.

There are a number of different types of security of tenure. Which of them applies to a particular tenancy will depend on a number of factors, including:

- the date the tenancy was granted
- whether the landlord is a local authority or a private person
- in some cases, what the landlord and tenant actually agreed.

SECURE TENANCIES

These are tenancies where the landlord is a public body, normally a local authority. The tenant can only be evicted if a court finds that the landlord has proved at least one of the **grounds for possession** listed in the legislation.

In most cases, the court will have to think it is reasonable to make a possession order; in some cases, the landlord will have to provide suitable alternative accommodation.

The main grounds are:

- failure to pay rent
- antisocial behaviour by the tenant or a person living with or visiting the tenant (eg, racial or sexual harassment)
- use of the property for illegal or immoral purposes (eg, for drug-dealing or prostitution)
- breakdown of a relationship caused by domestic violence
- allowing the condition of the property to deteriorate
- overcrowding in the property
- the landlord's intention to demolish, redevelop or sell the property.

HUMAN RIGHTS

Local authorities are public bodies, which must not:

- act contrary to the principles of public administrative law
- act unreasonably or irrationally
- fail to comply with the principles of natural justice.

Where they do act in such a way, a person affected by such an act or decision may be able to challenge it by means of judicial review proceedings.

Public bodies are also under a duty to comply with the requirements of the *Human Rights Act 1998*. This means that a local authority landlord must ensure that the tenant's home and private life are respected. The authority may therefore be open to criticism if it has breached the tenant's human rights. This is a new and quickly developing area of UK law and professional legal advice should be sought before seeking to challenge a decision on human rights grounds (see CHAPTER 16: HUMAN RIGHTS ACT).

INTRODUCTORY TENANCIES

A local authority can decide that all its new tenancies will be **introductory**, or **probationary**, tenancies for their first year, during which full **security of**

tenure will not apply, making it considerably easier for the landlord to obtain a **possession order**. An introductory tenancy automatically becomes a secure tenancy if the tenant has not been evicted within the probationary year.

ASSURED TENANCIES

These are tenancies from a private landlord or a **housing association** (now called a **registered social landlord**). Assured tenancies operate like secure tenancies, but the grounds for possession are a little different and in some cases it will not matter whether or not the court considers that the claim is reasonable.

The most common of these grounds are if:

- the landlord previously occupied the property as his only or principal home and has served notice to that effect at the beginning of the tenancy
- the landlord intends to demolish all or part of the property and the works cannot reasonably be carried out with the tenant in residence
- at both the date of the notice and the date of the hearing, there is rent unpaid for at least two months (if rent is payable monthly) or eight weeks (if payable weekly or fortnightly).

Other grounds for possession, where the court does have power to refuse an order if it is not reasonable to make one, include:

- where there is suitable alternative accommodation available for the tenant
- arrears of rent or persistent lateness in paying rent
- breach of an obligation under the terms of the tenancy
- allowing the condition of the property to deteriorate
- antisocial behaviour by the tenant.

In some cases, **registered social landlords** may be considered public bodies to which the points made above about human rights may be applied.

A tenancy can now only be an assured tenancy if, before the tenancy is entered into, the landlord gives the tenant a notice saying so. Otherwise it will be an **assured shorthold tenancy**. If the tenancy was granted before 28 February 1997, however, the reverse is the case: it will be an assured tenancy unless the landlord gave the tenant notice that it was an assured shorthold tenancy.

> *ASSURED SHORTHOLD TENANCIES* are tenancies with little security of tenure. The landlord may simply give two months' written notice to the tenant, and then obtain a court order. Provided the tenancy is more than six months old (or, if for a fixed term, provided that term had run out), the court has no power to refuse a possession order.

RENT ACT TENANCIES

The *Rent Acts* provided the old form of security of tenure for private sector tenants but have been phased out since 15 January 1989 when **assured tenancies** were introduced (although in a small number of cases – for example, when a tenant agrees to move or is moved by court order to alternative accommodation – a new **Rent Act tenancy** may still be granted). A Rent Act tenancy which started before 15 January 1989, will normally still be a Rent Act tenancy.

Under the *Rent Acts*, the concept of residence is slightly different: it does not require residence as an only or main home, merely as *a* home.

Otherwise, security is similar in substance.

- The landlord must prove a ground for possession in court
- In most cases the court will have to consider whether it is reasonable to make an order (and sometimes alternative accommodation will have to be provided).

The main grounds for possession against a **Rent Act tenant** are similar to those applicable against **secure tenants** and **assured tenants** (where the court has no reasonableness discretion).

EXCLUSIONS FROM SECURITY OF TENURE

Certain types of lettings and properties are excluded from **security of tenure**. These exclusions vary from scheme to scheme, but there is some overlap. In particular, lettings where the landlord is resident in the same building will not enjoy **security of tenure** (unless very old indeed – from 1974). Obviously, this does not apply to secure tenancies from local authorities, or assured or **assured shorthold tenancies** from registered social landlords, because they are 'bodies' rather than 'people', they cannot 'reside'. The same is true of any landlord which is a company, trust or society.

Generally, the following will not attract **security of tenure** as **assured, assured shorthold** or **Rent Act tenancies**:

- properties with a high rateable value or rent
- properties with a low, or no, rent
- business tenancies
- licensed premises
- agricultural lettings (though these may be covered separately)
- lettings to a student of student accommodation
- holiday lettings
- lettings where the landlord is the Crown (unless managed by the CROWN ESTATES COMMISSIONERS)
- lettings where the landlord is a local authority.

Most of the exclusions listed above are also exclusions from the secure tenancy scheme. Other types of lettings excluded from that scheme include:

- long leases (21 years or more)
- premises occupied by local authority employees in connection with their employment, policemen and firemen
- land acquired for redevelopment which is now to be carried out
- accommodation used for housing the homeless
- accommodation that is leased to the local authority by a private landlord
- temporary accommodation during works
- almshouses.

Eviction

With a small number of exceptions (**excluded licences** and **excluded tenancies**), a court order is needed to evict any former tenant, whether they have security of tenure or not.

If you are a **secure** or **assured tenant**, any threat of eviction proceedings will have to have been preceded by a formal notice setting out the grounds on which possession is sought against you and, where relevant, offering an opportunity to make amends (eg, pay any rent arrears, repair damage, or evict a lodger who has been behaving antisocially towards neighbours).

For a **Rent Act tenant**, there is no such formal requirement, although the landlord will have had to terminate your contract of tenancy, but in practice you will have been warned.

An **assured shorthold tenant** must, before possession proceedings are brought, be served with a notice that states that possession of the premises will be sought.

If threatened with eviction, you should always take advice. Leaving aside the possibility that you will be able to defend the proceedings because of your security, a landlord must take a number of procedural steps, which your adviser should check. Failure by the landlord to comply with procedural steps may defeat his claim for possession.

A landlord cannot generally simply evict or exclude a tenant from the property, nor use force to do so. Likewise, it is illegal for a landlord to do anything short of actual eviction that interferes with the tenant's enjoyment of the property (eg, by cutting off the water or gas, threatening the tenant, coming into the tenant's rooms without consent, etc) and is intended to cause the tenant to leave. These acts will amount to unlawful eviction and/or harassment.

The tenant could bring legal proceedings against the landlord in order to regain occupation of the premises and/or seek compensation. In the event that you believe that you have been unlawfully evicted, you should contact a solicitor and detail all the circumstances surrounding your eviction.

Transfer of tenancies

SUCCESSION AND SURVIVORSHIP

> The death of a tenant does not necessarily bring the tenancy to an end. If there is only one tenant, and she/he dies, the tenancy will generally pass to their personal representatives.

A deceased tenant's spouse, cohabitee or family member may also acquire the tenancy, provided certain conditions are met (this is called **succession**).

If there is a joint tenancy, the deceased tenant's interest will automatically pass to the remaining joint tenants (this is called **survivorship**).

Where a person is entitled to succeed to a tenancy, the tenancy will pass to that person even if the deceased tenant left the tenancy to someone else in their will.

The conditions that must be met vary between the different schemes of security of tenure, but are in general as follows.

- Only one transfer by succession is usually allowed. The exception to this is **Rent Act tenancies**, under which there may be two successions. If there is a joint tenancy, and the deceased tenant's interest passes to the remaining joint tenant(s), this counts as a succession.

- A legal spouse usually only has to have been living in the property with the deceased tenant at the time of their death to be allowed to succeed.

- In the case of a cohabitee or other family member, they must also normally have lived at the property at the time of the tenant's death, with the deceased tenant, for at least 12 months before their death.

If you think that you may be entitled to succeed to a tenancy, you should seek legal advice.

ASSIGNMENT

Theoretically, fixed term and periodic tenancies can be transferred by way of **assignment** to one or more other people.

This, however, is subject to the terms of the tenancy agreement and to various statutory provisions. For example, the tenancy agreement may prohibit assignment altogether, or may require that the landlord's consent be obtained first. In addition, statute has, in some instances, limited the circumstances in which an assignment can be made.

In particular, secure tenants can only assign in very restricted circumstances:

- to a person who would be entitled to succeed on the tenant's death

- to another secure tenant where both tenants wish to swap homes (**mutual exchange**)

- under a court order on the breakdown of a relationship.

It is not possible to assign a **Rent Act tenancy** unless the landlord is also a party to the agreement.

The matter is very often complex, so you should seek legal advice if you are thinking of assigning your tenancy or taking an assignment of a tenancy.

Sub-letting and lodgers

SUB-LETTING

A tenant is, in theory, entitled to sub-let their property to someone else. A tenant's entitlement to sub-let will, however, be subject to any terms contained in the tenancy agreement: very often sub-letting is prohibited altogether or else made conditional on the landlord's consent being obtained.

> You should be aware before sub-letting that it may adversely affect your **security of tenure**, and in some cases will remove it entirely. This would make it easier for the landlord to terminate the tenancy and recover possession of the premises. The precise impact sub-letting will have on security of tenure will depend on the type of tenancy held by the tenant.

SECURE TENANCY

A secure tenant will lose **security of tenure** if they sub-let all of the property. Once lost, the security of tenure is gone for ever. It will not be recovered even if the tenant evicts the sub-tenant(s) and starts to live in the property again. A secure tenant can, however, sub-let part of the premises and not lose security of tenure if the landlord has given written permission. The landlord cannot unreasonably refuse to give permission.

ASSURED (INCLUDING ASSURED SHORTHOLD) TENANCY

In order to enjoy **security of tenure**, an **assured tenant** must occupy the premises as their only or principal home. If the tenant has granted another person a sub-tenancy of the whole of the premises, security of tenure could be lost and the tenancy determined. Unlike secure tenants, however, an assured tenant can regain security of tenure by going back to live in the premises again as their only or principal home. An assured tenant can sub-let part of the premises unless the tenancy agreement says otherwise.

RENT ACT TENANCY

Unless prohibited or made conditional on the landlord's consent by the terms of the tenancy, a **Rent Act tenant** will be entitled to sub-let their home. Continued security of tenure will depend on the tenant occupying the premises as their residence. This is not likely to be the case if the result of the sub-letting is that the tenant is no longer in occupation. As to sub-letting part of the premises, this requires permission from the landlord.

LODGERS

Provided there are no terms in the tenancy agreement to the contrary, a tenant is entitled to take in lodgers. A lodger has no legal interest in the property and merely occupies by permission granted by the tenant (or owner). A lodger is a type of **licensee**. Taking in lodgers, provided it is done in accordance with any terms contained in the tenancy agreement, will not jeopardise the tenant's security of tenure and enjoyment of their home.

Other forms of occupation

WHEN IS AN OCCUPIER NOT A TENANT?

An occupier is not a tenant either when they are an owner/occupier, or when they are a **licensee** or **trespasser**.

LICENCES

Sometimes people are permitted to occupy property informally, temporarily, or for a limited and specific purpose. These arrangements may not be intended to create a legally binding relationship, such as when a person stays with friends or family as a lodger for a few weeks. They may be purely temporary, such as hostel accommodation. These arrangements, with permission but without the formality of tenancy, are known as **licences**.

As with any agreement, a licence can be subject to various terms, very often about the period the occupation is to last and what the charge will be. Like tenancies, licences can be periodic: they last for a period of time, which keeps repeating until either party gives notice.

TENANCY / LICENCE

It can be difficult to distinguish between a **tenancy** and a **licence**. The distinction is, however, an important one. A **tenant** has many more rights than a **licensee**. It is, therefore, crucial to know whether you are a tenant or a licensee. Where there is a dispute, the matter can be referred to court, where the circumstances will be considered and a decision made.

NO SECURITY OF TENURE

Licensees have fewer rights than tenants and in general have no security of tenure (the exception to this being **secure licences**, which have the same security as secure tenancies). It is therefore easier to terminate a licence and recover possession of the property than it is with a **tenancy**.

In order to terminate a **licence notice** must be give in accordance with the terms of that licence, if there are any. Where there are no terms about notice, a reasonable period of time should be given to the licensee to leave the property. If the licence is a periodic one, however, a written formal notice to quit must be given. This notice must give at least 28 days' notice to the licensee.

EXCLUDED LICENCES

Once notice has expired and the licence is terminated, the licensor can generally only recover possession by way of court proceedings.

Licences will be excluded from this requirement in the following circumstances, where:

- an occupier shares accommodation with the licensor or a member of his family
- a licence has been granted as a temporary measure to a trespasser
- the property is holiday accommodation
- the licence was granted other than for money
- the property is hostel accommodation provided by the local authority or other specified public body.

EXCLUDED TENANCIES

Even if a **tenancy** may be excluded – so that it is not strictly necessary to evict by a court order – if it fulfils the same criteria.

This is a very difficult area. There are various criminal offences that can be committed in relation to eviction from occupied premises. It is therefore always best to obtain a court order for possession whenever the property is occupied residentially, and to have that order enforced by the appropriate authorities. If in doubt, take advice.

TRESPASS

Trespass will be committed where any person enters onto another's property without any right, permission or licence to be there. Squatters are trespassers and court proceedings can be brought on a relatively speedy basis to evict them. If a squatter occupies land openly and without force they are said to be in **adverse possession** of it. If a squatter is in adverse possession of land for more than 12 years, they may acquire the title to that land.

> The way in which title to property is acquired by **adverse possession** is to change in 2003: in order to acquire title the squatter will have to be registered as the owner (the **proprietor**) of the land at the LAND REGISTRY. The squatter will only be entitled to be registered if they have been in adverse possession of the land for more than ten years.

Termination

SURRENDER

A tenant, or all the joint tenants acting together, can agree with the land-lord to give up the tenancy. This is called a **surrender**, and must be in writing. One joint tenant cannot surrender a tenancy unilaterally, unless all the others agree. A surrender may also occur by law if the tenant leaves the property in circumstances from which it is clear that they are giving up the tenancy, and if the landlord takes some positive action from which it is clear that they have accepted the giving up of the tenancy.

TENANT'S NOTICE TO QUIT

The tenant or a joint tenant can also terminate the tenancy by giving a **notice to quit** to the landlord. In this case, it is not necessary for all the joint tenants to act together; any one of them may act alone to bring the tenancy to an end.

> A joint tenant is entitled to terminate the tenancy without the consent of the remaining tenant(s) by giving the landlord a tenant's **notice to quit** (a notice to the landlord that the departing tenant intends to give up the tenancy). If the departing tenant does this, the whole tenancy comes to an end and the remaining tenant(s) will lose the right to remain in the property.

ABANDONMENT

Contrary to popular belief, a tenant cannot terminate the tenancy simply by abandoning the property, except in circumstances that are capable of amounting to a **surrender** by operation of law. Otherwise, the abandoning tenant will remain liable to pay the rent and under other relevant terms of the tenancy agreement unless and until the tenancy is terminated properly.

RELATIONSHIP / CO-OWNERSHIP BREAKDOWN

When a domestic relationship breaks down, or one or more of the joint tenants fall out, and the tenant or one of the joint tenants leaves, a range of rights exist. Married couples and cohabitees can prevent a departing tenant from terminating the tenancy, and have the tenancy transferred from her/his name. Legal assistance should be sought in such matters.

Rent and other charges

Generally, the occupier will pay rent. The amount of rent, and when it should be paid must be expressly agreed as part of the tenancy agreement. The level of rent, and how often and by how much it can be increased, are, however, commonly controlled by law. The amount of control will depend on the type of occupation/tenancy.

SECURE TENANCIES

Those who occupy local authority accommodation will, generally, pay less rent for their homes than those occupying similar accommodation in the private sector. Local authorities are bound by statute to charge reasonable rents, which they must review from time to time. In deciding what is reasonable, the local authority will take into account various economic factors, such as:

- expenditure
- inflation
- the level of subsidy they receive from central government
- their statutory obligation to balance their accounts relating to their housing functions.

ASSURED / ASSURED SHORTHOLD TENANCIES

The starting point is that the rent will be what has been agreed. Generally a **market rent** is agreed (unlike Rent Act tenancies). Where there is fixed-term assured tenancy, the rent can only be varied in accordance with the terms of the tenancy agreement. Once the fixed term comes to an end, a periodic tenancy will, by law, come into existence. The terms of this **statutory periodic tenancy** will be the same as those under the original fixed-term tenancy, including the terms about rent. They can, however, be varied within one year of the fixed term expiring, by application to a RENT ASSESSMENT COMMITTEE.

In other cases, including all **periodic assured tenancies** and **assured shorthold tenancies**, the landlord can increase the rent either by agreement with the tenant or by serving a formal notice on the tenant which the tenant can, in response, refer to the Rent Assessment Committee. This option is not available if a periodic tenancy agreement contains its own provisions for increase: those provisions will apply instead.

> If your landlord is seeking to increase your rent and you are in doubt as to whether or not this is legal, you should seek legal advice as soon as possible, as otherwise you may lose the right to refer the proposed increase to the Rent Assessment Committee.

Assured shorthold tenants can also refer their rent to the Rent Assessment Committee, even though the landlord has not sought to increase it. If the assured tenancy began after 28 February 1997, the reference must be made within the first six months of the tenancy. In relation to assured shorthold tenancies beginning before that date, a reference can only be made on one occasion and during the initial fixed term (all earlier assured shortholds had to be fixed term).

RENT ACT TENANCIES

All **Rent Act tenants** enjoy a protected rent, which is set by the rent officer and is known as the **fair rent**. In setting the fair rent certain circumstances are disregarded including the scarcity value of the property (ie, the competition for accommodation, which causes rents to increase). This produces much lower rents.

Once the fair rent is decided in relation to the property, the rent is **registered**. The fair rent is the maximum rent that can be recovered by the landlord, no matter what the tenancy agreement might say. An application for a new rent to be registered can be made two years after the last registration.

If either the tenant or the landlord is dissatisfied with the level of rent registered, they may appeal to the Rent Assessment Committee, which will consider the matter again. If you are concerned by a proposed rent increase, you should seek advice about it as soon as possible.

SERVICE CHARGES

Almost all long leases, some short-term residential tenancy agreements, and even some freeholds (where purchased under the right to buy, and benefiting from communal services), contain terms that entitle the landlord to recover from the tenant the costs incurred in providing repairs, insurance and other services. The cost to the tenant is known as the **service charge**. The lease may well treat these service charges as an additional rent.

REGULATION OF SERVICE CHARGES: A SUMMARY

Service charges can generally only be recovered if they are reasonable.

- It must have been reasonable for the landlord to incur the costs for which the charges are claimed.
- The charges themselves must be reasonable for the services provided.
- Any work carried out and charged for must have been of a reasonable standard.

If there is dispute, the matter can be resolved by the court or by a body called the **leasehold valuation tribunal**.

> Landlords must consult tenants about any proposed major works to their premises and/or the building of which they form a part. Tenants are also entitled, if they ask their landlord, to information about their service charges and the accounts relating to them. It is a criminal offence for a landlord to fail, without reasonable excuse, to comply with such a request.

A tenants' association can also appoint a properly qualified chartered surveyor to advise and assist them on matters relating to service charges.

Anti-social behaviour

Antisocial behaviour and/or the general condition of neighbouring properties may unreasonably interfere with your use and enjoyment of your property. What can be done, if anything, will depend on the nature and level of the disturbance and the surrounding circumstances, but it may be that the interference constitutes a nuisance.

If you feel brave enough, you should complain to your neighbour, as they may not even realise that there is a problem. If this does not work, there are a number of different options.

- If the neighbour is a tenant, you could complain to their landlord and ask that the covenants in the neighbour's tenancy agreement should be enforced by means of possession proceedings.

- If the neighbour is a council or registered social landlord tenant, you could ask the council or registered social landlord to seek a court injunction against the neighbour to stop the behaviour.

- The council, registered social landlord, and/or the police could apply for an **anti-social behaviour order** against the neighbour. Such an order is particularly useful if the person behaving antisocially is a child, as a normal injunction may not be available against someone who is not an adult.

NOISY NEIGHBOURS

In noise nuisance cases, you could complain to the environmental health department of your local authority, which may investigate the complaint and which has power to issue **abatement notices** or, in extreme circumstances, to seize hi-fi equipment.

Alternatively, in all cases, you could apply to the court for an **injunction to restrain** the activities that are causing a nuisance.

THE CONDITION OF NEIGHBOURING PROPERTY

If the house next door (or flat upstairs, etc) is not kept in good condition, so that it damages your own property, you will probably also have a right to an injunction and/or compensation.

Repairs

Whether you own your home or rent it, you may be under an obligation to keep the property in a reasonable state of repair. If you own your property with the benefit of a mortgage, the mortgage lender may require you to ensure that the property is kept in good structural repair. It is also almost always a requirement of your mortgage, and in any event advisable, that your house is insured against structural damage.

REPAIRING OBLIGATIONS

If you rent your home and there is a written tenancy agreement, it may state who is responsible for repairing, decorating and maintaining your home. These obligations are divided between you as the tenant and your landlord. Generally, you will be responsible for repairing and decorating the inside of your home and your landlord will be responsible for the structure and exterior of the building. Both parties will be obliged to comply with whatever is stated in the written agreement.

IMPLIED REPAIRING OBLIGATION

Where the tenancy was initially granted for less than seven years, which includes all **periodic tenancies** even if they have lasted for longer than seven years, further obligations on the landlord will be implied into the tenancy agreement by law, where there is no written agreement, and will override any written agreement to the contrary.

The landlord will be obliged to:

- keep in repair the structure and exterior of the dwelling and/or the building in which the dwelling is situated

- maintain in proper working order equipment for the supply of water, gas, electricity, sanitation (including basins, baths and lavatories), heating and hot water.

NOTICE OF DISREPAIR

If your premises are suffering from disrepair, you should inform your landlord as soon as possible. It is also advisable to keep a written record of:

- any disrepair that occurs in the premises

- how and when the landlord was informed of the problem

- what was the landlord's response.

REMEDIES FOR DISREPAIR

If your landlord fails to carry out repairs for which they are responsible, within a reasonable time of being notified of the problem, they will be in breach of the tenancy agreement.

You will then have the right to commence proceedings in the county court seeking both compensation for any loss or inconvenience suffered and an order that the landlord carry out the necessary works.

Deciding whether or not to exercise that right may depend on your security of tenure. If you have none (eg, if you are an **assured shorthold tenant**) there is a risk – not to say likelihood – that the landlord's response will be to terminate your right of occupation. This may not be a bar to compensation, but it may render the exercise academic or even self-defeating from your point of view. On the other hand, if you have full security, there is rarely any reason not to exercise these rights.

It is advisable to seek legal advice and representation if you intend to commence proceedings against your landlord, not least because the definition of **repair** and **disrepair** can be complex. Often, solicitors undertake these proceedings on a fixed or **conditional fee basis** and you should ask what this means and how much it will cost you before committing yourself to litigation.

> Landlords' repairing obligations are rarely as wide-ranging as most tenants would like. The premises can be damp and mouldy yet not in a state of disrepair, as the damp may be caused by inadequate heating of the premises or by condensation rather than anything that qualifies as actual disrepair. Without disrepair, the landlord will not be in breach of his repairing obligations.

If the landlord is in breach, however, any action for works to be done can be accompanied by a claim for damages:

- for actual damage to possessions
- for damage to health
- for discomfort.

Such a claim may arise in the course of a landlord's action for possession for arrears (of rent): there is nothing wrong with seeking to reduce arrears (a failure of the tenant's obligations) by pointing to (and setting off against) disrepair (a failure of the landlord's).

STATUTORY NUISANCE

Regardless of the landlord's contractual repairing obligations (whether in the agreement or implied by law), the premises may still be in such a state as to be prejudicial to health. If this is so, it is deemed a **statutory nuisance**. You can complain to the local authority, which will then take steps to investigate the complaint and prevent the nuisance. If the landlord is your local authority, you can, after first having given your landlord 21 days' notice of your intention to do so, complain to the magistrates court. The magistrates' court may order the authority:

- to carry out any necessary works within a specified timescale
- to pay compensation for any damage caused by the statutory nuisance
- to pay any costs incurred by you in making the complaint.

DEFECTIVE PREMISES

A landlord also has a duty to take reasonable care to prevent the condition of the premises causing injury to people using them, or damage to their property.

Right to buy

Once a person has been a secure tenant of a local authority for the requisite period of time, they will acquire the **right to buy** the property they live in at a discount. The requisite period is, at present, two years but this may increase as a result of propsed changes to the law. It is not necessary that the tenant has lived in the same property for all of those two years. The right to buy can be exercised either individually or with other family members. The discount is calculated by reference to the number of years that the tenant has been a secure tenant, up to a maximum of 60 per cent for a house and 70 per cent for a flat.

Some assured tenants of **registered social landlords** may also be entitled to the right to buy, either because they used to be secure tenants or because the landlord offers them the right to buy as a contractual term of the tenancy.

If you are not sure whether you have the right to buy your home, you should seek legal advice.

Private sector housing standards

Local authorities have a range of powers and duties to ensure that premises used for residential accommodation within their area are only used if they reach acceptable standards. Measures can be taken by local authorities in order to promote and ensure the provision of adequate housing in their area:

- in relation to a house or flat
- in relation to large residential areas.

Local authorities have powers and duties in relation to all residential accommodation in their district: houses, flats, **houses in multiple occupation (HMOs)**.

What is stated in this part, in relation to housing standards and HMOs, is a summary of how these areas are currently regulated. The law in these areas is in the process of change. A new method of assessing the risk of harm to the health and safety of occupants of residential premises is to be devised and the type of action that local authorities can take in order to control and maintain standards will also be changed.

FIT FOR HUMAN HABITATION

A person's home should be:

- structurally stable
- free from serious disrepair
- free from damp that is prejudicial to health
- have adequate lighting, heating, ventilation, plumbing, sanitation
- facilities for the storage, preparation and cooking of food
- adequate drainage and waste installations.

TYPES OF ACTION

If a local authority is satisfied that a property is unfit for human habitation, it is obliged to do something about it. The options are as follows.

- A **repair notice** may be served on the person who has control of the premises.

- A **closing or demolition order** could be served on the owner (and mortgagee) of the premises.

- A **purchase notice** could be served on the owner of the premises. If the owner will not agree to sell the premises, it could be compulsorily purchased by the local authority.

- A **deferred action notice** could be served. This will state that the local authority considers the premises to be unfit and what works are necessary to improve them. The notice does not actually require the person to carry out those works, but gives them the opportunity to do so.

The local authority will pursue whichever type of action is the most satisfactory in the circumstances. The person served with a notice has a right of appeal to the local county court, which must be brought within 21 days of receiving the notice. The court hearing the appeal may, depending on the evidence, dismiss it or quash or vary the notice.

> Failure to comply with any notice served (unless appealed) is a criminal offence and may be prosecuted by the local authority. Those who lose their homes as a result of any of the measures referred to above will generally have rights of rehousing and compensation.

GRANTS

Local authorities provide grants for improvements, repairs and alterations to residential premises. Each authority has its own, local scheme of grant aid, but all local authorities must pay disabled facilities grants in circumstances prescribed by parliament. You should contact your local authority in order to find out more about the availability of such grants.

OVERCROWDING

Local authorities will also try to ensure that residential accommodation within their area is not overcrowded. Overcrowding will, in law, occur in two situations:

- when there are so many people in a house that two or more people, over the age of ten, of opposite sexes and not living together as a couple, have to sleep in the same room. That room may be either a bedroom or a living room, and for these purposes a kitchen (at least one big enough to contain a bed) may well count as a living room. A property will therefore not be overcrowded where the situation could be avoided by a person sleeping in the living room or even the kitchen (but not the bathroom).

- when there are too many people for the size of the accommodation. There are two ways in which the law assesses this, by specifying:
  - the maximum number of people who can occupy a property according to the number of rooms in that property
  - the maximum number of people who can occupy a property according to the size of the rooms.

When any one of these standards is infringed (even if the others are not), the property will be overcrowded in law.

There will normally be no overcrowding when a standard is offended as a result of **natural growth** (eg, a child reaching a relevant age) if – but only if – the occupier has taken all reasonable steps to avoid it – for example, where it would be reasonable to evict a lodger.

> It is a criminal offence, for both landlords and occupiers, to permit premises to be overcrowded. They should, in any event, notify the local authority of the overcrowding once they learn of it.

Illegal overcrowding may result in both **Rent Act** and **secure tenants** losing their security of tenure. In either case, their landlords may, as a consequence, be able to terminate their tenancies and will be entitled, upon proceedings being commenced, to a **possession order**. In practice, however, the occupier and family will, by one route or another, be entitled to rehousing from the local authority.

HOUSES IN MULTIPLE OCCUPATION (HMOs)

A house or flat may be designed or converted to accommodate more than one household. If occupied in this way, the premises will, in law, be a **house in multiple occupation**. Whether there is more than one household occupying a property will depend on factors such as:

- whether the occupants moved in as a single group or arrived independently and sporadically

- to what extent the facilities are shared
- whether the occupants are collectively responsible for the whole premises or each individually responsible for their own part
- whether individuals occupy a room to the exclusion of others and can lock and secure it
- the size of the property.

REGULATION AND MANAGEMENT

Local authorities have duties to ensure that such properties are properly managed and safe. Types of action include:

- statutory nuisance (see above)
- overcrowding controls
- registration schemes
- execution of works
- management of regulations
- control orders.

OVERCROWDING CONTROLS

A notice may be served specifying:

- the maximum number of people who can sleep in each room in the house
- (if necessary) the age of those people
- what rooms are unsuitable for sleeping.

REGISTRATION SCHEMES

A registration scheme may be adopted by an authority for all **HMOs** within its locality, or for those of a specified type or within a particular area, so as to aid the enforcement of standards.

Registration schemes are also used to manage and control **HMOs**. Registration can be conditional on certain requirements being met or works being carried out to the property in question. Sometimes registration can be revoked or made conditional upon, for example, the management of the premises or the behaviour of its occupants.

MANAGEMENT REGULATIONS

These are intended to ensure that a person managing an **HMO** observes proper standards of repair, maintenance, cleanliness and good order, for:

- water supply
- drainage
- ventilation
- escape from fire
- disposal of rubbish.

The authority can enforce these regulations by serving a works notice.

WORKS NOTICES

A notice requiring specified works may be served on the person in control of the **HMO**, relating to:

- the storage and preparation of food
- sanitation and bathroom facilities
- means of escape from fire and other fire precautions.

CONTROL ORDERS

A **control order** can be made if:

- the steps referred to above either could have been pursued, or have been pursued but have not remedied the problem
- it appears to the local authority that the living conditions in the property are such that the protection, safety, welfare or health of people living in that property are at risk.

A **control order** has the effect of giving the local authority control of the property. The authority will take possession of it and have the right to manage it, including granting tenancies and charging rent. This is the most draconian order the authority can make in relation to an **HMO**. The order comes into effect as soon as it is made and the authority can immediately take possession of the property, taking whatever steps are necessary to protect the safety, health and welfare of those in occupation.

All of these orders may be appealed or challenged at law, usually by appeal to the county court, which may vary an order, quash it or confirm it. Non-compliance may in some circumstances be a criminal offence.

If you are unsure what you should do in relation to any notice served by the local authority about a property you own, are responsible for, or live in, you should seek legal advice.

Changes in the law on this area are underway. A new licensing scheme for (some) HMOs is proposed together with (what is expected to be) more effective methods of enforcing and maintaining standards for local housing authorities.

Homelessness and allocations

Local authorities have a number of duties relating to the provision of accommodation for those who require housing, including homeless people. Inevitably need and demand for such assistance outstrip the resources that are available and, as a result, local authorities have been required by law to establish schemes to determine how, and in what order, the available housing is to be allocated.

A local authority may only allocate accommodation in accordance with its allocation scheme by:

- providing a person with a home from the local authority's housing stock – a secure tenancy or an introductory tenancy of the property will be granted
- nominating a person to be a secure or introductory tenant of another local authority
- nominating a person to be an assured (or assured shorthold) tenant of a registered social landlord.

Local authorities are also obliged to assist those within their areas who are homeless. This assistance will be provided in a variety of ways ranging from the provision of accommodation to providing information and advice only.

The arrangements for allocating housing to those who qualify for it under an allocation scheme, and the provision of assistance for homeless people, are intended to run in parallel, so that a homeless person will receive only temporary assistance for as long as it takes to be allocated long-term accommodation from the authority's housing register.

ALLOCATIONS

Local authorities must allocate accommodation according to their allocations scheme. This must be framed so as to make sure that preference is given to those in the greatest need – for example, people or families:

- occupying insanitary or overcrowded housing

- occupying temporary accommodation

- with dependent children or who are expecting a child

- with special social or economic circumstances

- who particularly need settled accommodation for medical or welfare reasons.

> Local authorities may exclude from their schemes, or decide not to give a preference to, people or members of their families who have been guilty of such unacceptable behaviour in the past that they are not suitable to become local authority tenants.

This refers to antisocial behaviour (which can include arrears of rent), sufficiently bad that it could have led to a possession order on one of the relevant grounds for possession (whether in fact it did so or not). If you are excluded on this basis, you can reapply as soon as you have any reason to consider that you should now be excused the effects of previous behaviour.

If the authority proposes to exclude you, it must:

- give you a statement of the facts on which it has based its decision

- allow an internal review

- notify you of the outcome of any such review

- give reasons if the original decision is upheld.

The only way of challenging a decision made on review is by issuing a claim for **judicial review** of that decision.

To apply for local authority accommodation, you should contact your local authority's housing department, which will provide you with further information and an application form.

HOMELESSNESS

Advice and assistance

> Every local authority is obliged to provide advice and information about homelessness and how to prevent it to any person in their area. Local authorities also have obligations to provide assistance and accommodation to those who apply and whom the authority has reason to believe may be homeless or threatened with homelessness (a person is threatened with homelessness if they will become homeless within 28 days).

Interim accommodation

If the local authority has reason to believe that an applicant may be homeless, eligible for assistance and in priority need, it must provide that person (and any person who resides, or who could reasonably be expected to reside, with them as a member of their family) with accommodation pending its decision as to what duty, if any, is owed to that person.

Full housing duty

Where the local authority is satisfied that the applicant is:

- homeless
- eligible for assistance
- in priority need
- and did not become homeless intentionally

it must provide that person (together with any person who lives with them as a member of their family) with suitable accommodation.

Homeless

Each of the four criteria referred to above is a legal concept which can raise complex issues. Briefly, an applicant would generally be considered to be homeless if:

- there was no accommodation available which they had some sort of right to occupy
- there was no accommodation which was also available to any other person who lived as a member of their family or could be reasonably expected to live with them.

The applicant would not be considered as having accommodation unless it was accommodation that was reasonable for them to continue to occupy. What is reasonable will depend on the circumstances. It would be unreasonable for a victim of domestic violence to continue to occupy the same property as the abuser.

Eligible for assistance

The circumstances in which a person is, or is not, eligible for assistance, are extremely complex. Generally, however, a person will not be eligible for assistance if they are a person from abroad and subject to immigration control.

It should be noted that asylum-seekers are now accommodated by the NATIONAL ASYLUM SUPPORT SERVICE, and not by local authorities.

Priority need

The following people (together with those that live with them or might be expected to do so) are examples of people in priority need:

- pregnant women

- people with dependent children

- people who are vulnerable as a result of old age, mental illness or handicap or physical disability or other special reason (eg, because they have been in care or have recently left prison)

- people who are homeless as a result of an emergency (eg, flood, fire or other disaster).

Intentional homelessness

A person will be intentionally homeless if they deliberately do something or fail to do something as a result of which they stop occupying accommodation which remains available for occupation, and where it would otherwise have been reasonable for them to continue to occupy it. Accommodation is only considered to be available to a person if it is also available to anyone who might be expected to reside with them.

> Any number of acts (or failures to act) may cause homelessness. A common cause is eviction for rent arrears. If you lose your home because of rent arrears the local authority may consider you to have become homeless intentionally.

Ultimately, however, it will depend on all the circumstances and the authority must consider what caused the rent arrears. If, for example, you could not meet the rent payments without going without food and clothing, it is unlikely that you could lawfully be considered to be intentionally homeless.

DUTIES TO THE HOMELESS

If the local authority is satisfied that you meet all of the above criteria, it must make sure that suitable accommodation is available for you and your family, or provide reasonable advice and assistance in order for you to secure available suitable accommodation for yourself. Accommodation provided by the authority under these homelessness provisions will not have any security of tenure. If accommodation is provided by a private landlord, the tenancy will generally be an assured shorthold and security will therefore be limited.

LOCAL CONNECTION

The local authority to which a person applies for assistance may refer them to another local authority if it considers it would be obliged to accommodate them as a homeless person but that they (or anyone who might be expected to live with them):

- do not have a local connection with the authority
- do have a local connection with another local authority
- are not at risk of suffering domestic violence in that other district.

ENQUIRIES

Local authorities are under a duty to make enquiries into applications (pending the outcome of which, temporary accommodation will usually be provided). The extent of the enquiries is up to the authority, but they must be sufficient to enable the authority to make a decision about the various issues referred to above. The benefit of any doubt is to be given to the applicant.

CHALLENGING DECISIONS

Once the enquiries are complete, the authority must notify the applicant of the decision and, if the decision is unfavourable, give reasons. If you are dissatisfied with the authority's decision about any of the following:

- your eligibility for assistance
- the duty (if any) it owes you
- the decision to refer your application to another local authority
- the duty that is owed following a referral
- the suitability of any property offered

you may seek a review of that decision. The review must be sought within 21 days of your being notified of the decision.

Once the review has been carried out, you will be notified of the decision of the review and of the reasons for it. There is a limited right of appeal from this decision to the county court, on the ground that the authority made some kind of error of law in reaching its decision (as opposed to asking the court if it simply agrees with the decision). This might be that the authority:

- misunderstood the law relating to your case
- made a wholly unreasonable decision
- deprived you of a proper chance to tell your side of the story.

An appeal should be brought within 21 days of your being notified of the review decision. The authority may, but is not obliged to, provide temporary accommodation for you while you exercise your rights of review or appeal.

> The review and appeal processes are complicated. If you want to pursue a review or appeal you should seek legal advice as soon as possible – you risk losing your entitlement to both if you delay.

Organisations i

National associations that should be able to provide you with advice or recommend a solicitor:

► **ADVICE UK (formerly THE FEDERATION OF INFORMATION AND ADVICE CENTRES)**
12th Floor
New London Bridge House
25 London Bridge Street
London SE1 9ST
Tel: 020 7407 4070
www.fiac.org.uk

► **ADVISORY SERVICE FOR SQUATTERS**
2 St Paul's Road
Islington
London N1 2QN
Tel: 020 7359 8814 or 0845 644 5814
advice@squat.freeserve.co.uk
www.squat.freeserve.co.uk

► **CENTREPOINT**
Neil House
7 Whitechapel Road
London E1 1DU
Tel: 020 7426 5300
Fax: 020 7426 5301
www.centrepoint.org.uk

► **CRISIS**
66 Commercial Street
London E1 6LT
Tel: 0870 011 3335
Fax: 0870 011 3336
enquiries@crisis.org.uk
www.crisis.org.uk

► **CROWN ESTATES COMMISSIONERS**
www.crownestate.co.uk
London Office:
The Crown Estate
16 Carlton House Terrace
London SW1Y 5AH
Tel: 020 7210 4377
Fax: 020 7210 4236
pr@crownestate.co.uk
Edinburgh Office:
The Crown Estate
6 Bell's Brae
Edinburgh EH4 3BJ
Tel: 0131 260 6070
cescotland@crownestate.co.uk

► **FEDERATION OF BLACK HOUSING ORGANISATIONS (FBHO)**
1 King Edwards Road
London E9 7SF
Tel: 020 8533 7053
Fax: 020 8985 9166
www.fbho.org.uk

► **FREE REPRESENTATION UNIT (FRU)**
Fourth Floor, Peer House
8–14 Verulam Street
London WC1X 8LZ
www.fru.org.uk
Please note that the FRU does NOT deal with members of the public directly.

► **FRONTLINE HOUSING ADVICE**
1st Floor
Elmfield House
5 Stockwell Mews
London SW9 9GX
Tel: 020 7501 9573

► **HOUSING CORPORATION CORPORATE SERVICES**
Maple House
149 Tottenham Court Road
London W1T 7BN
Tel: 020 7393 2000
Fax: 020 7393 2111
enquiries@housingcorp.gsx.gov.uk
www.housingcorp.gov.uk

► **LAND REGISTRY**
See website for contact details:
www.landreg.gov.uk

► **LAW CENTRES FEDERATION**
Duchess House
18–19 Warren Street
London W1T 5LR
Tel: 020 7387 8570
Fax: 020 7387 8368
info@lawcentres.org.uk
www.lawcentres.org.uk

► **LAW SOCIETY**
113 Chancery Lane
London WC2A 1PL
Tel: 020 7242 1222
Fax: 020 7831 0344
info.services@lawsociety.org.uk
www.lawsoc.org.uk

► **NATIONAL ASSOCIATION OF CITIZENS ADVICE BUREAUX (NACAB)**

Myddelton House
115–123 Pentonville Road
London N1 9LZ

Tel: 020 7833 2181
www.nacab.org.uk

Adviceguide: the National Association of Citizens Advice Bureaux offers fact sheets covering issues such as employment, housing and taxation
www.adviceguide.org.uk

► **NATIONAL ASSOCIATION OF ESTATE AGENTS (NAEA)**

Arbon House
21 Jury Street
Warwick CV34 4EH

Tel: 01926 496800
Fax: 01926 400953
info@naea.co.uk
www.naea.co.uk

► **NATIONAL ASYLUM SUPPORT SERVICE (NASS)**

Frank Corrigan
27 Old Gloucester Street
Bloomsbury
London WC1N 3XX

info@asylumsupport.info
www.asylumsupport.info

► **NATIONAL DISABLED PERSONS HOUSING SERVICE (HoDIS)**

17 Priory Street
York YO1 6ET

Tel: 01904 653888
Fax: 01904 653999
info@hodis.org.uk
www.hodis.org.uk

► **NATIONAL HOMELESS ALLIANCE**

Homeless Link
First Floor, 10–13 Rushworth Street
London SE1 0RB

Tel: 020 7960 3010
www.homeless.org.uk

Membership organisation for those providing services to homeless people.

► **SHELTER**

88 Old Street
London EC1V 9HU

Tel: 020 7505 4699

Free helpline for housing help and advice:
0808 800 4444

info@shelter.org.uk
www.shelter.org.uk

Government departments with responsibility for housing issues:

► **OFFICE OF THE DEPUTY PRIME MINISTER (ODPM)**

Tel: 0207 944 4400
www.odpm.gov.uk

► **DEPARTMENT FOR WORK AND PENSIONS (DWP)**

Adelphi
1–11 John Adam Street
London WC2N 6HT

Tel: 020 7962 8000
www.dwp.gov.uk

You may need to contact your local authority, which will be listed in the local telephone directory. In London contact:

► **GREATER LONDON AUTHORITY (GLA)**

City Hall
The Queen's Walk
London SE1 2AA

Tel: 020 7983 4000
www.london.gov.uk

Further reading

The following are useful, introductory texts to this area of law.

Arden and Hunter, *Manual of Housing Law*, 6th edn (Sweet & Maxwell, London)

Arden and Hunter, *Homelessness and Allocations* (LAG, London)

Baker, Carter and Hunter, *Housing and Human Rights Law* (LAG, London)

Carter and Dymond, *Arden & Partington's Quiet Enjoyment*, 6th edn (LAG, London)

16 Human Rights Act

The *Human Rights Act*, **which only came into force in October 2000, is having dramatic and far-reaching effects on almost every aspect of our daily lives. The aim of this chapter is to explain the rights guaranteed by the Act.**

The Human Rights Act and the European Convention on Human Rights

The UK was one of the first countries to ratify the *European Convention on Human Rights* in 1951 but it has only been since the *Human Rights Act* came into force that individuals have been able to complain to British courts that their rights under the *European Convention* have been infringed. Whatever your particular cause of legal complaint, you need to ensure that your lawyer has taken this dimension on board.

WHAT IS THE EUROPEAN CONVENTION ON HUMAN RIGHTS?

The *European Convention on Human Rights* is an international treaty concluded by the countries that make up the COUNCIL OF EUROPE. The European powers created two *separate* institutions: the EUROPEAN ECONOMIC COMMUNITY (EEC) to promote economic stability in Europe, and the COUNCIL OF EUROPE to encourage respect for the rule of law and human rights.

The COUNCIL OF EUROPE drafted the *Convention for the Protection of Human Rights and Fundamental Freedoms (the European Convention on Human Rights)*, which entered into force on 3 September 1953. It established a EUROPEAN COURT OF HUMAN RIGHTS in Strasbourg to hear interstate cases or those brought by individuals against states.

Additional rights are protected by *protocols to the Convention*. States that have signed and ratified these protocols are also bound to protect the rights contained within them. The UK has ratified both the *first* and *sixth protocols*.

HUMAN RIGHTS ACT 1998

> The *Human Rights Act (HRA)* incorporates into English law articles 2–12 and 14 of the Convention, and the rights contained in the first and sixth protocols, and these are referred to collectively as Convention rights.

The *HRA* protects Convention rights in three ways:

DUTY ON THE COURTS TO INTERPRET LAW TO PROTECT CONVENTION RIGHTS

Under the *HRA*, all courts and tribunals must interpret laws in a way that is **compatible** with the rights contained within the Convention and protocols. Whenever it is argued that a law restricts a Convention right, the courts must consider, though not necessarily follow, cases decided by the European Court and Commission on Human Rights when deciding the meaning of the law.

Courts and tribunals covers a wide number of bodies including:

- magistrates' courts, crown courts, county courts
- the higher courts, the High Court, Court of Appeal
- the House of Lords
- employment tribunals
- the social security appeal tribunal
- tax tribunal
- immigration adjudicator and appeal tribunals

In theory, all settled principles developed through case law can now be challenged on the basis that they fail to respect human rights. In practice, however, most settled case law is likely to be compatible with the Convention rights.

Where the higher courts decide that it would be impossible to interpret a British statute in a way which is compatible with Convention rights, they cannot (unlike, for example, the US Supreme Court) simply strike the legislation down. They only have the power to make a **declaration of incompatibility**, or a statement that the law is in conflict with a Convention right. Parliament can then amend the law. However, a declaration of incompatibility does not affect the validity of the law, and the court must apply the law to the facts of the case even though it offends the Convention right.

PARLIAMENTARY RESPONSIBILITY

All legislation enacted since 1998 must be scrutinised by parliament for compliance with Convention rights. Each enacted statute now carries a **compatibility statement**, affirming that parliament considers that it complies with the Convention rights, or that it does not but parliament nevertheless wishes to enact the legislation.

ACTIONS AGAINST PUBLIC AUTHORITIES

A **public authority** must respect an individual's Convention rights. A public authority includes:

- central government departments, local authorities
- police, prison, immigration officers, the armed forces
- NHS hospitals
- Customs and Excise
- courts and tribunals

but *not* the House of Commons or Lords. The *HRA* extends the definition of a public authority to include private bodies which perform a public function, such as:

- National Rail Authority, Group 4 Security, British Telecom
- housing associations
- the Football Association, the Jockey Club
- some charities.

> A victim (a person or legal entity such as a company or association, directly, indirectly or potentially affected) may bring a claim against a public authority or defend themselves in court by complaining that their Convention rights have been or will be restricted.

The *HRA* does not create any special courts. The appropriate court or tribunal will therefore depend upon the nature of the case or subject matter.

SPECIALIST LEGAL ADVICE

Lawyers are only just starting to become familiar with the *European Convention*. If you believe that your Convention rights have been or are restricted by a public authority, seek advice from the general advice centres or from lawyers who specialise in the field (see CHAPTER 1: FINDING AND MEETING YOUR LAWYER).

It is important to note that, in the vast majority of cases, causes of action against public authorities already exist. A claim under the *HRA* is therefore to complement existing causes of action.

Remedies and just satisfaction

If a court or tribunal finds that a Convention right has been infringed, it can award a victim **just satisfaction** or the appropriate relief. Again, the relief granted by a court will depend upon the circumstances, but can include:

- damages (money)
- an order to the public authority to stop acting in a way which could or does infringe the Convention right (eg, not to deport someone, or not to interfere with a prisoner's correspondence)
- an order to the public authority to take steps to ensure that the right is protected or that they should take action to ensure this (eg, continue to provide medical treatment, rehouse someone, give them their job back).

The courts are limited to using their existing powers in granting any relief.

TIME LIMITS

Any claim against a public authority must be brought within one year of the act restricting the Convention right, although shorter time limits may apply where the claim under the *HRA* is included with other claims (eg, **judicial review** claims, which must be made within three months). Claims for acts prior to 2 October 2000 are unlikely to proceed.

Where, however, proceedings are brought against a person by a public authority (for example, a criminal prosecution by the CROWN PROSECUTION SERVICE, the police or proceedings brought by local authorities) and the defendant relies upon a Convention right as a defence, there is no such time limit.

The Convention rights

The Convention is, unlike domestic law, subject to different rules of interpretation.

- It is a 'living instrument' and must be interpreted in the light of modern social and cultural attitudes.

- The words in the Convention must be interpreted in the light of their **object and purpose**.

- The public authority must guarantee the rights not only in theory but in practice.

- Some rights are absolute and can never be restricted.

- Other rights may be limited. Any restriction on a Convention right must be set out in clearly defined and accessible laws.

- Any restriction on a Convention right must **pursue a legitimate aim**. There must be a justification for the restriction upon the right.

  Examples include:

  - national security
  - preventing crime
  - the economic well-being of the country
  - protecting health or morals
  - protecting the rights and freedoms of others.

- A public authority can only restrict the rights to the extent that this is **necessary** and **proportionate**.

Right to life

Article 2 protects against the arbitrary deprivation of life by the state, and covers cases of both deliberate and accidental killing. The Convention permits the use of lethal force by the police or armed forces only in very limited circumstances:

- in defending a person from violence
- in making an arrest
- in preventing an escape from custody
- in suppressing a riot or insurrection.

This does not mean that the state can kill intentionally in such cases.

> Lethal force may only be used when it is *absolutely necessary* and where it is a *proportionate* response to the actions of the victim.

Article 2 also imposes a duty to take steps to safeguard the lives of those who are at risk. Where a public authority is aware, or ought to be aware, of a specific, real and immediate threat to an individual's life, it is under a positive obligation to take reasonable steps to ensure that the person comes to no harm. The authorities may therefore be responsible for:

- the death in custody of a known suicide risk
- the death of a person with a known medical condition, if they fail to provide assistance
- the failure of social services adequately to protect the life of a child known to be at risk.

Where a person dies in custody (eg, police custody, psychiatric hospital), even if they take their own lives, the right to life obliges the authorities to carry out a thorough, effective and impartial investigation into the circumstances surrounding the death. Inquests generally fulfil this obligation, although they have recently been criticised for their failure to ensure that family members are able to participate effectively in the proceedings, and more generally for their inability to determine the liability of the authorities in whose custody a person dies (see CHAPTER 18: INQUESTS).

> The right to life does not extend to the unborn foetus, which has no viable life outside the mother.

Torture

The *Convention* protects against all forms of serious ill-treatment. It is never permissible for the police to detain and seriously ill-treat suspected terrorists or criminals, regardless of what they are alleged to have done or information they may have. The prohibition is absolute, but only the most serious kinds of ill-treatment are absolutely prohibited. When assessing ill-treatment, the characteristics of the victim are highly relevant: their age, their sex and their physical and mental condition.

- **Torture** is defined as **deliberate or intentionally inflicted inhuman treatment causing very serious and cruel suffering**, and includes custodial rape.

- **Inhuman treatment** or punishment is that which causes **intense physical and mental suffering**.

- **Degrading treatment** or punishment is that **arousing in the victim a feeling of fear, anguish and inferiority, which humiliates or debases the victim**, possibly breaking their physical or moral resistance.

Like *Article 2*, the authorities are **positively obliged** to ensure that a person under their control does not suffer any form of ill-treatment. Similarly, where an allegation of serious ill-treatment is made, public authorities are obliged to carry out an effective and impartial investigation into the allegation. The burden rests with the public authority to provide a plausible explanation for any injuries (see CHAPTER 5: ACTIONS AGAINST THE POLICE).

A **civil action against the police** for ill-treatment is already available to persons who make such a complaint. *Article 3* reinforces the duty on the police to investigate allegations of ill-treatment and ensure that only proportionate force is used as a last resort.

> To assist in making either a **civil claim** or a claim under the *HRA*, ensure that:
> - a complaint is made to a custody sergeant shortly after the alleged assault
> - an independent medical report is obtained
> - clear photographs are taken of the injuries.

A number of cases concerning the corporal punishment of children have been taken to the European Court in Strasbourg, with parents arguing that such treatment is inhuman and degrading. Prison conditions may also violate *Article 3*.

Where the police or social services fail to protect the victims of domestic violence or vulnerable children, an action for negligence before a county court may be supported by reference to *Article 3* (see CHAPTER 14: FAMILY).

Article 3 has also been invoked by asylum-seekers where there is a serious risk that they will suffer serious ill-treatment if they are returned. Where the evidence points to such a risk, they cannot be removed from the UK. The *Immigration and Asylum Act 1999* makes provision for such cases to be heard by the **IMMIGRATION APPELLATE AUTHORITY** (see CHAPTER 17: IMMIGRATION AND REFUGEES).

Slavery

> The *Convention* prohibits slavery (implying ownership of another), servitude and compulsory labour. Military service, prison work and work in times of public emergency are exceptions to this prohibition. There has been little case law generated on this article of the Convention.

Liberty of the person

Article 5 protects individuals against all forms of arbitrary detention. Liberty may only be deprived in accordance with a procedure set out in law and in clearly defined circumstances. Most commonly, a person is deprived of their liberty after they have been arrested by the police on reasonable suspicion that they have committed a criminal offence, or where a court sentences a person to a period of imprisonment following conviction. But *Article 5* applies to all forms of detention, including detention of:

- children
- the mentally impaired

- drug addicts or alcoholics
- the homeless
- those seeking to enter the country illegally.

Article 5 sets out the minimum **procedural** safeguards anyone who is detained must receive.

> *Anyone* detained, whether on suspicion of having committed a criminal offence or otherwise, must be advised in a language they understand, at the time of their arrest or detention, of the reasons for their detention and of any criminal charges against them.

CRIMINAL CASES

In such cases a person:

- may be arrested only where there is objective evidence giving rise to a suspicion that they have committed an offence
- must be offered legal advice before they are questioned
- must be brought to court in order that their detention may be authorised
- is entitled to bail unless there are **relevant and sufficient reasons** for bail to be withheld.

A suspect's legal representatives should be supplied with details of the evidence used to justify continued detention, in order for an effective challenge to be made.

All persons who are detained must be offered:

- an opportunity to bring proceedings before a court, with power to order their release, to challenge whether their continued detention is lawful
- meaningful legal representation.

> Any violation of the right to liberty under the Convention gives rise to a right to compensation.

It is important to appreciate that almost all of the procedural requirements of *Article 5* are already in force in cases where a person is detained. In the criminal context, the *Police and Criminal Evidence Act (PACE)* demands that a person must be advised of the reasons for their arrest at the time they are arrested. *PACE* ensures that a person arrested by the police is made aware of their right to consult with a legal representative and for that representative to be present during questioning. A failure to comply with these provisions may give rise to a **civil action against the police**. (See CHAPTER 5: CIVIL ACTIONS AGAINST THE POLICE.)

Those arrested must be brought before a magistrate, who may grant bail or order their detention. The *Bail Act*, setting out the conditions in which bail should be granted, mirrors **EUROPEAN COURT** case law.

Successful challenges have been made in cases where the criminal law automatically denies bail or automatically provides for a life sentence because serious offences have been committed in the past. The courts have also found that there is a duty to ensure that sentences are commensurate with the gravity of offences, which will include taking into consideration the particular circumstances of the offender. Police powers to stop and search individuals may be considered to violate *Article 5*, although the point has not been resolved (see CHAPTER 8: CRIMINAL LAW).

There have been a number of actions brought by those detained under the provisions of the *Mental Health Act*, particularly in connection with the length of time taken by the **MENTAL HEALTH REVIEW TRIBUNAL** to review the grounds for continued detention (see CHAPTER 22: MENTAL HEALTH).

Fair trial

The **right to fair trial**, perhaps the most litigated of all the Convention rights, sets out the minimum **procedural** safeguards anyone in a court or tribunal can expect to receive.

The safeguards apply to any proceedings involving civil rights, a wide phrase covering all types of legal action, including:

- contracts
- commercial law
- wills
- insurance

- family law

- negligence claims

- disciplinary hearings before professional governing bodies.

> The right to a fair trial does not apply in decisions made by
> the authorities that are **public** in character. For example, the
> categorisation of prisoners, the issue of a passport, or asylum and
> immigration proceedings, as these are regarded by the EUROPEAN
> COURT in Strasbourg as purely 'administrative' measures.

The right to a fair trial also applies to criminal cases, where the safeguards
have been carefully particularised. The overriding obligation is to ensure
that all civil and criminal proceedings are fair.

The principle of fairness demands that a party to either criminal or civil
proceedings:

- has a right to have their case heard – a right of **access to court**

- has notice of the hearings in advance

- is able to be present at the hearing

- has a proper opportunity to put their case

- is entitled to the evidence or documents relied upon by their opposing
  party

- is given a reasoned decision.

Hearings should, unless there are special reasons, be held in public. The fair
trial provisions apply throughout the proceedings as a whole, and include
preliminary hearings, costs hearings and the enforcement of judgements.

Any individual is entitled to trial before an **independent** (free from executive influence) and **impartial** (free from bias) court, in fact as well as in
appearance. The proceedings must also take place within a reasonable
period of time, but certain kinds of cases (eg, those involving children)
should be determined quickly. Time runs from the date of the institution of
civil proceedings or the point at which a defendant was charged.

In criminal cases, the safeguards include the right of defendants:

- to be presumed innocent until proven guilty

- not to be forced to answer questions or produce documents that tend to incriminate them

- to be provided with full details of the case against them, and in particular documentary evidence

- to be legally represented

- to have time to prepare a defence, including the right to consult with lawyers in private, prior to questioning

- to cross-examine any **crown witnesses**

- to have an interpreter, if they require one.

Special measures must be taken when vulnerable groups (eg, children or the mentally ill) are tried in criminal courts.

Retroactive criminal offences

The Convention prohibits absolutely the creation of new **criminal offences**, which have **retrospective application**, as well as the imposition of additional penalties or sentences on those already convicted. More generally, it implies that the criminal law must be clear and that proscribed conduct must be carefully defined.

Respect for private and family life

> The *Convention* protects against arbitrary interference by the authorities in our private lives. **Private life** implies anything that is not done in public. What an individual does in private, with his or her family, in his or her home and in private correspondence, should not be subject to any interference by the authorities.

However, the right to respect for private life is not absolute and is subject to restrictions. Any restrictions must be **lawful, pursue a legitimate aim** and be **necessary and proportionate**. The essence of *Article 8* (and similarly *Articles 9,*

10 and *11*) is to ensure that a proper balance is struck between the individual's right to private life on the one hand and the general interest on the other. Much will depend on the individual circumstances in a case.

The protections provided by the right to private life cover a very large number of situations, for example:

- sexual relations and identity
- privacy
- protection of the home
- environmental protection
- moral and physical integrity
- family life

The right applies to many areas of law, including family, prisoners, mental health, environment, media, land and employment.

Freedom of thought

The *Convention* protects the right to hold religious beliefs, to change one's religion and to manifest those beliefs in worship, teaching, practice and observance. The essential underlying principle is that individuals are free to develop their own belief system, without interference. While the right to **freedom of thought** is absolute, implying that no one can be subject to enforced indoctrination, the right to manifest beliefs may be subject to proportionate restrictions.

A great many cases brought before both the European and British courts have concerned the rights of members of minority communities and faiths to practise their religious beliefs.

> The right to **freedom of conscience** also includes the rights of atheists and agnostics, as well as those with strong convictions, such as vegans and pacifists.

Freedom of expression

The *Convention* guarantees not only the right to hold opinions, but also the right to receive and impart information. The **EUROPEAN COURT** in Strasbourg has explained that freedom of expression is an essential cornerstone of democracy, and applies to information and ideas favourably received, as well as those that offend, disturb and shock. The essence of the right lies in pluralism, tolerance and broad-mindedness, without which there can be no democratic society. However, the right is not absolute and is subject to lawful, legitimate and proportionate restrictions by the authorities.

Article 10 protects many kinds of expression:

- political expression, journalistic freedoms, artistic expression and even commercial expression

- words, pictures, images, demonstrations and actions expressing an idea or imparting information, as well as new forms of communication such as email and internet.

In practice, the protection accorded to political expression, the freedom of journalists and others who criticise politicians and public figures, is the widest. Often, press freedoms come into conflict with the right to respect for privacy, and a number of recent cases have shown a greater willingness on the part of the courts to protect the private lives of public figures.

An **interference** with the right to freedom of expression may arise in many forms, for example:

- libel and slander proceedings against writers and publishers

- a refusal to issue a licence to broadcasters

- injunctions upon newspapers preventing them from publishing stories

- banning works of art or books

- arrests at public protests.

Irrespective of the manner in which the right to freedom of expression is restricted, the courts must examine whether any limitations are lawful, pursue a legitimate aim and strike a fair balance between the general interest and the rights of the individual.

> The right to freedom of expression also includes the right to receive information, which may extend to obtaining personal records from local authorities or government departments about the past or health.

Freedom of association

The protection provided by *Article 11* concerns three rights:

- to peaceful assembly, including public marches and demonstrations
- to associate freely with others
- to join any kind of association or trade union for the protection of an individual's interests.

The underlying principle is that each individual may choose with whom they wish (and do not wish) to associate. The right is not absolute, and is subject to legitimate and proportionate restrictions.

The right to assemble overlaps with the right to freedom of expression. The purpose of a demonstration is irrelevant so long as the intention is to hold a peaceful demonstration. Protests that impede the actions of others are protected and the police must take reasonable and appropriate measures, in the face of disruption or disorder from others, to ensure that protestors are able to demonstrate. Permission to hold a protest may be required, and demonstrations on public highways can be restricted to ensure that others have unimpeded access. (See CHAPTER 26: PUBLIC ORDER.)

All kinds of associations are protected: for example, political parties, pressure groups and professional governing bodies, which are free to regulate their membership and activities. Banning groups is permissible only where there is cogent evidence that the association calls for the use of violence.

Trade union members have a general right to put their demands to their employers. While the right to strike is not expressly mentioned in *Article 11*, subject to reasonable restrictions, it is recognised as an important means by which trade unions can protect their members' interests.

Special restrictions are imposed upon the police, the army and civil servants in the formation of associations and trade unions.

The right to marry

The right under *Article 12* provides that men and women are free to marry in accordance with British law. Prisoners, despite being deprived of their liberty, are entitled to marry, but homosexuals are not.

Article 12 also protects the right to found a family, implying a right to have children.

Effective remedy

Article 13 guarantees the right of all persons to a **remedy for an arguable violation of a Convention right before a national authority**. *Article 13* is **not** included among the Convention rights given effect by the *Human Rights Act* because the *HRA* itself, by allowing an individual to enforce their rights before British courts, is itself guaranteeing an effective remedy.

Discrimination

Discrimination presupposes that a person is treated differently without good reason, when compared with another in the same situation. *Article 14* prohibits discrimination on a very wide variety of grounds, including:

- sex
- race
- political opinion
- association with national minority
- any other status.

The list of grounds included in *Article 14* is not exhaustive. While most international and regional human rights treaties prohibit discriminatory treatment, *Article 14 only* prohibits discrimination in **the enjoyment of a Convention right**. It is *not* a free-standing prohibition against discrimination.

A cause of action for sex or race discrimination lies under the *Sex Discrimination and Race Relations Act*, and the protection provided by this Act provides greater protection than *Article 14* (see CHAPTER 10: DISCRIMINATION).

Interpretation

Articles 15–18 do not provide specific Convention rights; rather they concern the interpretation of the Convention.

> *Article 15* explains that, even in times of war and public emergency, these absolute rights may *never* be compromised:
> - the protection of life (*Article 2*) (other than deaths arising in war)
> - the prohibition on torture (*Article 3*)
> - the prohibition on slavery and servitude (*Article 4*)
> - freedom from retroactive legislation (*Article 7*).

Article 16 permits restriction of rights to free expression, association and discrimination in relation to the political activities of non-UK nationals.

Articles 17 and *18* explain that the Convention may not be interpreted so as to provide a right to groups or persons which would destroy the rights protected under the Convention, and that the restrictions permitted under the Convention must not have an ulterior motive.

Right to property

Article 1 Protocol 1 concerns the right of individuals and companies to the peaceful enjoyment of their possessions.

The term **possessions** is widely interpreted and includes: houses and land, leases, inheritance rights, licences, and, in certain circumstances, an obligation to pay contributions to a social security scheme.

Possessions may not be deprived arbitrarily, although a public authority is entitled to control the use of property in accordance with the general interest, and to secure the payment of taxation or other contributions or penalties. Any restrictions on property must pursue a legitimate aim and be proportionate, striking a fair balance between the general interest and the right of the property owner. Ultimately, the case law on *Article 1* reflects the right of a state to organise its economy and exercise control over property in a way that reflects its political and social aspirations.

Many complaints may be generated from restrictions imposed by public authorities on the control and use of property. Control on its use must be in the public interest and have a specific aim. For example, a refusal to grant planning permission for an extension or for a particular purpose may be justified by the need to protect neighbours from incursions upon their right to enjoy their own property.

The EUROPEAN COURT in Strasbourg has ruled that there is a distinction between contributory pension schemes which create an individual share in a pension fund, and non-contributory schemes creating only an expectation of a benefit. Where legislation deprives a contributor of an entitlement to that pension, it may offend *Article 1*. Where benefits and allowances are available to widows but not widowers, it is likely to amount to discrimination, contrary to *Article 14*.

In addition, decisions made by public authorities affecting property must be procedurally fair and ensure that the right to a fair hearing is properly respected (see *Article 6*).

Right to education

Article 2 is primarily concerned with the rights of primary and secondary education for children. It also protects the right of parents to have their children educated in a way that reflects their own philosophical and moral convictions. The European Court has restricted the application of *Article 2* to the extent that it avoids unreasonable public expenditure.

There is no obligation on the part of the government to subsidise or fund minority schools, home education or particular kinds of special needs education. However, where state funding is available to certain denominational schools but not to others, that may amount to discriminatory treatment and be contrary to *Article 14*.

> Local education authorities must ensure that adequate facilities are available to provide schooling where a child is expelled or suffers from a disability.
>
> Schools must also respect the religious and philosophical convictions of the parents or pupils – for example, their religion, attitudes to sex education and corporal punishment.

Free and fair elections

The *Convention* obliges states to hold free and fair national parliamentary elections at reasonable intervals and by secret ballot, in order to ensure the free expression of the opinion of the electorate in the choice of legislature. It includes the right to vote and stand for elections, but does not include a duty to introduce a specific system of voting (eg, proportional representation).

Abolition of the death penalty

Protocol 6 is exclusively concerned with the abolition of the death penalty. The death penalty was abolished by the UK in 1965 for all serious offences other than treason, piracy and a number of offences under military law. By ratifying *Protocol 6*, the government is obliged:

- not to impose the death penalty for any of these offences
- never to reintroduce its enactment
- never to deport or extradite a person to face the death penalty in another country.

The *HRA* will continue to have an extensice influence on national law and how it impinges on our daily lives.

Organisations   i

▶ **ADVICE ON INDIVIDUAL RIGHTS IN EUROPE**
The AIRE Centre
3rd Floor, 17 Red Lion Square
London WC1R 4QH
Advice line: 020 7831 3850
info@airecentre.org
www.airecentre.org

▶ **AMNESTY INTERNATIONAL**
99–119 Rosebery Avenue
London EC1R 4RE
Tel: 020 7814 6200
Fax: 020 7833 1510
information@amnesty.org.uk
www.amnesty.org.uk

► **CHARTER 88**

18a Victoria Park Square
London E2 9PF

Tel: 020 888 6088
Fax: 020 8880 6089
info@charter88.org.uk
www.charter88.org.uk

► **CHILDREN'S LEGAL CENTRE**

University of Essex
Wivenhoe Park
Colchester
Essex CO4 3SQ

Advice line: 01206 873820
www.essex.ac.uk

► **INTERIGHTS**

Lancaster House
33 Islington High Street
London N1 9LH

Tel: 020 7278 3230   or   020 7278 4334
ir@interights.org
www.interights.org

► **JUSTICE**

59 Carter Lane
London EC4V 5AQ

Tel: 020 7329 5100
Fax: 020 739 5055
admin@justice.org.uk
www.justice.org.uk

► **LAW CENTRES FEDERATION**

Duchess House
18–19 Warren Street
London W1T 5LR

Tel: 020 7387 8570
Fax: 020 7387 8368
info@lawcentres.org.uk
www.lawcentres.org.uk

► **LIBERTY**

21 Tabard Street
London SE1 4LA

Tel: 020 7403 3888
Fax: 020 7407 5354
info@liberty-human-rights.org.uk
www.liberty-human-rights.org.uk

► **NATIONAL ASSOCIATION OF CITIZENS ADVICE BUREAUX (NACAB)**

Myddelton House
115–123 Pentonville Road
London N1 9LZ

Tel: 020 7833 2181
www.nacab.org.uk

Adviceguide: the National Association of Citizens Advice Bureaux offers fact sheets covering issues such as employment, housing and taxation
www.adviceguide.org.uk

► **NATIONAL CIVIL RIGHTS MOVEMENT (NCRM)**

14 Featherstone Road
Southall
Middlesex UB2 5AA

Tel: 020 8574 0818   or   020 8843 2333
Fax: 020 8813 9734
info@ncrm.org.uk
www.ncrm.org.uk

► **STATEWATCH**

PO Box 1516
London N16 0EW

Tel: 020 8802 1882
Fax: 020 8880 1727
info@statewatch.org
www.statewatch.org

Research papers/regular bulletins on policing, immigration, prisons, Europe, etc.

Further reading

Wadham and Mountfield, *Blackstone's Guide to the Human Rights Act 1998* (Blackstone Press, 1999)

Keir Starmer, *European Human Rights Law* (Legal Action Group, 1999)

17 **Immigration and refugees**

Immigration law is one of the most complex, least understood and frequently changing areas of law, with the potential for very serious, sometimes fatal, consequences for those who are making immigration applications.

Types of application

Broadly, immigration law covers applications for:

- leave to enter or remain in the UK as a visitor, student, relative or unmarried partner of a person settled in the UK, and for business or employment purposes
- asylum
- leave to live, work or study in the UK, made under the *EC Treaty* or an *EC Association Agreement*
- leave to enter or remain in the UK on the basis that requiring the applicant to return to his or her home country would amount to a breach of their human rights contrary to the *European Convention on Human Rights*
- British citizenship.

Sources of immigration law

The breadth and complexity of immigration law is partly a result of the various overlapping and sometimes conflicting sources of domestic and international law. The following are just some of the legal instruments that set out an individual's rights and the state's obligations:

- *Immigration Act 1971*

- *Immigration Act 1988*

- *Asylum and Immigration Appeals Act 1993*

- *Asylum and Immigration Act 1996*

- *Special Immigration Appeals Commission Act 1997*

- *Human Rights Act 1998*

- *Immigration and Asylum Act 1999*

- *Nationality, Immigration and Asylum Act 2002*

- *Immigration Rules (HC 395)*

- *1951 Convention Relating to the Status of Refugees*

- *1967 Protocol Relating to the Status of Refugees*

- *UNHCR Handbook on Procedures and Criteria Relating to the Status of Refugees*

- *European Convention on Human Rights*

- *Convention Relating to the Status of Stateless Persons*

- *Treaty on European Union*

- *Council directive 64/221/EEC*

- *Council regulation (EEC) 1612/68*

- *Dublin Convention*

- various *EC Association Agreements*

Making an application to enter or remain

Because immigration law is so complex it is essential that when faced with an immigration issue you obtain advice from lawyers who are specialists. Many immigration applications are unsuccessful because the individual or their adviser does not fully understand the relevant law or is not able successfully to challenge an unlawful HOME OFFICE decision.

The application forms provided by the HOME OFFICE, or British embassies abroad, are usually complicated and if filled in incorrectly may lead to an application being turned down. Financial consequences follow, since a non-refundable fee is required with most applications.

Appeals

If your application for leave to enter or remain in the UK is refused by the HOME OFFICE or BRITISH EMBASSY, in many instances, but not all, you will have a right of appeal to the IMMIGRATION APPELLATE AUTHORITY. In some cases, your remedy will be a claim for **judicial review** in the High Court.

Your appeal will usually be heard in the first instance by an **adjudicator** and then if that fails you may appeal to the IMMIGRATION APPEAL TRIBUNAL. However, because the time limits for appeal are very stringent and the documentation that needs to be completed, which includes the **grounds of appeal**, is very difficult, it should not be attempted without the assistance of a specialist.

Legal advice

Because people with immigration problems are often in a vulnerable position, and may not have a thorough understanding of English, a number of unscrupulous advisers offer immigration advice in return for vast sums of money, and invariably provide a very poor service. In order to help counteract the problem the government recently created an **Immigration Services Commissioner**, whose duty is to promote good practice on the part of those who provide immigration advice.

Although there is no certain way of ensuring that a solicitor can provide you with the level of specialist advice you require, positive indicators include:

- membership of the IMMIGRATION LAW PRACTITIONERS ASSOCIATION

- the holding of a **public funding contract** that has been awarded to the firm by the LEGAL SERVICES COMMISSION.

Good quality specialist advice is also provided by:

- some law centres

- REFUGEE LEGAL CENTRE

- ASYLUM AID.

Legal aid is available for advice and representation in immigration matters (see CHAPTER 2: LEGAL AID).

Organisations   i

▶ **ADVICE UK (formerly THE FEDERATION OF INFORMATION AND ADVICE CENTRES)**
12th Floor
New London Bridge House
25 London Bridge Street
London SE1 9ST
Tel: 020 7407 4070
www.fiac.org.uk

▶ **ASYLUM AID**
28 Commercial Street
London E1 6LS
Tel: 020 7377 5123
Fax: 020 7247 7789
advice@asylumaid.org.uk
www.asylumaid.org.uk

▶ **EUROPEAN COUNCIL ON REFUGEES AND EXILES**
ECRE Secretariat, Clifton Centre
Unit 22, 3rd Floor, 110 Clifton Street
London EC2A 4HT
Tel: 020 7729 5152
Fax: 020 7729 5141
ecre@ecre.org

▶ **FREE REPRESENTATION UNIT (FRU)**
Fourth Floor, Peer House
8–14 Verulam Street
London WC1X 8LZ
www.fru.org.uk
Please note that the FRU does NOT deal with members of the public directly.

▶ **HOME OFFICE**
Customer Information Service
7th floor, 50 Queen Anne's Gate
London SW1H 9AT
General enquiries (9.00am–5.00pm):
0870 0001585
www.homeoffice.gov.uk

▶ **IMMIGRATION ADVISORY SERVICE**
County House
190 Great Dover Street
London SE1 4YB
Tel: 020 7967 1200
Fax: 020 7378 0665
www.iasuk.org

▶ **IMMIGRATION APPEAL TRIBUNAL**
(see IMMIGRATION APPELLATE AUTHORITY)

► **IMMIGRATION APPELLATE AUTHORITY**
Arnhem House
PO Box 6987
Leicester LE1 6ZX
Tel: 0845 6000 877
Fax: 0116 249 4130
webmaster@courtservice.gsi.gov.uk
www.iaa.gov.uk
For general queries concerning asylum cases, leaflets and customer complaints.

► **IMMIGRATION LAW PRACTITIONERS ASSOCIATION**
Lindsey House
40–42 Charterhouse Street
London EC1M 6JN
Tel: 020 7251 8383
Fax: 020 7251 8384
info@ilpa.org.uk
www.ilpa.org.uk

► **IMMIGRATION SERVICES COMMISSIONER**
Fleetbank House
2–6 Salisbury Square
London EC4Y 8JX
Tel: 020 7211 1500
Fax: 020 7211 1553

► **JOINT COUNCIL FOR THE WELFARE OF IMMIGRANTS**
115 Old Street
London EC1V 9RT
Tel: 020 7251 8708
Fax: 020 7251 8707
info@jcwi.org.uk
www.jcwi.org.uk

► **LAW CENTRES FEDERATION**
Duchess House
18–19 Warren Street
London W1T 5LR
Tel: 020 7387 8570
Fax: 020 7387 8368
info@lawcentres.org.uk
www.lawcentres.org.uk

► **LEGAL SERVICES COMMISSION**
85 Gray's Inn Road
London WC1X 8TX
Tel: 020 7759 0000
www.legalservices.gov.uk
www.justask.org.uk
Regional telephone helplines on various legal subjects.

► **NATIONAL ASSOCIATION OF CITIZENS ADVICE BUREAUX (NACAB)**
Myddelton House
115–123 Pentonville Road
London N1 9LZ
Tel: 020 7833 2181
www.nacab.org.uk
Adviceguide: the National Association of Citizens Advice Bureaux offers fact sheets covering issues such as employment, housing and taxation
www.adviceguide.org.uk

► **REFUGEE LEGAL CENTRE**
Nelson House
153–157 Commercial Road
London E1 2DA
Tel: 020 7780 3200
General enquiries:
RLC@refugee-legal-centre.org.uk
www.refugee-legal-centre.org.uk

► **STATEWATCH**
PO Box 1516
London N16 0EW
Tel: 020 8802 1882
Fax: 020 8880 1727
info@statewatch.org
www.statewatch.org
Research papers/regular bulletins on policing, immigration, prisons, Europe, etc.

► **UNITED KINGDOM PASSPORT SERVICE**
Tel: 0870 521 0410
www.ukps.gov.uk

18 **Inquests**

The aim of this chapter is to explain what an inquest seeks to achieve, and to help you find the best advice and representation should this be necessary.

What is an inquest?

An inquest is an inquiry into a death by a special kind of judge called a **coroner**. An inquest is held when the coroner judges that a death was not from natural causes but was violent or sudden and suspicious.

(For odd historical reasons, coroners also decide questions about **treasure trove** – valuables that are found when their owner is not known.)

There is a **coroner** for each local authority area, and more than one for larger cities. Inquests are held in special coroner's courts or, in some areas, the coroner borrows a court room from the local magistrates' or crown court.

The purpose of an inquest is to determine:
- who the deceased was
- how
- when
- and where they met their death.

The verdict

The inquest hears evidence then decides on a verdict. The verdict of the inquest gives the cause of death: this is what goes on the death certificate. Verdicts include:

- **accident** (which is the same as misadventure)
- **suicide**
- **neglect**
- **unlawful killing**
- **open verdict** (where the court cannot come to a conclusion).

The coroner will hear evidence from:

- eyewitnesses to the death or surrounding events
- medical and emergency service staff
- a **pathologist** who has been ordered by the coroner to carry out a postmortem – a medical examination of the body to find out the medical cause of death. Sometimes the coroner also orders other tests (eg, to check body samples for signs of drink or drugs).

> The **pathology report** is one of the few documents you can request and obtain from the coroner at an early stage. You may also consider engaging an independent pathologist to provide your own report.

The verdict is not supposed to decide any question of **civil** or **criminal liability** – in other words it won't say directly who is to blame for the death. (This rule and other aspects of the inquest process are currently under review by the government.) Because of this an inquest will often be disappointing for the family of the dead person, but it can provide some answers about what led to the death. The coroner can also make recommendations to public authorities about what ought to be done to reduce the risks of a particular type of death happening again.

Juries

The coroner usually hears the evidence alone and decides on a verdict, but a coroner has to call a jury to hear the evidence and decide the verdict if the death was:

- in prison
- in police custody, or resulting from an injury caused by a police officer
- caused by a notifiable accident, poisoning or disease – for example, an accident at work where the HEALTH AND SAFETY EXECUTIVE has to be notified
- in circumstances where there is a risk that other people may be harmed in a similar way.

Inquest juries are drawn from the same pool of people called to do jury service at the crown court (see CHAPTER 3: LAWYERS AND THE COURTS).

Representation

Unlike civil or criminal trials, an inquest doesn't have **parties of sides** (defence and prosecution), although the coroner may allow people involved with the case to be represented (eg, the family of the person who has died, the employer in a work accident, the prison service in a death in custody).

The coroner decides what questions can be asked by legal representatives. The coroner also has sweeping powers over what witnesses and documents the inquest should consider and what, if any, evidence should be revealed before the inquest starts.

> Press hard for **advance disclosure** of all statements of witnesses the coroner intends to call. Some coroners can be difficult about this, so ensure your lawyer has the **Home Office guidelines** on this topic and can challenge any decision.

Inquest procedure is likely to be changed as a result of the *Human Rights Act* so as to allow some allocation of blame. In particular, there may be substantial changes where the death may have been caused by the state – in prison cases or cases where public servants failed to do something to prevent the death (see CHAPTER 16: HUMAN RIGHTS ACT).

Practicalities

CORONER'S OFFICER

This is a policeman allocated to work for the coroner. The coroner's officer acts as an administrator and communicates with the family and witnesses about when the inquest will be held.

ADJOURNMENT

Sometimes the inquest will be postponed if:

- the coroner needs further information

- a witness has to be traced

- someone is being prosecuted for a criminal offence in connection with the death (usually the inquest is adjourned until after a criminal trial).

Legal aid

There is currently no automatic legal aid to pay for families of the deceased to be represented at inquests, although this is under review by the government.

If there is a civil case being pursued (eg, for medical negligence) for which legal aid has been granted, that may cover the cost of having a lawyer's representative at the inquest. Other personal injury cases are no longer covered by legal aid, but lawyers who operate under so-called **no win no fee** agreements may also arrange for a representative to attend an inquest.

In exceptional cases, some committed lawyers will represent families **pro bono** (for free), and where the inquests arise from a major disaster the **LORD CHANCELLOR'S DEPARTMENT** (now the **DEPARTMENT FOR CONSTITUTIONAL AFFAIRS**) will make an ex gratia payment for legal representation.

Do I need a lawyer?

Until it happens to you, few people give the circumstances of an unusual death a second thought. When it does, there are feelings of enormous grief, anger, recrimination and guilt, which often make it difficult to focus and appreciate what is going on. Combined with this, some coroners withhold information and fail to treat families with courtesy and respect. Some, of course, do, but it is often the luck of the draw which type of coroner you get. Given the power they wield, and the fact that most interested parties (police and medical authorities) will be represented at the inquest, the 'need to know' must predominate. It is essential you have someone to act on your behalf who knows the ropes and can get the questions you want asked put before the coroner.

SPECIALIST LAWYERS

Inquests are a fairly specialised area and many high street solicitors will not have experience of them. If you do go to a local solicitor, ask how often and when they last represented someone at an inquest (see CHAPTER 1: FINDING AND MEETING YOUR LAWYER).

In June 2003, the Home Office published a review of the whole inquest system, which has existed for over eight hundred years. It contains 122 recommendations for change, providing stronger rights for bereaved families and fuller verdicts on the causes of death. The principal intended improvement is access to information and **legal aid** for families and the replacement of coroners by judges in complex cases. A less acceptable proposal is a reduction in the use of juries. This can be seen as another aspect of the general attack being mounted on the jury system, particularly in the criminal arenas where verdicts adverse to the vested interests of the state are being characterised as 'perverse'.

Organisations [i]

▶ **CRUSE – BEREAVEMENT CARE**
126 Sheen Road
Richmond
Surrey TW9 1UR
Helpline: 0808 808 1677
www.crusebereavementcare.org.uk

▶ **DEPARTMENT FOR CONSTITUTIONAL AFFAIRS**
Selborne House
54–60 Victoria Street
London SW1E 6QW
Tel: 020 7210 8500
general.queries@dca.gsi.gov.uk
www.dca.gov.uk

▶ **HEALTH AND SAFETY EXECUTIVE**
Postal enquiries:
HSE Infoline
Caerphilly Business Park
Caerphilly CF83 3GG
Infoline (Monday to Friday, 8.30am to 5.00pm):
08701 545500
Fax: 02920 859260
hseinformationservices@natbrit.com
www.hse.gov.uk

▶ **HER MAJESTY'S STATIONERY OFFICE (HMSO)**
www.hmso.gov.uk

▶ **HOME OFFICE**
Customer Information Service
7th floor, 50 Queen Anne's Gate
London SW1H 9AT
General enquiries (9.00am–5.00pm):
0870 0001585
www.homeoffice.gov.uk

▶ **INQUEST**
89–93 Fonthill Road
London N4 3JH
Tel: 020 7263 1111
Fax: 020 7561 0799
www.inquest.org
Advises families and sometimes arranges free representation at inquests.

▶ **THE SAMARITANS**
Helpline: 08457 90 90 90
jo@samaritans.org
www.samaritans.org.uk

▶ **SUPPORT AFTER MURDER AND MANSLAUGHTER (SAMM)**
Cranmer House
39 Brixton Road
London SW9 6DZ
Tel: 020 7735 3838
Helpline: 0845 3030 900
enquiries@samm.org.uk
www.samm.org.uk

▶ **TRADES UNION CONGRESS (TUC)**
Congress House
Great Russell Street
London WC1B 3LS
Tel: 020 7636 4030
info@tuc.org.uk
www.tuc.org.uk
Trade unions will often provide direct help, particularly in connection with accidents at work, but there will also sometimes be legal expenses cover for members which may pay for representation at an inquest.

▶ **VICTIM SUPPORT**
Cranmer House
39 Brixton Road
London SW9 6DZ
Tel: 020 7735 9166
contact@victimsupport.org
www.victimsupport.com
Victim Support has centres throughout the UK.

Further reading

Information for Families of Homicide Victims. The Home Office produces this information pack. Local police stations should be able to provide copies or telephone 020 7273 2066 to order a free copy.

19 **Intellectual property**

This chapter sets out the basis for the protection of intellectual property and where to turn to protect your creative innovation.

Protecting innovation and creativity

The law encourages creativity and innovation by trying to provide a fair level of protection to those who create and innovate. This protection comes in the form of a variety of different rights, collectively known as **intellectual property rights**, which either create a monopoly or protect from imitation.

The owner of these rights can stop others from copying, or making things, with their creation or innovation. This is a rapidly expanding area, partly because of the need to have laws that protect new and developing technology, and partly due to the increased value of intellectual property.

CONTRACTS

Contracts are used to control exploitation of intellectual property rights. For instance, contracts are used in the music industry to govern the production of CDs of a particular performer's music and to impose obligations on others to do or not to do certain things. Performers or musicians may, through their contract with a record company, be obliged to make a specified number of CDs, appear at events and not participate in sports or activities that could endanger their health. Within reason, the record company can regulate aspects of the performer's life. The same applies to professional sportsmen. A club can, through the contract with the sportsman, regulate aspects of that player's life, both on and off the field.

WHAT DO INTELLECTUAL PROPERTY RIGHTS PROTECT?

- Inventors can protect their novel inventions for products and the methods of making them, through **registered patents**.

- Names and logos of businesses or products, and the reputation and goodwill generated under them, can be protected by **registered trademarks** and the **law of passing-off**.

- Secret or confidential ideas and information can be protected through the *law of confidential information*.

- Designs for things can be protected by **design rights**.

- Literary or artistic works, such as songs, computer software and drawings, can be protected by **copyrights**.

- There are also **database rights**, protecting things such as tables or charts.

These various rights overlap and the different areas of intellectual property law are frequently used together in order to protect a brand, a novel product or some other work which has been created.

HOW ARE THESE RIGHTS CREATED?

Many of these rights exist automatically once the work has been created, including **copyrights**, **design rights**, **database rights** and **rights in performances**.

> Once the design, literary or artistic work has been put onto paper then a right to prevent copying of that work is created. The first owner of the rights that subsist in the work is the author, or the employer if created in pursuance of the author's employment.

Other rights, such as **registered trademarks**, **patents** and **registered designs**, need to be applied for and are granted by a national or European administrative body. It is your choice whether to apply for protection in the UK alone or across Europe. For UK intellectual property rights contact the PATENT OFFICE. Although called the PATENT OFFICE, it deals with registered designs and trademarks as well as patents.

Alternatively, for Europe-wide registered design rights or trademarks contact the OFFICE FOR HARMONIZATION IN THE INTERNAL MARKET (OHIM). For Europe-wide patents contact the EUROPEAN PATENT OFFICE (EPO).

To obtain a registered design, trademark or patent:

- you need to fill in a form and pay a registration fee
- the administrative body then processes the application and will search its records to see whether there is an earlier conflicting right
- if granted, the design right, trademark or patent is put onto a register and a document will be sent to you stating that such a right exists and that you own it.

The advantage of a registered right is that the owner has a document to wave at potential licensees or infringers rather than having to go to court to prove that such a right exists in the first place. However, just because a registered right has been granted does not mean that it will remain registered, as the courts have the power to revoke the registration.

Patents

A **patent** protects a new product or a new method of doing something that is better than the products or methods that existed before.

A patent can also protect improved products or methods that are better for the same reasons as those on which the original patent was based. You need to make your application to the PATENT OFFICE or the EPO.

Applying for and obtaining patent protection across Europe is an expensive exercise and enforcing those rights can also be expensive. A UK patent is cheaper to obtain and enforce, but provides protection in the UK only. Applying for a patent, for the UK or across Europe, is a technical operation and the patent application is usually written and made by **patent attorneys**.

Patent attorneys sometimes give half an hour of advice for free and in that time you will get some guidance on whether the application is likely to be granted. There are plenty of patent attorneys in the UK who have knowledge of a wide variety of technical fields. Patent attorneys need to be members of the governing body, which is called the CHARTERED INSTITUTE OF PATENT ATTORNEYS (CIPA). CIPA provides:

- a list of all patent attorneys
- information about patents and how to apply for them
- free clinics.

> Once granted, a patent confers a monopoly right. In other words, it is a right to stop others from doing what is described in the patent, whether or not they came up with the same idea independently.

A patent is an effective means of protecting a particular area and it is considered to be the most draconian of intellectual property rights.

Trademarks

> A **trademark** is a sign that acts as an indication of the source of goods or services. When consumers see the brand, they believe they know what they are getting.

Collectively businesses spend billions of pounds promoting their brands in the hope of making them familiar to the relevant market for that type of product. The law tries to protect legitimate traders from the attempts of other traders to 'piggyback' on the success of other trade names or product logos.

If you want a registered trademark to cover the whole of Europe, then make your application to OHIM. If you want protection in the UK alone then make your application to the PATENT OFFICE. **Trademark attorneys** often make the application for a registered trademark on behalf of their clients, although there is not the same need for a specialist adviser as there is with a patent application. The governing body for trademark attorneys is called the INSTITUTE OF TRADEMARKS ATTORNEYS (ITMA). ITMA provides:

- a list of trademark attorneys in the UK
- information about trademarks and how to apply for them.

Passing-off

In addition to a registered trademark, the law has evolved a separate right protecting traders who have traded under a name or logo to the extent that they have a reputation and goodwill in that name or logo.

> The law protecting the reputation and goodwill of a trader under a particular name or logo is called the *law of passing-off*.

There is no need to register such a right. It is a form of protection generated as a result of trading under a particular name or logo. The law will provide protection even with limited trading over a short period of time. What matters is whether:

- there are customers or members of the trade who recognise the name or logo as denoting your business
- there is another person leading the trade or potential customers into believing that they are somehow connected with your business.

Copyright

> **Copyright** protects the expression of someone's ideas, be they literary, artistic or musical, by creating a right in the expression of that idea. It will be infringed if someone else reproduces that work or a substantial part of it without the consent of the owner of that right.

There is an important distinction in copyright between the expression of the idea, which is protected by copyright, and the idea itself, which is not protected by copyright.

For instance, a photograph taken of a landscape will give rise to a copyright in the photograph, but that copyright cannot prevent someone else from taking another picture of the same landscape from the same place. In other words, the idea of the subject matter of the photograph will not be protected by copyright. Taking another picture of that same landscape will give rise to another, distinct copyright. Both photographers will own separate copyrights in photographs of the same subject matter and both photographers can prevent copying of their respective photographs.

Copyright:

- is created automatically when pen is put to paper or an idea is somehow set down, be it on a computer, by the release of a camera shutter, or in some other form

- does not need to be applied for

- will subsist regardless of artistic, literary or musical merit.

As long as a work originates from an author, in that they created it, then it is likely that copyright will subsist and the author will own it.

Design rights

WHAT IS A DESIGN RIGHT AND HOW DO I GET ONE?

There are two types of design right: **unregistered** and **registered**. Unregistered design rights protect designs from being copied. Registered designs grant the owner the exclusive right to use the design and any design which does not produce on the informed user a different overall impression.

A registered design right can be UK or European wide. Recent changes in the law make it now possible to register a wide variety of designs such as handicraft items, logos and the colours of products. However, to qualify for a registered design right the design needs to be new. You need to apply to The PATENT OFFICE for a United Kingdom registered design and to OHIM for a European registered design.

There are two types of unregistered design right which arise provided certain conditions are met. UK design right protects the shape and configuration of a design, or part of it, from copying by others. For instance, the design of a teapot will have design right in the various aspects of its design like the spout, handle or body. It exists automatically once a design has been put onto paper or once something has been made to a design and can subsist either in the United Kingdom or across Europe. Design right protects copying of the design but, like copyright, it will not protect the concept or the underlying idea of the design.

A European community design right protects a design that is new and has individual character. It has a shorter lifespan of three years whereas the UK design right can last for up to fifteen years. However, it gives a wider scope of protection than the UK design right because it can protect the colours, materials and texture as well as the design contours, lines and configuration.

Database rights

> *DATABASE RIGHT* protects a database where there has been a substantial investment in collating and verifying the information that forms that database. The person who was responsible for creating the database will own it.

A database right exists automatically once the investment has been put into creating the database and so there is no need to make an application or fill in any forms. The investment required does not have to be financial, and an investment of time and effort will suffice. A spreadsheet on a computer may well take time to put together and can contain information about almost anything. Obtaining the data that is the content of that spreadsheet and working out how best to present that data in a meaningful way will take time and effort. It is this time and effort which the database right protects.

The person, or persons, responsible for that work will own the database right, which will enable the owners to prevent others from extracting or utilising substantial parts of that database without permission.

Confidential information

Information that is secret or confidential can be kept confidential so long as:

- the information is not publicly available

- the person to whom the confidential information has been given appreciates that it is confidential and that they must keep it confidential.

You do not need to register the confidential information and it does not have to be of significant financial value, although most disputes seem to relate to financially valuable information. People, such as celebrities, try to keep photos and stories about them from being published by using the *law of confidential information*.

Further information

Further information about intellectual property can be obtained online from www.intellectual-property.gov.uk

The PATENT OFFICE will also provide help and guidance by telephone and through their website.

Organisations i

A government site that offers advice on this subject can be found at: www.intellectual-property.gov.uk

► **CHARTERED INSTITUTE OF PATENT ATTORNEYS**
95 Chancery Lane
London WC2A 1DT
Tel: 0207 7405 9450
mail@cipa.org.uk
www.cipa.org.uk

► **EUROPEAN PATENT OFFICE**
Erhardstrasse 27
D-80331 München
Germany
Tel: ++ 49 89 23 9 90
www.epo.org

► **INSTITUTE OF TRADEMARKS ATTORNEYS**
Canterbury House
2–6 Sydenham Road
Croydon
Surrey CRO 9XE
Tel: 0208 686 2052
Fax: 020 8680 5723
www.itma.org.uk.

► **OFFICE FOR HARMONIZATION IN THE INTERNAL MARKET (OHIM)**
Avenida de Europa 4
E-03080 Alicante
Spain
Tel: ++ 34 965 139 100
www.oami.eu.int

► **PATENT OFFICE**
Concept House
Cardiff Road
Newport
South Wales NP10 8QQ
Tel: 08459 500 505
enquiries@patent.gov.uk
www.patent.gov.uk

20 **International issues**

This chapter deals with many issues that may occur during your visit to a foreign country or involve your relations with legal authorities abroad, such as:

- adoption from abroad
- abduction, including children
- crimes, including theft, assault, rape and murder
- forced marriage
- kidnap
- marriage abroad
- missing persons
- prisoners abroad.

The first thing to do if anything goes wrong is to contact your relatives and friends at home. They can then take action within the UK. Any British national who gets into difficulty overseas can seek help from the nearest BRITISH DIPLOMATIC MISSION. They should be available 24 hours a day. Where there is no British representative in a country, you should instead contact the nearest EU MISSION.

Adoption from abroad

The procedures for adopting a child from overseas vary significantly depending on the nationality of the child you wish to adopt. The **DEPARTMENT OF HEALTH**'s website contains detailed information on inter-country adoptions:
www.doh.gov.uk/adoption/intercountry/index.htm

Abduction

If someone in your family has not returned from a visit overseas and you suspect they may have been abducted, you should seek help immediately.

Try the **NATIONAL MISSING PERSONS HELPLINE** or contact the **COMMUNITY LIAISON UNIT** of the Foreign Office. They will then contact the relevant **HIGH COMMISSION** or **EMBASSY** on your behalf, which will then try to make contact with the person and see whether they need any help. Give as many details as possible about where they went, when they were due back and when you last heard from them.

CHILD ABDUCTION

If your child has been taken or kept overseas by the other parent without your consent, or you suspect this might happen, you must seek urgent advice. Before you call anyone, be prepared to provide the following information:

- ☑ your child's name, age, date of birth, description, passport details and nationality (dual nationality is often automatic when one parent was born in another country)
- ☑ details of the abducting parent and their relatives, both in the UK and overseas
- ☑ the country to which you think the child has been abducted, when they were due back and when you last heard from them
- ☑ details of any court orders giving you residence or contact.

These are various courses of action you can take:

POLICE

If your child is missing, the police can contact INTERPOL on your behalf, which can work with overseas police forces to locate the child and check they are safe and well.

PORT ALERT

A **port alert** provides the child's details via a 24-hour computer system (operated by the POLICE NATIONAL COMPUTER) to all ports. If the threat of abduction is real and imminent (your child is likely to be taken overseas within 48 hours), a solicitor should ring the local police station. A court order is not necessary. The police will contact the NATIONAL PORTS OFFICE which will issue a port alert to all UK points of departure to try to prevent the abduction.

LEGAL ADVICE

Abduction, depending on the circumstances, is a criminal offence in the UK under the *Child Abduction Act 1985*, so legal advice is imperative. See a suitably qualified family lawyer if you are unsure about your legal position in relation to your child (see CHAPTER 1: FINDING AND MEETING YOUR LAWYER and CHAPTER 14: FAMILY). You may need to get a **residence order** (custody) or **preventative order** to stop your child being taken out of the country, or else have your child made a **ward of court**.

FOREIGN AND COMMONWEALTH OFFICE (FCO)

Contact the CONSULAR DIVISION and speak to the **consular desk officer** for the country concerned. They can give advice and tell you whether the country to which your child has been abducted is a member of the *Hague Convention on Child Abduction*.

The FCO should be able to:

- ☑ provide a list of overseas lawyers
- ☑ give practical help when dealing with authorities overseas
- ☑ provide travel advice and help with finding safe accommodation locally
- ☑ make informal translations of key documents

☑ obtain a welfare report once the child is located and, with the other parent's consent, press the courts overseas to handle a court case as quickly as possible in the best interests of the child.

The FCO cannot:

☒ provide legal advice

☒ get your child back for you – this will be for the courts overseas to decide

☒ intervene in the legal system of another country

☒ pay legal costs or fund air travel

☒ obtain visas.

UK CENTRAL AUTHORITIES

If your child has been abducted to a country that is a member of the *Hague Convention on International Child Abduction*, the UK central authorities will handle your case and may be able to process the legal action to have your child returned to the UK. Contact the CHILD ABDUCTION UNIT in the LORD CHANCELLOR'S DEPARTMENT (now renamed the DEPARTMENT FOR CONSTITUTIONAL AFFAIRS).

UNITED KINGDOM PASSPORT SERVICE

This can provide information on issuing or withholding passports for children. Ask them not to grant a British passport to your child without your consent. They can only do this in certain circumstances. If the other parent of your child is not a British national, this will not prevent them from obtaining a passport for the child from their own embassy, high commission or consulate in this country. In that case, you or your lawyer should write to these offices asking them not to issue a passport to your child. They are not obliged to agree to your request, but they may do so voluntarily.

REUNITE

This is a charity which provides practical advice and information to parents and guardians whose children have been, or might be, abducted overseas. It also has a list of lawyers specialising in family law in both the UK and overseas.

HAGUE CONVENTION

Because of the problem of international child abduction, the *Hague Convention* and the *Euopean Convention* provide procedures for tracing a child and returning it. These two conventions are incorporated in the *Child Abduction and Custody Act 1985*.

> The *Hague Convention* seeks to return an abducted child to the country where she/he is **habitually resident** (ie, normally lives) so issues of residence (custody) and contact (access) can be decided by the courts of that country.

For example, if your child is abducted to Spain, a **UK central authority** may be able to help you get a court order in Spain under the *Hague Convention* to have your child brought back to the UK. The UK courts will then decide on arrangements for the child's residence.

> The *Hague Convention* is successful in returning children to the UK in approximately 50–60 per cent of cases.

The *Hague Convention* contains articles that describe the objectives, define a wrongful removal or retention, determine to whom the Convention applies, how the application should be handled and what the court must do. It protects rights of custody, whereas the *European Convention* facilitates the recognition and enforcement of decisions relating to custody.

CONTRACTING STATES

The *Hague Convention* only applies between the UK and other countries that have also incorporated the Convention into their law. These are known as **contracting states**, and include: Argentina, Australia, Austria, the Bahamas, Belize, Bosnia and Herzegovina, Burkina, Canada (only certain specified territories), Chile, Colombia, Croatia, Cyprus, Denmark, Ecuador, Federal Republic of Yugoslavia, Finland, France, Georgia, Germany, Greece, Honduras, Hungary, Iceland, Republic of Ireland, Israel, Italy, Luxembourg, Macedonia, Mauritius, Mexico, Monaco, the Netherlands, New Zealand, Norway, Panama, Poland, Portugal, Romania, Slovenia, South Africa, Spain,

St Kitts-Nevis, Sweden, Switzerland, USA, Venezuela and Zimbabwe.

The following are the contracting states to the *European Convention*: Austria, Belgium, Cyprus, Denmark, Finland, France, Germany, Greece, Iceland, Republic of Ireland, Italy, Liechtenstein, Luxembourg, Netherlands, Norway, Poland, Portugal, Spain, Sweden and Switzerland.

WRONGFUL REMOVAL AND RETENTION

Article 3 of the HAGUE CONVENTION provides that the removal and retention of a child is wrongful where:

> *'It is in breach of rights of custody attributed to a person, an institution or any other body, either jointly or alone, under the law of the State in which the child is habitually resident immediately before the removal or retention'* and *'at the time of removal or retention those rights were actually exercised, jointly or alone, or would have been so exercised but for the removal or retention'.*

Article 4 of the HAGUE CONVENTION provides:

> *'The Convention shall apply to any child who was habitually resident in a Contracting State immediately before any breach of custody or access rights. The Convention shall cease to apply when the child attains the age of 16.'*

The term **habitual residence** is not defined in the *Child Abduction and Custody Act* or the *Hague Convention*. Habitual residence is similar to the concept of **ordinary residence**. Decisions from previous cases (not just family law) show that the important factors are that the person was present in a place or country:

- voluntarily
- for settled purposes and with a settled intention.

Whether a person will be habitually resident in a particular country depends on the particular facts of the case, taking into account all the circumstances. Case law has also referred to the person being resident for **an appreciable period of time** – however, no clear guidance is available as to how long or short a period of time is necessary. Again, it will depend on the individual facts of the case.

To commence a case under either Convention a formal request must be transmitted from the **central authority** of the country from which the abduction occurred to the central authority of the country where the child is located. The central authority for the UK is the LORD CHANCELLOR'S

DEPARTMENT (now renamed the **DEPARTMENT FOR CONSTITUTIONAL AFFAIRS**). The usual procedure is for the 'innocent' parent to contact a lawyer in the country where the abduction occurred, who will then make the formal request to the local central authority.

The central authority will then contact a specialist solicitor who deals with child abduction and the solicitor will deal with the case and commence proceedings in the High Court by issuing the appropriate application, which is known as an **originating summons**. Depending on the particular facts of the case, the solicitor will apply for the appropriate orders.

COSTS

If a UK central authority processes your application under the *Hague Convention*, it will help you locate a lawyer overseas. You may not need to pay for your overseas lawyer, depending on the legal aid system in the foreign country, but you may still have to pay for a lawyer in the UK.

ABDUCTION TO A NON-CONVENTION COUNTRY

Where a child has been abducted to a non-Convention country, the parent who is attempting to secure the child's return is often faced with many problems. In these circumstances, try to come to an amicable settlement with the other parent.

If this is not possible, your only option will be to apply for custody and permission to bring your child back to the UK through the courts overseas. Return of your child is not guaranteed. In some Islamic countries, non-Muslim mothers have very little chance of winning custody, and return of your child may not be an option.

> Pursuing litigation in the country to which the child has been abducted is very difficult, and expensive, as legal aid is not available. Legal systems vary from country to country and many Non-Convention countries do not apply the same rules of justice as the English courts.

To locate the child, as much information as possible should be obtained from family, friends, neighbours, employer. Also checks should be made with relevant passport agencies, airlines and travel agents. Enquiries should be made of the DEPARTMENT FOR WORK AND PENSIONS as benefits can be paid overseas for a short period of time.

Once the child has been located, the parent must decide whether to instruct a lawyer in the UK or in the foreign country. The relevant embassy in the UK will be able to provide a list of English-speaking lawyers. The procedure and process for commencing a case in the other country will depend on the law of that country. Unfortunately, orders made by English courts as to the residence of the child will not automatically be recognised or enforceable.

Crimes abroad

In cases of real difficulty such as:

- arrest and detention
- serious accident or illness
- risk of physical harm
- death

the BRITISH CONSUL in the country concerned should take action.

Consuls can:

☑ contact your relatives and friends and, with your permission, let them know what has happened

☑ ask them to help you with money or tickets

☑ tell you how to transfer funds

☑ help you get in touch with lawyers, interpreters and doctors

☑ at most posts, in an emergency, advance up to £100 in local currency against a sterling cheque supported by a valid cheque guarantee card

☑ as a last resort, and provided certain strict criteria are met, make a repayable loan to return you to the UK.

Consuls cannot:

☒ investigate a crime or give legal advice

☒ pay your hotel, legal, medical or travel costs

[X] get better treatment for you in hospital than is provided for local nationals

[X] intervene in court cases.

> If you have been the victim of a crime overseas, or a friend or relative has been the victim of violent death, it is important to seek legal advice. Help is also available in the UK.

THEFT

[✓] Make a list of the items stolen

[✓] Tell the local police as soon as possible and insist on a police report (needed for any insurance and/or compensation claim)

[✓] Cancel your credit cards and rebook your travel tickets

[✓] Contact the BRITISH CONSULATE, especially if your passport has been stolen – the consul, after some checks, will issue you with another.

> ### INSURANCE
>
> Ask your insurance company what your travel insurance covers before travelling. Your policy may provide limited cover for theft and may also cover personal injuries received as a result of a crime. A personal accident or sickness policy may cover medical expenses within financial and geographical limits. The policy almost always requires that you report the incident to the police in the relevant country at the time.

ASSAULT

[✓] Tell the local police as soon as possible and insist on a police report (needed for any insurance and/or compensation claim)

[✓] Inform the BRITISH CONSULATE, especially if you have been arrested or have ended up in hospital

[✓] Contact VICTIM SUPPORT, which has centres throughout the UK and contacts with other victim support groups across the world.

COMPENSATION

Courts abroad may be able to order the offender to pay compensation for your injuries and/or losses in certain circumstances, either following conviction in a criminal court or as a result of a civil action. Some countries have a state-funded compensation scheme to cover physical or psychological injuries sustained as a result of a violent crime, which may apply to foreign nationals injured in that country. A police report will be essential. Local lawyers should be able to provide information about how to claim compensation.

RAPE

> Contact a friend, a doctor or even someone at home in the UK.
> It can be vitally important that you talk to someone straight away as you may be suffering from rape trauma (a type of shock). You can ask your friends or family to contact the RAPE CRISIS FEDERATION, which has centres throughout the UK and may be able to refer you to an organisation abroad.

You may not want to report a rape attack to the police, but if you change your mind later, forensic evidence may have been lost. If at all possible, do not:

- ☒ shower or take a bath
- ☒ change your clothes
- ☒ take any alcohol

until someone arrives to advise you. At least try to keep soiled clothes in a clean container.

Contact the BRITISH CONSULATE or embassy where you are staying. The consul should accompany you to the police and arrange for an interpreter, if necessary, and for you to see a doctor who can give advice on sexually transmitted diseases, including AIDS, and on pregnancy or abortion.

MURDER

The death of a relative or friend because of a violent act is always painful. If the death has occurred a long way from home, it is doubly difficult.

Bringing the body home may be delayed in order to have an overseas inquest and post-mortem. You may need to fly out or get help from the UK. If a relative or friend is the victim of murder overseas, you should:

- contact the BRITISH CONSULATE, which can advise on local burial/cremation or refer you to an experienced international undertaker to bring the body home

- register the death with the local authorities

- register the death with the BRITISH CONSULATE – you do not have to do this, but by doing so you can obtain a UK death certificate and the death will be registered in the UK (British Consulates cannot issue UK death certificates in: Australia, Canada, New Zealand, Republic of Ireland, South Africa and Zimbabwe).

The Consul can provide details of local lawyers but cannot become directly involved in any legal action, investigate a crime or follow up a murder.

> You can ask your friends or family to contact: SUPPORT AFTER MURDER AND MANSLAUGHTER (SAMM) or CRUSE – BEREAVEMENT CARE.
> The HOME OFFICE has an information pack called *Information for Families of Homicide Victims*.

Arrest/imprisonment

There are hundreds of Britons detained overseas. If you are arrested:

- try to stay calm and co-operate

- insist that the BRITISH CONSUL be notified – *it is your right*

- tell relatives or friends to contact the local BRITISH CONSUL or the FOREIGN AND COMMONWEALTH OFFICE (FCO) in London or PRISONERS ABROAD.

The consul should:

☑ contact you after being notified by the local authorities of your arrest

☑ visit you as soon as possible – if that is what you want

☑ give you information on suitably qualified English-speaking local lawyers and the legal system – this will include details of legal aid (if available) and prosecution, remand, bail and appeal procedures, so that you know what is happening and are aware of your rights

☑ tell you about the prison system, visiting arrangements, mail and censorship, privileges, work possibilities and social and welfare services

☑ pass a message to your family if you want – to save money, your family can find out what is happening to you by contacting the CONSULAR DIVISION at the FCO in London

☑ ensure that any medical problem you have is brought to the attention of the prison doctor, and if necessary ask for independent medical advice

☑ take up (at your request) any justified complaint about ill-treatment or discrimination with the police or prison authorities

☑ make representations to the local authorities if your trial is unreasonably delayed, or is not conducted according to due process

☑ help you find an interpreter to ensure that you understand the charges against you and can understand what is being said at court hearings, in accordance with international human rights standards.

In the longer term, the consul should:

☑ continue to visit (this should be at least once a year, and in countries where the prison conditions are difficult can be more often)

☑ make sure you have a lawyer, or know how to change the one you have if you are not satisfied with the existing arrangement

☑ send you money from your family

☑ provide information on how to apply for transfer to a UK prison if you are in a country that does this.

The consul cannot:

☒ get you better treatment than is given to locals

☒ give or pay for legal advice, start court proceedings on your behalf, or interfere in local judicial procedures to get you out of prison

☒ investigate a crime

☒ formally assist dual nationals in the country of their other nationality – scope for action may be limited by the laws and practices of the other country (but the consul should provide protection for all British passport holders who normally live in the UK, regardless of whether or not they are dual nationals)

☒ pay for prison comforts – if you do not have money or are unable to earn money working in prison, your family and friends can send money directly to you or via the consul (if your family cannot send you money and you are really in need, PRISONERS ABROAD may be able to provide you with a small grant)

☒ forward parcels to you on behalf of family and friends (the system has been abused in the past when drugs have been sent into prisons).

WHAT YOU CAN DO FOR YOURSELF

Prison life can be difficult, but there are things that you can do to make it easier:

Language: Prison guards may be more helpful if you try to learn the language. If you cannot get the books you need inside the prison, or from its shop, ask the prison staff to get them for you.

Legal advice: Your local lawyer is familiar with local laws and should provide legal advice on your case, although you may need to seek legal advice in the UK as well.

Work: You may not be able to work while you are on remand, but you may find that work helps to pass time more quickly.

Mail: Make sure you know how many letters you are allowed to send. It is important to get your affairs in order before a trial. In some countries, restrictions on sending mail are imposed after sentencing.

Health: If you fall ill, contact the prison doctor in the first instance. If you think you are not getting adequate treatment, contact the BRITISH CONSUL.

AIDS: If you are HIV-positive or have AIDS, you should tell the consul. Consuls can ensure you get medical treatment.

DRUGS

Many British nationals are detained abroad for drugs offences (over half the total). The British government co-operates with other governments to stop traffickers and smugglers. If you are arrested for a drugs offence, it is likely that the local police will contact the police in the UK.

VIOLENT / SEX OFFENCES

The local police may contact the police in the UK if you are arrested for a violent offence or a sexual offence.

TRANSFER TO THE UK

In some countries, prisoners can apply to serve part of their sentence in the UK. You can only apply for transfer after all local appeals have been heard and fines paid. The FCO has produced a leaflet which explains how this works: *British Prisoners Abroad – Can I Be Transferred Home?*

Advice for relatives

Prisons overseas can have extremely varied conditions, and staying in touch can also be frustrating. The legal process, imprisonment and even the return home can be difficult.

USEFUL INFORMATION

Relatives should try to obtain:

- ☑ the full postal address of the prison
- ☑ details of the prisoner's legal representative
- ☑ information about the authorities responsible for the court proceedings
- ☑ the address, telephone and fax numbers of the BRITISH CONSULATE nearest to the prison.

> For help and support, contact PRISONERS ABROAD, which gives practical support and advice, with no moral judgements, on all aspects, especially relieving isolation, plus help for released prisoners; and FAIR TRIALS ABROAD, which seeks justice and fair legal representation for EU citizens outside their country of residence, by providing legal advice and gathering evidence.

VISITING

Arrangements vary from country to country. Relatives should make an appointment to visit before setting off on a long journey. The consul will be able to tell you how the visiting system works and whether special arrangements apply for parcels.

MONEY FOR PRISON COMFORTS

■ Arrangements for making money available to prisoners vary from country to country. The FCO can help to transfer money to British prisoners overseas.

■ You must include the full name of the prisoner, their personal number, the address of where they are being held and the name of the sender.

■ The money will be sent as quickly as possible to the nearest Consulate, which will ensure it is passed on to the prisoner in local currency. It will normally take two to three weeks to reach the prisoner.

Prison transfers

British citizens sentenced to a term of imprisonment abroad may be able to transfer home to serve the rest of their sentence in a prison in the UK. The following is not a statement of your legal rights, so always contact a lawyer.

WHO IS ELIGIBLE FOR TRANSFER?

You must:

☑ be a British citizen or have close family ties with the UK (normally through permanent residence in the UK)

☑ have completed all criminal proceedings in the foreign country – you cannot be transferred if you are awaiting trial or the outcome of an appeal against your conviction and/or the length of your sentence

☑ normally have at least six months of your sentence left to serve when you make your application for transfer

☑ have been convicted of an offence that is criminal in the part of the UK to which you wish to be transferred (ie, England, Wales, Scotland or Northern Ireland)

☑ have no outstanding fines or other non-custodial penalties.

HOW ARE TRANSFERS ARRANGED?

The UK government has signed international agreements that allow British prisoners to be transferred from certain countries to the UK.

MAKING A TRANSFER APPLICATION

You should normally make your application to the prison authorities in your place of detention, or you can write to the nearest BRITISH CONSULATE, which will pass on your letter to the relevant UK authorities. They will then make an application to the foreign authorities on your behalf. Making an application for transfer does not commit you to going ahead with it. Your formal consent is required before the transfer can proceed.

WHO AGREES THE TRANSFER?

The transfer must be agreed by:

- the authorities in the country in which you are serving your sentence

- the **Home Secretary**, if you are seeking to be transferred to England or Wales

- you, or someone authorised on your behalf.

You cannot be transferred unless *all three of these parties* agree to the transfer.

TRANSFER COSTS

Most of the costs of the transfer are the responsibility of the UK and foreign authority. However, you will be responsible for the cost of your own airfare. This can be paid in advance or you can give an undertaking to repay the cost as soon as possible after your arrival in the UK. If you choose the second option, your passport will be retained until repayment is made.

HOW LONG WILL IT TAKE?

The length of time varies from case to case. It can sometimes take up to two years. Do not be over-optimistic about a speedy transfer.

LENGTH OF SENTENCE IN UK

Your UK sentence will be calculated by deducting the time you have already served abroad from the original sentence (including time spent on remand where the foreign authority takes this into account) and any remission to which you are eligible for this period.

Once you have been transferred, you will be treated as if you had been sentenced under UK law, so you will be entitled to be considered for discretionary, early or automatic release.

WILL I BE LIABLE TO PROSECUTION FOR OTHER OFFENCES IF I RETURN?

You cannot be prosecuted in the UK for the offence for which you are sentenced. You will, however, be liable to detention or prosecution in connection with any other alleged offence committed in the UK.

Forced marriage

A small number of people find themselves being forced into marriage by their families when they go abroad.

> A marriage should be entered into with the free and full consent of both parties. You have the right to legal protection. If someone is forcing you into a marriage they may be in breach of the law in the UK and other countries.

In order to protect yourself think carefully before you decide to go. Once you are abroad, you may:

- be isolated or face emotional pressure
- be watched all the time
- have no money, passport or ticket
- be a long way from a telephone.

Before you travel, contact the FCO'S COMMUNITY LIAISON UNIT. Leave the following details with the unit, in confidence, or with a trusted friend:

- your name as shown on your passport
- your passport number, date and place of issue
- your date of birth
- a recent photograph of yourself
- your parents' names
- your address and telephone number in the UK
- the address and telephone number of the place and relatives in the country you are visiting
- the date you are expecting to return to the UK
- details of a trusted and reliable friend or relative in the UK.

In addition:

- ☑ obtain the FCO leaflet on *Forced Marriages Abroad – Your Right to Choose*. Fill in and detach the card at the end of the leaflet. Keep it in a safe place and take it with you when you travel
- ☑ make a note of the address and telephone number of the BRITISH HIGH COMMISSION/EMBASSY in the country you are visiting
- ☑ take some money with you (for telephone calls or for transport).

If you fear you are going to be forced into a marriage while you are abroad you should contact your relatives, a friend or the nearest BRITISH HIGH COMMISSION/EMBASSY. They will:

- try to get you back to the UK
- issue an emergency passport if necessary
- provide you with safe accommodation and transport.

You or a friend will need to provide money for your ticket home (in exceptional circumstances a loan can be arranged) and your passport details.

If you have been forced into a marriage overseas and wish your 'spouse' to be refused a visa to the UK, you need to be prepared to make public the fact that you do not want him to join you in the UK.

Kidnap

It is very rare for a person to be kidnapped abroad. Even if the worst occurs, most kidnapped people return home safely. Reduce the risk of becoming a target for kidnappers:

- avoid areas of high risk by reading guide books and talking to friends and travel agents about the country you are to visit

- respect local customs and do not be too conspicuous. Don't carry expensive cameras, jewellery or other equipment that might signal you are foreign and/or wealthy

- change your daily routine and don't be too predictable. Register with the nearest BRITISH HIGH COMMISSION/EMBASSY. Always let people know where you are and for how long, especially if travelling to remote areas.

In the event of the kidnap of a British national overseas, the British government will make the following points to the government of the country concerned:

- the safety of the hostages is paramount

- the British government does not make substantive concessions to hostage takers and never pays ransoms

- the government of the country in which the kidnap takes place is responsible for resolving the situation.

There are organisations that maintain regular contacts with the families and employees of hostages, offering up-to-date information, support and advice on media handling.

MISSING PERSONS

If you are concerned that a person in your family, or a friend, has gone missing overseas, you should contact:

- the BRITISH CONSULATE – it cannot trace your son/daughter/friend but can keep a lookout for them and, where there are serious grounds for concern, contact local authorities that may be able to help

- the NATIONAL MISSING PERSONS HELPLINE.

Marrying abroad

If you are thinking of getting married overseas, either check with a British lawyer or the relevant embassy or high commission in London whether the marriage is legal in the UK. If you marry under local law, the local authorities will issue a marriage certificate. You will not get a British marriage certificate from the embassy. If your spouse gets a visa to settle in the UK with you, he/she will become eligible to apply for naturalisation after three years of residence in the UK.

Organisations   i

▶ **AMNESTY INTERNATIONAL UK**
99–119 Rosebery Avenue
London EC1R 4RE
Tel: 020 7814 6200
Fax: 020 7833 1510
information@amnesty.org.uk
www.amnesty.org.uk

▶ **CENTRAL AUTHORITY FOR ENGLAND AND WALES**
The Child Abduction Unit
Lord Chancellor's Department
81 Chancery Lane
London WC2A 1DD
Tel: 020 7911 7045/7047
www.offsol.demon.co.uk

▶ **CENTRAL AUTHORITY FOR NORTHERN IRELAND**
Northern Ireland Courts Service
Windsor House
9–15 Bedford Street
Belfast BT2 7LT
Tel: 02890 328594
www.nics.gov.uk

▶ **COMMUNITY LIAISON UNIT**
G55 Foreign and Commonwealth Office
Old Admiralty Building
London SW1A 2PA
Tel: 020 7008 0230/0135
clu@fco.gov.uk
www.fco.gov.uk

▶ **CRUSE – BEREAVEMENT CARE**
126 Sheen Road
Richmond
Surrey TW9 1UR
Helpline: 0808 808 1677
www.crusebereavementcare.org.uk

▶ **DEPARTMENT FOR CONSTITUTIONAL AFFAIRS**
Selborne House
54–60 Victoria Street
London SW1E 6QW
Tel: 020 7210 8500
general.queries@dca.gsi.gov.uk
www.dca.gov.uk

▶ **DEPARTMENT OF HEALTH**
Richmond House
75 Whitehall
London SW1A 2NL
Tel: 020 7210 4850
dhmail@doh.gsi.gov.uk
www.doh.gov.uk

▶ **DEPARTMENT FOR WORK AND PENSIONS (DWP)**
Adelphi
1–11 John Adam Street
London WC2N 6HT
Tel: 020 7962 8000
www.dwp.gov.uk

▶ **FAIR TRIALS ABROAD**
Bench House
Ham Street
Richmond
Surrey TW10 7HR
Tel: 020 8332 2800
Fax: 020 8332 2810
www.f-t-a.freeserve.co.uk

▶ **FOREIGN AND COMMONWEALTH OFFICE**
King Charles Street
London SW1A 2AH
Consular enquiries (not visas):
020 7008 0218
Travel advice: 020 7008 0232 / 0233
Visa enquiries: 020 7008 3838
www.fco.gov.uk

▶ **HM PRISON SERVICE**
www.hmprisonservice.gov.uk

▶ **HOME OFFICE**
Customer Information Service
7th floor, 50 Queen Anne's Gate
London SW1H 9AT
General enquiries (9.00am–5.00pm):
0870 0001585
www.homeoffice.gov.uk

▶ **INTERPOL**
www.interpol.int

▶ **NATIONAL MISSING PERSONS HELPLINE**
0500 700 700
If you are calling from outside the UK:
++ 44 20 8392 4545

▶ **NORTHERN IRELAND PRISON SERVICE**
Prison Service Headquarters
Operational Management Division
Dundonald House
Upper Newtownards Road
Belfast BT4 3SU
Tel: 028 9052 5065
info@niprisonservice.gov.uk
www.niprisonservice.gov.uk

▶ **PRISONERS ABROAD**
89–93 Fonthill Road
Finsbury Park
London N4 3JH
Tel: 020 7561 6820
Fax: 020 7561 6821
info@prisonersabroad.org.uk
www.prisonersabroad.org.uk

▶ **REUNITE INTERNATIONAL**
P.O. Box 7124
Leicester
LE1 7XX
Advice line: 0116 2256 234
reunite@dircon.co.uk
www.reunite.org

▶ **THE SALVATION ARMY**
The Salvation Army HQ
101 Newington Causeway
London SE1 6BN
Tel: 020 7367 4500
Helpline: 0845 634 0101
thq@salvationarmy.org.uk
www.salvationarmy.org.uk

▶ **THE SAMARITANS**
National helpline: 08457 90 90 90
jo@samaritans.org
www.samaritans.org.uk

▶ **SUPPORT AFTER MURDER AND MANSLAUGHTER (SAMM)**
Cranmer House
39 Brixton Road
London SW9 6DZ
Tel: 020 7735 3838
Helpline: 0845 3030 900
enquiries@samm.org.uk
www.samm.org.uk

▶ **UNITED KINGDOM PASSPORT SERVICE**
Tel: 0870 521 0410
www.ukps.gov.uk

▶ **VICTIM SUPPORT**

National Office
Cranmer House
39 Brixton Road
London SW9 6DZ

Tel: 020 7735 9166
Fax: 020 7582 5712
contact@victimsupport.org
www.victimsupport.com

Victim Support has centres throughout the UK and contacts with other victim support groups across the world.

Further reading

Information for Families of Homicide Victims. The Home Office produces this information pack. Local police stations should be able to provide copies, or telephone 020 7273 2066 to order a free copy. Also recommended if the death has taken place abroad.

British Prisoners Abroad: Can I Be Transferred Home? available from the Foreign and Commonwealth Office.

Forced Marriages Abroad

21 **Libel**

This chapter outlines the laws of libel and what kind of remedies are available to a person whose reputation is attacked.

There are three main claims available:

- Libel **relates to publications in permanent form – in a newspaper, broadcast or film.**
- Slander **covers publication by spoken words or in some other temporary form, such as sounds or gestures.**
- Malicious falsehood **applies where false allegations are published, maliciously causing loss to the person attacked.**

Libel

To establish **libel** it is necessary to prove publication:

- to someone other than the person attacked
- of material containing an untrue imputation (accusation)
- which is likely to lower the reputation of the person attacked in the view of right-thinking members of society.

Slander

In order to succeed in a claim for **slander** it is also normally necessary to show that damage has resulted from the slander.

Libel and **slander** cases are normally decided by a jury, although they may be decided by a judge if the subject matter of the case is thought to be complex.

The rules on drafting claims are highly technical. It is a defence to show that the words complained of were **true** or that they constituted **fair comment** on a matter of public interest. So, for example, a newspaper could argue that it is in the public interest to publish details of the financial misdeeds of a politician.

Fair comment

The defence of **fair comment** protects only comment, not factual allegations. The defendant simply has to show that the comment was based on the honest belief of its author. Alternatively the defendant may choose to defend the claim with the argument that the person attacked had no reputation to lose because of previous behaviour (other than the original libel).

Utterances in parliament or in a law court are absolutely privileged and protected from litigation.

Qualified privilege

In some circumstances comments may be the subject of **qualified privilege**. This means a claim can only succeed if the person attacked can show **malice** (spiteful accusation). This applies to communications such as job references and reports of the courts or parliament.

The courts have recently been prepared to accept that the defence of qualified privilege may be available where the media is reporting on matters of legitimate public interest. Where it can be shown that a defendant has acted responsibly in reporting a matter of genuine public interest, the defendant may be able to rely on the defence of qualified privilege regardless of whether the allegation is true. The law in this area is still developing and it remains somewhat unpredictable as to when a court will allow a defendant to invoke qualified privilege in cases of this kind.

Malicious falsehood

This claim can be brought where the words used by the defendant are false, even if they are not likely to lower the reputation of the claimant, provided that the claimant can prove:

- that they were published maliciously

- that **special damage** has followed as a direct and natural result of their publication – special damage has been defined as *loss which is capable of being estimated in money* (eg, loss of employment or loss of business).

Section 3(1) of the *Defamation Act 1952* specifies that in an action for malicious falsehood it is unnecessary to show special damage:

- if the words on which the action is based are calculated to cause financial damage to the plaintiff and are published in writing or other permanent form

- if the words are calculated to cause financial damage to the claimant in respect of any office, profession or business carried on by them at the time of the publication.

Time limits

A claim for **libel**, **slander** or **malicious falsehood** must normally be brought within one year, but the court can extend this period in special circumstances.

Funding

Public funding is not available to claimants or defendants in libel actions. This has always made **libel/slander** proceedings a rich man's game. However, it is possible to mount a defence despite this hindrance.

For example, the McLibel Two defended themselves against McDonald's with the help of volunteer lawyers and donations for a period of five years.

Anyone considering a claim should think long and hard before venturing into the courts. Potential claimants should also note that the level of damages in libel/slander cases has been dramatically reduced recently so that the old-style jackpot wins of Jeffrey Archer and others are no longer likely.

The *Defamation Act 1996* does provide a new **summary procedure** which allows a judge to dismiss a claim or to give judgement in favour of the claimant where the merits of the claim are clear either way. Where there is a clear conflict of evidence, the court will not adopt this procedure.

Representation

Most solicitors have little or no expertise in **libel/slander**. If you are considering making a claim it is vital that you consult a solicitor who is a specialist in this area. THE LAW SOCIETY will provide a list of specialist solicitors in your area.

You should ask any solicitor advising you:

- how many claims for libel/slander they have previously dealt with
- how many actions they have actually taken to court
- how many they have settled successfully.

You should also ensure that you get an estimate of your potential liability for costs before instructing any solicitor (see CHAPTER 1: FINDING AND MEETING YOUR LAWYER).

Complaints

In the case of a newspaper article a complaint can be made to the PRESS
COMPLAINTS COMMISSION (PCC).

The PCC will consider complaints about articles that are either:

- untrue
- unfair
- based on an unjustifiable infringement of privacy
- in breach of the **codes of guidance** for newspapers.

If the complaint is upheld, the judgement of the PCC should be given
similar prominence to the original item of news in the relevant newspaper.
The PCC has no power to award damages or legal costs.

The BROADCASTING STANDARDS COMMISSION (BSC) fulfils a similar role for
sound or television programmes broadcast by the BBC or IBA and adjudi-
cates on complaints of unjust or unfair treatment or infringement of privacy.
The BSC can require a broadcaster to publish a summary of the complaint
and its findings.

> The laws of libel are a civil matter but **racial hatred** is a criminal
> offence. Either
>
> - using threatening, abusive or insulting words or behaviour or
>   displays
> - or possessing, publishing, distributing or performing racially
>   inflammatory material
>
> with the intention of stirring up racial hatred is an offence under the
> law. It cannot be prosecuted if the offences occur in a dwelling but it
> can be if they can be heard or seen from that dwelling. (See CHAPTER
> 8: CRIMINAL LAW.)

Organisations ⓘ

► **ADVICE UK (formerly THE FEDERATION OF INFORMATION AND ADVICE CENTRES)**
12th Floor
New London Bridge House
25 London Bridge Street
London SE1 9ST
Tel: 020 7407 4070
www.fiac.org.uk

► **BROADCASTING STANDARDS COMMISSION**
7 The Sanctuary
London SW1P 3JS
Tel: 020 7808 1000
Fax: 020 7233 0397
bsc@bsc.org.uk
www.bsc.org.uk

► **LAW CENTRES FEDERATION**
Duchess House
18–19 Warren Street
London W1T 5LR
Tel: 020 7387 8570
Fax: 020 7387 8368
info@lawcentres.org.uk
www.lawcentres.org.uk

► **THE LAW SOCIETY**
113 Chancery Lane
London WC2A 1PL
Tel: 020 7242 1222
Fax: 020 7831 0344
info.services@lawsociety.org.uk
www.lawsoc.org.uk

► **LEGAL SERVICES COMMISSION**
85 Gray's Inn Road
London WC1X 8TX
Tel: 020 7759 0000
www.legalservices.gov.uk
www.justask.org.uk
Regional telephone helplines on various legal subjects.

► **NATIONAL ASSOCIATION OF CITIZENS ADVICE BUREAUX (NACAB)**
Myddelton House
115–123 Pentonville Road
London N1 9LZ
Tel: 020 7833 2181
www.nacab.org.uk
Adviceguide: the National Association of Citizens Advice Bureaux offers fact sheets covering issues such as employment, housing and taxation
www.adviceguide.org.uk

► **PRESS COMPLAINTS COMMISSION (PCC)**
1 Salisbury Square
London EC4Y 8JB
Tel: 020 7353 3732
pcc@pcc.org.uk
www.pcc.org.uk

22 **Mental health**

Often there is a lack of definition to problems in the area of mental health. There may be a general feeling of fear or concern over loss of power, or a disagreement about treatment, but no specific legal problem. Frequently, problems are to do with clinical decisions, not having enough information, or concerns about policy issues. In many of these situations a lawyer is unlikely to be able to help. Other avenues such as complaints procedures or enlisting the help of an advocate might be more appropriate.

When do you need a mental health lawyer?

The *Mental Health Act 1983* is the legislation that controls compulsory hospital admission and treatment. People who are admitted to hospital under the Act are often referred to as having been:

- **compulsorily admitted**
- **detained**
- **sectioned**.

The Act also deals with the management of the property of people who are unable to manage it themselves. It allows for people to be detained and treated against their will and so it is important that it is used properly.

Most people who use mental health services will never be detained under the *Mental Health Act*. People who are admitted to hospital voluntarily are usually referred to as **informal patients**. Some of the Act's provisions do apply to informal patients.

Solicitors who specialise in mental health law provide the best option for challenging decisions made under the Act, and should be able to provide advice and assistance in relation to:

- assessment, admission and discharge from hospital
- treatment and consent
- capacity (to understand and make a decision).

Mental health lawyers are particularly valuable at tribunal hearings. They will not normally deal with complaints against doctors.

WHEN DO YOU NEED A DIFFERENT SORT OF LAWYER?

There are many other areas that do not raise questions of mental health law but directly affect people who have mental health problems. Of particular significance are the areas of:

- disability discrimination
- community care
- human rights
- suing a doctor for negligent treatment.

These are all specialist areas of law and a mental health solicitor will not necessarily be qualified to take them on.

> Although in many situations a solicitor will be able to help in more than one area of law, it will be useful if you try to identify what your main problem is and approach a solicitor who specialises in that field.

Public funding is usually only available through a solicitor with a **specialist contract** in that area. Do not be afraid to ask about a person's experience if you need help in more than one area of law. If the main problem is not mental health law there may still be mental health issues that are relevant. You should feel free to ask the solicitor about any mental health implications, or contact MIND, which will also provide information to solicitors.

Lawyers can provide advice and representation, and should be used if:

- specialist legal knowledge is required
- there are technical legal issues

- you need to instruct an independent expert or a barrister

- there is a lot of correspondence or paperwork

- the matter is complicated

- there is a hearing where witnesses will be questioned and you need to give evidence.

Finding a lawyer

The questions to ask when seeking legal assistance in relation to mental health law are:

? whether the solicitor has experience and expertise in this area of law

? if you will have to pay for your legal help or if public funding is available

? if you do have to pay, how much is it likely to cost.

> It is possible to get funding from the LEGAL SERVICES COMMISSION for advice and representation in mental health cases. Before solicitors can provide free services they must have a legal services commission contract in mental health and have achieved the **Specialist Quality Mark**. The contract will cover work done in relation to mental health law and under the *Mental Health Act 1983*, including representation before a MENTAL HEALTH REVIEW TRIBUNAL. It will not cover work in relation to clinical negligence or personal injury.

Where the primary problem is another area of law you will need to approach a solicitor with expertise in that area, even if there are mental health issues as well.

A list of firms that offer services in a particular field is available from the LEGAL SERVICES COMMISSION. There is also a LAW SOCIETY specialist mental health panel (list available), and a solicitor who wants to represent people at a tribunal must be on this panel. MIND keeps a list of solicitors who are part of their legal network and work in mental health law, and also those who will take on related cases in other areas of law.

The Mental Health Act

Most people receive psychiatric care and treatment in exactly the same way as they would receive treatment for a physical condition. They will usually see their GP, who may or may not make a referral to a psychiatrist. Following that, they may be admitted to hospital if that is felt to be the most appropriate way of dealing with their problem at the time.

Admission to hospital does not give medical staff any added powers in relation to treatment, and the patient is entitled to leave hospital or refuse treatment if they want.

> There are some powers under the common law that allow for a person to be treated without their consent, if they are:
> - not capable of giving consent
> - not capable of validly withholding consent
> - in need of treatment in their best interests.
>
> This will apply to patients whether or not they are detained under the Act.

Compulsory admission

A person can only be admitted under the *Mental Health Act* if they are, or are thought to be, suffering from a **mental disorder**. This is defined as:

- mental illness
- arrested or incomplete development of mind
- psychopathic disorder
- any other disorder or disability of mind.

For many of the provisions of the Act a person must have been diagnosed as suffering from one of four categories of mental disorder, which are further defined within the Act. In addition to this diagnosis, the compulsory admission must be justified or necessary in order to protect the health and safety of the person suffering, or for the protection of others.

There are different sections of the Act which deal with admission in various circumstances. The most commonly applied sections are *Section 2* and *Section 3*.

- *Section 2* enables a person to be admitted for a period of up to 28 days for assessment.

- *Section 3* allows for admission for treatment and lasts initially for a period of up to six months.

Both of these sections also allow for **compulsory medical treatment** for the mental disorder. Once a person is **sectioned** they will be liable to be detained in hospital and can be brought back there if they abscond.

ADMISSION PROCESS

- Compulsory admission is arranged following assessment by doctors and social workers, who then have to complete forms setting out the grounds for admission.

- The application will be made by an approved social worker or by the nearest relative.

- When a person is admitted to hospital under a section, the people who are technically charged with receiving them are the hospital managers. The hospital managers have to keep the use of the powers under the *Mental Health Act* under review, and they can refuse to admit someone if they are not satisfied with the grounds of the application.

- Detained patients and their nearest relatives have some rights to apply to the hospital managers if they think they should be discharged from their section.

THE CRIMINAL JUSTICE SYSTEM

The Act also contains provisions allowing for admission or transfer to hospital from the criminal justice system. The courts can order admission as part of a sentence after conviction or when a person is on remand. If a person is in prison and needs to be in hospital, they can be transferred there on medical recommendation if a bed is available for them. Despite these provisions, there are a large number of people with mental health problems in prison. A lawyer specialising in mental health will be able to represent people detained in hospital, even though they have arrived there via the criminal system.

Treatment

> Under general law, medical treatment can only be given if a person consents to it. There is a limited exception to this when a person is unable to consent. Treatment may be given without consent if it is necessary and in the patient's best interests. Nobody can consent on behalf of another adult.

The assessment of a person's ability to **consent** (capacity to understand and make a decision) is made for the particular decision required. For people *with* capacity, treatment may be given to which they consent, but consent may be withdrawn at any time.

The *Mental Health Act* contains provisions enabling medical staff to give people treatment even though they do not consent. The patient must be detained under one of the sections to which the treatment provisions apply. The Act applies to medical treatment for a mental disorder, so a detained patient can refuse treatment for a physical illness. Medical treatment includes medication and nursing care.

There are certain treatments that can only be given if a different doctor gives a second opinion that the treatment is appropriate, having consulted with other people involved in the care of the patient. Electroconvulsive therapy (ECT) and medication for more than three months require a second opinion if a patient does not consent. Treatments covered by this safeguard can only be given without the second opinion in urgent situations.

Mental Health Review Tribunal

Most people who are detained under the Act are entitled to apply to the MENTAL HEALTH REVIEW TRIBUNAL for an independent review of their detention. The tribunal is the body that hears applications by people who feel they should be discharged from their section.

A tribunal has three members: a lawyer, a doctor and someone with professional experience of the psychiatric system. They will:

■ hear evidence from the people involved in the patient's care, as well as from the patient

- give an opportunity to ask questions or cross-examine the other side.

The tribunal should discharge the section if they are not satisfied that certain criteria for continued detention are met. They must give reasons for their decision. Although the hearings are supposed to be quite informal, the rules are based on law and the tribunal will be looking out for specific points before making their decision.

> Even though it is possible to attend the hearing on your own it is generally very useful to have someone to represent you who understands the law, so they can make sure all the right questions are asked. Legal representation is provided free of charge; representing people at tribunals is one of the most significant areas of a mental health lawyer's practice.

Mental health hospitals will usually have a list of local solicitors who do this work. The person wanting advice and representation is not obliged to use one of the solicitors on the list. The solicitor they do use must have a **contract in mental health** with the LEGAL SERVICES COMMISSION to provide a free service. Because of this there may be a limited choice of solicitors in some areas.

Guardianship

There is a power under the Act to make an application for **guardianship** for a person over 16 years old. This is not an avenue for admission to hospital but will enable the guardian (which is usually the local authority) to require the patient to live at a certain place or to attend for training or treatment.

> Guardianship does not allow another person to give consent on the patient's behalf, nor can the patient receive compulsory treatment under the Act.

A person may be received into guardianship if:

- they are suffering from one of the four categories of mental disorder to a degree that warrants the application

- it is necessary in the interests of their welfare or for the protection of others.

Guardianship lasts for a period of up to six months initially and can be renewed for a further period of six months, then at yearly intervals. A nearest relative may apply for discharge of a guardianship order.

Patient rights

The *Mental Health Act Code of Practice* is a document for the benefit of staff who apply the *Mental Health Act*. It provides guidance to hospital staff about the implementation of the Act. The Code is not legally binding but can be taken into account when someone questions the standard of care given under the Act, or the correct interpretation of the Act. It applies to all patients, whether they are detained or informal. Doctors, nurses and social workers should all have regard to the Code in their dealings with patients. It should also be considered by others working in health and social services (including the independent and voluntary sectors) and by the police.

LEGAL HELP ON BEHALF OF OTHER PEOPLE

Frequently, a friend or relative will be seeking legal advice on another person's behalf. This does cause difficulties because solicitors act on behalf of their client only, and a concerned third person cannot instruct a solicitor for someone else. If a person is unwilling to instruct a solicitor then the solicitor will not be able to act for them. This can be particularly frustrating for people close to them. It may be possible for a friend or relative to act as **litigation friend** for a person who does not have capacity to instruct a solicitor. This will not be possible if there is any conflict of interest between them and the person without capacity. A litigation friend cannot take action on behalf of a person who does have capacity, even if the decisions they make are perceived to be against their own interests. You should seek legal advice if you want to take legal action on behalf of someone else.

> If somebody *does* instruct a solicitor, the person's family does not have a right to be involved, or to have access to information about the case, unless that person consents. This is the case even if the family does not think the person is making the right choices.

Occasionally the family might have a legal right of their own, for which they can seek legal assistance. The *Human Rights Act* may provide an opportunity for challenge where a decision of a public authority directly affects the family's rights. The most likely article to be invoked in this way is *Article 8* (the right to respect for private and family life), although this right is not absolute (see CHAPTER 16: HUMAN RIGHTS ACT).

Nearest relatives

The nearest relative of a detained patient is given certain rights under the *Mental Health Act*. They are entitled to:

- receive certain information
- apply for the admission of their relative
- apply for their discharge from section.

A person who is the nearest relative of a detained person may need access to a solicitor in relation to their rights and duties.

Nearest relative has a particular meaning under the Act and is determined by reference to set criteria. A person has no choice about who can take this role. The lack of choice about who can be a nearest relative has been subject to legal challenge. The government did agree to change the law so that people would have some choice about who would take this role, but they have not yet done so. A further legal challenge has recently been heard by the courts and this part of the *Mental Health Act* has been declared to be incompatible with the *Human Rights Act (Article 8)*. If there is a new Mental Health Act it will probably allow people to nominate a person of their choice. The role of nearest relative neither gives any right to take legal action on behalf of the patient, nor an automatic right to access confidential information about them or their treatment. In certain situations, a relative may be entitled to information if it is necessary in order for their own rights under the *Human Rights Act* to be upheld, or to carry out their functions as nearest relative. This will always be balanced against the patient's right to privacy.

In some situations a local authority can apply to have a nearest relative displaced. The nearest relative should take legal advice if this happens, or if they are told it will happen if they try to exercise their rights.

MANAGEMENT OF THE AFFAIRS OF A PERSON WITHOUT CAPACITY

A person *with* mental capacity can make an **enduring power of attorney** appointing someone else to manage their legal, financial or property affairs should they lose their mental capacity in the future. They must be able to understand the terms of the power they are granting. When a person has lost their mental capacity the appointed attorney(s) should apply to the PUBLIC GUARDIANSHIP OFFICE (the administrative arm of the COURT OF PROTECTION) to have the power registered.

If a person has not granted an enduring power of attorney or is incapable of doing so, an application must be made to the COURT OF PROTECTION for a **receiver** to be appointed. Medical evidence will be required and there are fees to pay when making the application.

The OFFICIAL SOLICITOR exists to provide legal representation for people without mental capacity where they are a party to legal proceedings. The OFFICIAL SOLICITOR can act in the COURT OF PROTECTION and in county and high court actions.

Clinical negligence claims

If you have a complaint about care that you have received in the past which has caused you real damage, you may be able to make a **claim of negligence**. Medical staff generally owe a **duty of care** to any person to whom they are providing services. This means that they have a duty to provide services of a reasonable standard. If they breach this duty and as a result a person suffers harm, the person may be able to bring a claim for damages against that person or body.

To bring this sort of claim you will need a solicitor who specialises in clinical negligence, rather than a mental health specialist. The unpredictable nature of psychiatric claims means that it is frequently difficult for people to find a solicitor to help them with this sort of problem. MIND has a list of solicitors who have said that they undertake psychiatric negligence claims.

> There is limited public funding for **clinical negligence claims** because they are expensive to bring. They also tend to be very difficult and can take a long time.

WHAT INFORMATION WILL THE SOLICITOR NEED?

A solicitor will need to know:

☑ if you have approached them on someone else's behalf, and if so why that person has not made direct contact

☑ what the problem is

☑ what information and documentation about your case is available

☑ if the person needing assistance is in hospital, and if they are detained under the *Mental Health Act* or informally admitted

☑ if the person is detained, under which section and when it was implemented.

If you have any documents relating to your case, you should take them with you. If there are a lot, you should try to put them in some order so that time is not wasted when you get there. Do not be surprised if the solicitor does not look at every document – they will often pick out what they need or read them later. On the other hand, if you think that the solicitor has missed something crucial to your complaint you should not be afraid to point it out.

WHAT SHOULD I ASK AT MY FIRST MEETING?

At your first meeting you will probably have all sorts of things you want to know. Do not be afraid to ask or to take notes of what the solicitor says. Although your main concern will usually be finding a solution to your problem, you should not forget a few formalities. You should ask:

? if they work in the area of law in which you are seeking help

? if they can provide that help for free

? if you have to pay, how much will it cost

? if you have a number of different problems, whether they will be able to deal with all of them or if you are likely to need to be referred to someone else for further advice.

At the end of the meeting make sure you know what you should do next. If you have agreed that they will take the next step, ensure you know what it is and how long they expect it to take. You should find out as soon as possible whether they think you have a strong case or a weak one. It is often useful to confirm whether they can put their advice in writing, especially if you find it difficult to concentrate or remember information.

The bodies that control the application of mental health law will nearly always be public authorities. This means that it may be possible to challenge their decisions by **judicial review** or under the *Human Rights Act*.

> The *Human Rights Act* is of huge significance in the field of mental health. You should contact a solicitor if you want to bring this sort of claim (see CHAPTER 16: HUMAN RIGHTS ACT).

Alternatives to legal action

Sometimes your problem will obviously be legal and you will know that you would benefit from the advice of a lawyer. At other times you may have a problem that you know is not a legal one but have no idea what you can do about it. Whatever the situation, it is useful to think about what sort of solution you are seeking.

- If it is an explanation or apology that is most important then it is often best to make a complaint through the health service or local authority complaints procedure. You should ensure that you use the correct avenue for complaining to the appropriate body.

- If that is unsatisfactory, you will be able to complain to the HEALTH SERVICES OMBUDSMAN (for health service complaints) or the LOCAL GOVERNMENT OMBUDSMAN (for local authority complaints).

- The MENTAL HEALTH ACT COMMISSION is responsible for investigating complaints of people who are detained under the *Mental Health Act*.

- Doctors and nurses are regulated by professional organisations such as the BRITISH MEDICAL ASSOCIATION (BMA) which will be responsible for investigating complaints about individuals.

If your concern is to do with mental health policy, either nationally or locally, there are several options. You can contact your local MP, organise publicity in the media, or contact campaigning bodies, such as MIND, which may be able to help.

Often, one of the main problems for mental health service users is accessing information and assistance, and getting themselves heard. There are an increasing number of advocacy services available across the country. An advocate can be a very useful resource whatever your problem, to help access the help you need.

Organisations · i

▶ **ACTION ON ELDER ABUSE**
Helpline: 0808 808 8141
aea@ace.org.uk
www.elderabuse.org

▶ **ADVICE UK (formerly THE FEDERATION OF INFORMATION AND ADVICE CENTRES)**
12th Floor
New London Bridge House
25 London Bridge Street
London SE1 9ST
Tel: 020 7407 4070
www.fiac.org.uk

▶ **BRITISH MEDICAL ASSOCIATION (BMA)**
BMA House
Tavistock Square
London WC1H 9JP
Tel: 020 7387 4499
Fax: 020 7383 6400
info.web@bma.org.uk
www.bma.org.uk

▶ **COURT OF PROTECTION PUBLIC GUARDIANSHIP OFFICE**
Archway Tower
2 Junction Road
London N19 5SZ
Tel: 0845 330 2900
Fax: 020 7664 7705
custserv@guardianship.gov.uk
www.guardianship.gov.uk

▶ **DEPRESSION ALLIANCE**
Tel: 020 7633 0557
www.depressionalliance.org

▶ **HEALTH SERVICE OMBUDSMAN**
Millbank Tower
Millbank
London SW1P 4QP
Tel: 020 7217 4051
Fax: 020 7217 4000
ohsc.enquiries@ombudsman.gsi.gov.uk
www.ombudsman.org.uk

▶ **JUSTICE**
59 Carter Lane
London EC4V 5AQ
Tel: 020 7329 5100
Fax: 020 7329 5055
admin@justice.org.uk
www.justice.org.uk

▶ **LAW CENTRES FEDERATION**
Duchess House
18–19 Warren Street
London W1T 5LR
Tel: 020 7387 8570
Fax: 020 7387 8368
info@lawcentres.org.uk
www.lawcentres.org.uk

▶ **LAW SOCIETY**
113 Chancery Lane
London WC2A 1PL
Tel: 020 7242 1222
Fax: 020 7831 0344
info.services@lawsociety.org.uk
www.lawsoc.org.uk
Ask for: Law Society specialist mental health panel

► **LEGAL ACTION GROUP**

242 Pentonville Road
London N1 9UN

Tel: 020 7833 2931
Fax: 020 7837 6094
lag@lag.org.uk
www.lag.org.uk

► **LEGAL SERVICES COMMISSION**

85 Gray's Inn Road
London WC1X 8TX

Tel: 020 7759 0000
www.legalservices.gov.uk
www.justask.org.uk

Regional telephone helplines on various
legal subjects.

► **LOCAL GOVERNMENT OMBUDSMAN**

www.lgo.org.uk

► **MENCAP**

123 Golden Lane
London EC1Y ORT

Tel: 020 7454 0454
Fax: 020 7696 5540
Free helpline: 0808 808 1111
Helpline Wales: 0808 8000 300
Helpline Northern Ireland: 0845 763 6227
Minicom: 0808808 8181
information@mencap.org.uk
www.mencap.org.uk

► **MENTAL HEALTH ACT COMMISSION**

Maid Marian House
56 Hounds Gate
Nottingham NG1 6BG

Tel: 0115 943 7100
Fax: 0115 943 7101
www.mhac.trent.nhs.uk

► **MIND**

15–19 Broadway
London E15 4BQ

Tel: 08457 660 163
contact@mind.org.uk
www.mind.org.uk

► **NATIONAL ASSOCIATION OF
CITIZENS ADVICE BUREAUX
(NACAB)**

Myddelton House
115–123 Pentonville Road
London N1 9LZ

Tel: 020 7833 2181
www.nacab.org.uk
Adviceguide: the National Association
of Citizens Advice Bureaux offers
fact sheets covering issues such as
employment, housing and taxation
www.adviceguide.org.uk

► **RETHINK (formerly THE NATIONAL
SCHIZOPHRENIA FEDERATION)**

30 Tabernacle Street
London EC2A 4DD

Tel: 020 7330 9100/01
Fax: 020 7330 9102

*National advice line (Monday–Friday,
10.00am–3.00pm):* 020 8974 6814

advice@rethink.org
www.rethink.org

23 Motoring

This chapter sets out the main offences you may be charged with, the sentences you could face, and suggests places to find further information and advice.

The law and your vehicle

In order to drive on the roads you must, by law, have:

- ☑ a vehicle with seat belts, lights, brakes, tyres, mirrors, horn, silencer, speedometer, wipers in good working order
- ☑ a driving licence – you must have passed a theory and driving test for the appropriate vehicle, declare any disability, and renew your licence every three years after the age of seventy
- ☑ an MOT if the vehicle is over three years old
- ☑ insurance (at least third party cover)
- ☑ a registration document proving proof of ownership
- ☑ a current tax disc.

> A police officer can stop a vehicle at any time for a spot check. The driver can ask for the check to be delayed for up to 30 days, but an officer who believes a vehicle may be in a dangerous condition can insist on an immediate inspection. If it is, the car may be prohibited from being driven.

Finding the right information

Even people who have otherwise managed to get through life without falling foul of the law can suddenly find themselves faced with a criminal charge – large or small – as a result of a driving offence. In this situation it is often vital to make swift decisions about what action to take.

You may find yourself:

- required to appear at the magistrates' court
- in possession of a fixed penalty notice.

You are then faced with the choice of pleading guilty to a minor charge in return for a fixed fine and possibly some points endorsed on your driving licence, or going to trial.

A decision about how to proceed will need to be made by the date indicated in the documents you are sent. Initial information sources include:

- the *Highway Code*, which contains some information about the rules of the road and the law, and can be bought at most bookshops
- your insurance company or motoring association, which may be able to provide advice by phone
- websites providing basic information about motoring law – but do consider whose website it is and whether they may have some sort of bias that could affect the information they offer
- *Anthony and Berryman's Magistrates' Court Guide* – this may be available in your local library.

There are also some very detailed specialist books that you might find in a library that has a good law section. These include *Blackstone's Criminal Practice, Stones' Justices Manual* and *Wilkinson on Road Traffic Offences*. Whatever your source of information, make sure that it is up to date because the law changes constantly.

Funding for legal representation

Public funding for legal assistance – commonly known as **legal aid** – may be available, especially in cases involving more serious offences where employment or even liberty are at stake. In general, if you can get such assistance, it is worth taking it. There may be factors that are relevant to your case of which you have not been informed, or that you don't realise are important. A trained professional may be able to help you identify these and to present your case in court, and help you keep your licence or avoid a heavy fine (see CHAPTER 2: LEGAL AID).

Offences and the courts

The most serious driving offences are only tried in the crown court, for example:

- **manslaughter**
- **causing death by dangerous driving** (whether or not under the influence of drink or drugs).

> **Dangerous driving** means that you are likely to cause either injury to a person or serious damage to property. These offences can carry sentences of up to ten years' imprisonment, with unlimited fines and obligatory disqualification from driving.

In such cases, the courts will impose the mandatory retesting of the driver by an extended driving test following their disqualification.

EITHER-WAY OFFENCES

These offences can be tried in the magistrates' or crown court. Common examples are:

- **dangerous driving**
- **taking a vehicle without consent** ('joyriding')
- **causing danger** to road users
- **failing to stop** after an accident
- **driving when disqualified**
- **speeding**
- traffic lights offences.

These can incur imprisonment, hefty fines or discretionary disqualification, or all three.

The defendant can choose to have such a case tried in the crown court, where a jury will decide the facts of the case, even if the magistrates consider the case to be less serious and therefore suitable to be tried in their court. However, sometimes the magistrates consider an **either-way offence** to be too serious or too complex for trial in the magistrates' court, and then the case will be sent to the crown court regardless of the defendant's wishes.

SUMMARY OFFENCES

The least serious offences can normally be tried only in the magistrates' court. These are referred to as **summary offences**. Occasionally, where a more serious charge is to be tried in the crown court, a summary offence related to it can also be sent to the crown court, for example:

- **failure to provide a breath specimen** when requested
- **driving without a licence**
- **driving without insurance**.

> Random breath-testing is not allowed. The police must have reasonable cause to suspect that you are over the limit – but you in turn must have a reasonable excuse not to comply. However, this is currently under review.

Many of the less serious offences are punishable only with a fine, but the court may – and sometimes must – also **endorse** your driving licence with points or **disqualify** you from driving for a period of time.

Sentencing and penalties

In the magistrates' court the maximum sentence is normally six months in prison and the maximum fine is £5000.

The crown court has much greater sentencing powers, with the maximum sentence varying from offence to offence. In cases where a prison sentence could be given, the court can also impose:

- a community sentence
- community punishment
- community rehabilitation (formerly known as probation)
- a fine.

FINES

The court will take into account your personal financial situation before deciding what fine to impose, and if the fine cannot be paid all at once, time will be allowed for payment.

CONDITIONAL DISCHARGE

In the least serious cases, and particularly where there are no previous convictions, a court may impose a **conditional discharge**. This means that no further sentence is imposed unless there is a further conviction within a specified period of time.

ABSOLUTE DISCHARGE

Rarely is an **absolute discharge** imposed. This is in effect not an actual punishment, but it does leave a conviction on your record.

DISQUALIFICATION AND ENDORSEMENT

Disqualification from driving is **mandatory** (obligatory) for some offences, and **discretionary** (optional) for less serious offences. You can also be disqualified if you have a series of minor driving offences. Even if disqualification is not imposed for one conviction, the penalty point system allows the fact of a driving conviction to be noted (**endorsed**) on a driving licence. The driver will not be disqualified unless further driving convictions follow.

> If 12 or more points are acquired on a licence within three years, the driver is automatically disqualified. The first disqualification under this system will be for six months, but a longer disqualification can be imposed for a subsequent conviction.

MANDATORY DISQUALIFICATION

Driving when under the influence of drink or drugs, or when there is more than a prescribed limit of alcohol in the blood, are among the offences that carry mandatory disqualification from driving. This can be catastrophic for those who rely on the use of a car for their day-to-day work.

However, when there is a disqualification from driving for 12 months or more in an alcohol-related case, the disqualification period can be reduced by up to a quarter by completing a special course for drink-drive offenders. Drivers reconvicted of a drink-driving offence within ten years of the course will be designated **high risk offenders**. Under this scheme your licence will not be returned unless the **medical adviser** of the DRIVER AND VEHICLE LICENSING AGENCY (DVLA) is satisfied that you do not have an ongoing drink problem.

SPECIAL REASONS

Normally disqualification cannot be avoided simply because losing your licence creates inconvenience or even problems with employment. However, if it is possible to show that there are **special reasons**, a court may choose not to impose a mandatory disqualification or endorse a driver's licence with penalty points, if they find:

- a **mitigating circumstance** – ie, something that tends to reduce the seriousness of the offence

- a factor other than an actual legal defence (if there was a legal defence there should not have been a conviction in the first place)

- something directly connected to the circumstances in which the offence was committed, not just the personal circumstances of the driver

- a factor that the court ought properly to take into consideration.

It is for the driver facing disqualification to prove that a special reason exists, and the court will hold a special hearing at which both sides can present evidence.

> Generally the courts take a hard line on offences involving alcohol, because of the high risks involved in driving while under the influence. Driving while disqualified is another offence looked on with particular disapproval, because it involves the flouting of the order of the previous court.

If you do find yourself in court for any driving offence, it pays dividends to adopt a friendly and respectful attitude to the court personnel and to remember that substantial credit may be given by the court, if deciding on a sentence, to people who plead guilty at an early opportunity. Of course, only you can decide, having received legal advice or having done your own homework, on whether to plead guilty or not in your specific case.

Finally, if going to court, *do take your licence with you*, since this will speed up the process. If no licence is available, the court may adjourn the case to get a printout of your driving record from the DVLA in Swansea.

Organisations   i

▶ **AUTOMOBILE ASSOCIATION (AA)**
Contact Centre
Carr Ellison House
William Armstrong Drive
Newcastle upon Tyne NE4 7YA
Tel: 0870 600 0371
(24 hours a day, seven days a week)
Fax: 0191 235 5111
www.theaa.com

▶ **DRIVER AND VEHICLE LICENSING AGENCY (DVLA)**
Customer Enquiries (**Drivers**) Unit
DVLC
Swansea SA6 7JL
Tel: 0870 240 0009
Fax: 01792 783071
drivers.dvla@gtnet.gov.uk
www.dvla.gov.uk

▶ **DRIVER AND VEHICLE LICENSING AGENCY (DVLA)**
Customer Enquiries (**Vehicles**) Unit
DVLC
Swansea SA99 1BL
Tel: 0870 240 0010
Fax: 01792 782793
vehicles.dvla@gtnet.gov.uk
www.dvla.gov.uk

▶ **LAW CENTRES FEDERATION**
Duchess House
18–19 Warren Street
London W1T 5LR
Tel: 020 7387 8570
Fax: 020 7387 8368
info@lawcentres.org.uk
www.lawcentres.org.uk

▶ **LEGAL SERVICES COMMISSION**
85 Gray's Inn Road
London WC1X 8TX
Tel: 020 7759 0000
www.legalservices.gov.uk
www.justask.org.uk
Regional telephone helplines on various legal subjects.

▶ **NATIONAL ASSOCIATION OF CITIZENS ADVICE BUREAUX (NACAB)**
Myddelton House
115–123 Pentonville Road
London N1 9LZ
Tel: 020 7833 2181
www.nacab.org.uk
Adviceguide: the National Association of Citizens Advice Bureaux offers fact sheets covering issues such as employment, housing and taxation
www.adviceguide.org.uk

▶ **RAC MOTORING SERVICES**
Great Park Road
Bradley Stoke
Bristol BS32 4QN
Legal help and information (Monday–Friday 8.00am–8.00pm, Saturday 9.00am–5.00pm):
Tel: 08705 533 533
Fax: 01454 208 222
www.rac.co.uk

24 **Prisoners' rights**

Prisoners retain all legal rights except for those taken away expressly or by implication as a consequence of their imprisonment. The *Prison Act 1952* and *Prison Rules 1999* both limit and grant rights. There are many areas of the *Human Rights Act* that apply to prisoners (see CHAPTER 16: HUMAN RIGHTS ACT).

> The **Prison Rules** give rights to:
> - food
> - clothing
> - exercise
> - a specified minimum number of visits and letters
> - a fair hearing in disciplinary procedures.

Allocation

Prisoners have no right to choose the prison or the location in which they will be held. However, a prisoner can ask for a transfer if an allocation causes severe problems – for example, to their family because of age, pregnancy or illness. You should provide material to support your case but if unsuccessful, you should seek legal advice. In extreme cases, the courts may review allocation or transfer.

Unconvicted prisoners

Unconvicted prisoners are:

- remanded
- awaiting extradition, deportation or removal from the UK as illegal entrants.

Unconvicted prisoners may still be disciplined.

Unconvicted prisoners are allowed:

- to wear their own clothes if they are suitable, clean and tidy. Clothes may be sent in from the outside or brought in by visitors and exchanged for dirty ones.
- as many visits as they wish, subject to conditions imposed by the Home Secretary. These do not need a visiting order and must:
  - be on at least three days each week
  - include at least one weekend visit
  - allow up to three adults and the prisoner's children in at any one time.
- to receive cigarettes, tobacco and toiletries via visitors or by post (only some prisons)
- to send and receive as many unread letters as they like (unless category A or on the escape list). Two second-class letters per week will be paid for by the prison, and any more from prison earnings or private cash. Letters to legal advisers normally have to be paid for, but if a prisoner has no private cash, the governor may allow letters essential to the defence to be sent by the prison
- to decide whether or not to work. If they do work they will be paid a small sum of money (the minimum weekly wage is £4). In practice, there is very little work available. Where no work can be found prisoners must be paid unemployment pay of £2.50 a week. If they refuse work when offered, this money will then be stopped and the prison is not obliged to offer any further work
- to be paid a very small sum to cover basics
- to receive money sent into the prison and spend it in the prison canteen
- to apply to be treated by the doctor or dentist of their choice at their own expense, although they can use the PRISON MEDICAL SERVICE.

Civil prisoners – in prison for not paying community charge, tax or maintenance – are in general treated in the same way as unconvicted prisoners.

Convicted prisoners

CATEGORISATION

On reception, prisoners are given a **security category** from A to D. Category A prisoners have extra security restrictions, including the vetting of their visitors by the police. Categorisation is reviewed periodically and prisoners can be moved to a higher or lower security category. There are procedural safeguards that should apply whenever categorisation decisions are taken. A failure to apply the safeguards may be challenged by **judicial review**.

CORRESPONDENCE

Prisoners can send and receive a letter on reception to prison and at least one a week after that. The total number of letters allowed will vary from prison to prison and special letters – extra letters intended to meet particular needs – may be available in certain circumstances.

There is no routine reading of mail at:

- category B prisons
- category C prisons
- open prisons
- designated women's prisons
- young offenders' institutions

and if this happens, the prisoner should be told and may be allowed to rewrite the letter in question.

All correspondence sent to or from prisoners who are:

- being considered for category A
- category A prisoners
- in units housing category A prisoners
- on the escape list

- detained as a consequence of proceedings under the *Protection from Harassment Act 1997*

will normally be read, except where it is legally privileged.

ACCESS TO LAWYERS

Prisoners have a right of access to a lawyer in criminal and civil proceedings. Prisoners who are involved in legal proceedings will not have correspondence with their legal advisers read or stopped, unless there is good reason to suspect that the correspondence does not relate to the proceedings.

Further advice can be sought from:

- a specialist solicitor (see CHAPTER 1: FINDING AND MEETING YOUR LAWYER)
- the COMMISSION FOR RACIAL EQUALITY, in cases of racial harassment or discrimination – prisons have a duty to apply racial equality to all prisoners (see CHAPTER 10: DISCRIMINATION)
- the PRISONERS' ADVICE SERVICE.

MEDICAL TREATMENT

The PRISON MEDICAL SERVICE is not currently part of the NHS, although prison healthcare will become part of the NHS over the next five years, starting in April 2003. Prison doctors and medical officers can refer prisoners to NHS hospitals, or ask specialists for a second opinion. The standard of treatment should in principle be equivalent to that provided by the NHS, although it is questionable whether this is true in practice. Treatment by opticians and dentists is available. All treatment in prisons must be with consent.

VISITS

A **visiting order** must be sent out to all visitors, which they should bring when they visit. Two visits are allowed in a four-week period, but this can be reduced to once a month by the Home Secretary. Additional visits can be awarded as a privilege.

Special visits may be allowed:

- to help conduct legal proceedings
- if there are personal or business difficulties following conviction

- if they are necessary for the welfare of you or your family
- on the advice of a medical officer if you are seriously ill.

Category A prisoners are subject to special procedures. Visits may not be stopped as part of a punishment, but may be deferred if the punishment includes a period of confinement to cell.

TRANSFERS

Prisoners may be transferred in the interests of **good order and discipline**, but transfers may not be used as a form of punishment. If the prison where a prisoner is held is a long way from friends and family, the prisoner may save up his visits and apply for a temporary transfer to a local prison in order that the visits can take place there (for transfers from abroad see CHAPTER 20: INTERNATIONAL ISSUES).

WORK

Convicted prisoners are required to do useful work for up to ten hours a day unless a medical officer excuses them, but the prison is under no obligation to provide work. It is a disciplinary offence:

- to fail to work properly on purpose
- to refuse to work.

Prisoners who work are entitled to a minimum weekly wage of £4. Where no work is available they are entitled to unemployment pay of £2.50. Prisoners who are short-term sick (up to four weeks) are entitled to £2.50 a week, and prisoners who are long-term sick are entitled to £3.25 a week. Prisoners who are on maternity leave or caring full-time for children are entitled to £3.25 a week.

Complaints

There is no need to make complaints internally before consulting with a solicitor/legal adviser. However, if you do take the internal route, requests or complaints should be made in the following order, if matters are not resolved satisfactorily, to:

- prison officer

- senior officer

- governor grade.

The complaint should be made in writing on the appropriate form.

You can bypass the internal procedure and go straight to the area manager if:

- the issue is about a **reserved subject** – for example, parole or a prison adjudication.

If this does not succeed, try:

- your local MP

- the MP in the constituency where the prison is located, who will refer it to the minister

- the PRISONS AND PROBATION OMBUDSMAN

- petitioning the Queen or parliament – prison staff should have copies of the procedures

- petitioning an MEP.

The *Human Rights Act* makes the *European Convention on Human Rights* part of UK law (see CHAPTER16: HUMAN RIGHTS ACT). A prisoner can bring a claim within six months of an incident occurring to the EUROPEAN COURT OF HUMAN RIGHTS after they have exhausted domestic legal remedies. In practice, this means that it will almost always be essential to apply to a domestic court before bringing a claim in the EUROPEAN COURT in Strasbourg.

Judicial review

Serious breaches of prisoners' rights can go before the courts for **judicial review**. The courts will in principle review any decisions by the prison authorities that are unfair or legally wrong, such as:

- censorship of mail
- disciplinary adjudications
- transfers
- separation of a mother from her baby.

Unless there are exceptional circumstances, applications for judicial review must be made within three months of the date of the decision in question.

Offences against prison discipline

Rule 51 of the *Prison Rules* lists offences against prison discipline. Prison governors deal with the less serious charges, more serious matters are referred to **independent adjudicators**, or to the police and CROWN PROSECUTION SERVICE (CPS) for prosecution in the outside criminal courts.

Prisoners must be:

- charged with any offence as soon as possible
- charged within 48 hours of the alleged offence being discovered (except in exceptional circumstances).

Prisoners should be:

- allowed to see statements or written material which will be used in evidence against them (medical reports may not be disclosed)
- given sufficient time to prepare for the hearing, if necessary by asking for an adjournment
- allowed a **McKenzie friend** (friend or adviser) or legal advice – in certain circumstances the *Human Rights Act* entitles a prisoner to representation before a governor.

Prison disciplinary charges should be referred to an independent adjudicator if a governor considers that a charge is so serious that additional days' imprisonment should be given as a punishment. Prisoners are entitled to legal representation for any charge heard by an independent adjudicator.

Prison disciplinary charges cannot be heard if:

- the case is referred to the CPS/police and a decision is made not to prosecute because of unsatisfactory evidence
- evidence has been presented in court by the CPS.

However, the governor may still bring a disciplinary charge if criminal charges are dropped for other reasons.

Punishment

A prisoner, if found guilty of a disciplinary offence, may be punished by:

- caution
- loss of visits
- loss of privileges for a maximum of 42 days
- loss of earnings for 82 days and of an amount not exceeding 42 days' earnings
- confinement to cell for a maximum of 14 days
- an award of up to an additional 42 days by an independent adjudicator
- exclusion from associated work for a maximum of 21 days.

(Different timescales apply for those in **Young Offenders' Institutions**.)

Appeal

A prisoner may appeal to the area manager, or apply for judicial review in the High Court:

- against the punishment imposed
- if the procedure was unfair, illegal or contained an error
- if the finding of guilt was unlawful or flawed.

Segregation

A prisoner should be segregated only:

- for the purpose of good order and discipline
- for no more than three days unless authorised by a member of the **board of visitors** or the **secretary of state**
- at their own request for their own protection.

The reasons should be clearly recorded.

Women prisoners

Women prisoners:

- may be allowed to keep their babies with them until the age of nine months or 18 months, depending on the prison (in exceptional circumstances children may remain with their mothers beyond these age limits)
- do not wear prison uniform
- cannot be forced to have their hair cut unless the medical officer makes an order
- are entitled to some toiletries, sanitary protection and clothing if they do not have enough of their own.

Young Offenders' Institutions (YOIs)

YOIs are governed by a separate set of rules, similar to the **Prison Rules**. If a prisoner is under 17 years they should have education or training for at least 15 hours within the normal working week.

Organisations

► **APEX CHARITABLE TRUST**

St Alphage House
Wingate Annexe
2 Fore Street
London EC2Y 5DA

Tel: 020 7638 5931
Fax: 020 7638 5977
jobcheck@apextrust.com
www.apextrust.com

► **ASSOCIATION OF PRISONERS**

www.associationofprisoners.org.uk
Campaigns for the civil and human
rights of prisoners.

► **CENTRE FOR ADOLESCENT REHABILITATION (C-FAR)**

Burdon Grange
Burdon Lane
Highampton
Devon EX21 5LX

Tel: 01409 231 665
Fax: 01409 231 593
info@c-far.org.uk
www.c-far.org.uk

► **COMMISSION FOR RACIAL EQUALITY (CRE)**

St Dunstan's House
201–211 Borough High Street
London SE1 1GZ

Tel: 020 7939 0000
Fax: 020 7939 0001
info@cre.gov.uk
www.cre.gov.uk

► **CROWN PROSECUTION SERVICE**

www.cps.gov.uk

► **HELP AND ADVICE FOR RELATIVES OF PRISONERS (HARP)**

Helpline (Tuesday–Friday, 10.00am–4.00pm;
Monday and Wednesday, 7.00pm–9.30pm):
0800 389 3003.
www.harpinfo.org.uk

► **HOWARD LEAGUE FOR PENAL REFORM**

1 Ardleigh Road
London N1 4HS

Tel: 020 7249 7373
Fax: 020 7249 7788
howardleague@ukonline.co.uk

► **JUSTICE**

59 Carter Lane
London EC4V 5AQ

Tel: 020 7329 5100
Fax: 020 7329 5055
admin@justice.org.uk
www.justice.org.uk

► **MISCARRIAGE OF JUSTICE ORGANISATION**

52 Octmore Road
Sheldon
Birmingham B33 OXL

Tel: 0121 789 8443 / 01902 731088
Fax: 0121 789 8443
mojuk@mojuk.org.uk
www.mojuk.org.uk

► **NATIONAL ASSOCIATION FOR THE CARE AND RESETTLEMENT OF OFFENDERS (NACRO)**

169 Clapham Road
London SW9 0PU

Tel: 020 7582 6500
www.nacro.org.uk

► **NATIONAL CIVIL RIGHTS MOVEMENT (NCRM)**

14 Featherstone Road
Southall
Middlesex UB2 5AA

Tel: 020 8574 0818 or 020 8843 2333
Fax: 020 8813 9734
info@ncrm.org
www.ncrm.org.uk

► **NATIONAL FEDERATION OF SERVICES SUPPORTING FAMILIES OF PRISONERS**

Unit 102, Riverbank House
1 Putney Bridge Approach
London SW6 3JD

Tel: 0207 384 1987
Fax: 0207 384 1855
www.prisonersfamilies.org.uk

► **PRISON ADVICE AND CARE TRUST (PACT)**

Lincoln House
1–3 Brixton Road
London SW9 6DE

Tel: 020 7582 1313
www.imprisonment.org.uk

► **PRISON REFORM TRUST**

15 Northburgh Street
London EC1V 0JR

Tel: 020 7251 5070
Fax: 020 7251 5076
prt@prisonreformtrust.org.uk
www.prisonreformtrust.org.uk

► **HM PRISON SERVICE**
(for PRISON MEDICAL SERVICE)

www.hmprisonservice.gov.uk

► **PRISONERS ABROAD**

89–93 Fonthill Road
Finsbury Park
London N4 3JH

Tel: 020 7561 6820
Fax: 020 7561 6821
info@prisonersabroad.org.uk
www.prisonersabroad.org.uk

► **PRISONERS' ADVICE SERVICE**

Unit 210, Hatton Square
16–16a Baldwins Gardens
London EC1N 7RJ

Tel: 020 7405 8090
Fax: 020 7405 8045
admin@prisoneradvice.demon.co.uk

► **PRISONERS' FAMILIES AND**
FRIENDS SERVICE

20 Trinity Street
London SE1 1DB

Tel: 0800 808 3444
Fax: 0207 357 9722
pffs@btclick.com

► **PRISONS AND PROBATION**
OMBUDSMAN

Ashley House
2 Monck Street
London SW1P 2BQ

Tel: 020 7035 2876   or   0845 010 7938
Fax: 020 7035 2860
mail@ppo.gsi.gov.uk
www.ppo.gov.uk

► **STATEWATCH**

PO Box 1516
London N16 0EW

Tel: 020 8802 1882
Fax: 020 8880 1727
info@statewatch.org
www.statewatch.org

Research papers/regular bulletins
on policing, immigration, prisons,
Europe, etc.

► **UNLOCK (NATIONAL ASSOCIATION**
OF EX-OFFENDERS)

35a High Street
Snodland
Kent ME6 5AG

Tel: 01634 247350
Fax: 01634 24735
info@unlockprison.org.uk
www.unlockprison.org.uk

► **WOMEN IN PRISON**

3b Aberdeen Studios
22 Highbury Grove
London N5 2EA

Tel: 020 7226 5879
Fax: 020 7354 8005
info@womeninprison.org.uk
www.womeninprison.org.uk

25 **Public inquiries**

This chapter sets out the what, why and where of public inquiries, giving guidance on how to initiate one, and where to get the best legal representation.

What is a public inquiry?

Also described as a **statutory inquiry,** a public inquiry is a device used by governments and local authorities to investigate important issues of public concern whilst enabling interested individuals or groups to participate.

Public inquiries are often held when a government is considering introducing significant changes to law or practice. The subject matter will vary greatly. It may range from the investigation of the death of an individual or individuals that involved some responsibility on the part of a public authority to allegations of corruption in a government department or questions of public health and welfare (such as the BSE inquiry).

In recent years many public inquiries have achieved an extremely high profile and have led to radical changes. These inquiries typically involve some form of state responsibility and include:

- *the inquiry into the death of Stephen Lawrence*, which led to significant changes in policing as well as being the catalyst for public bodies recognising and attempting to address the problem of institutional racism

- *the Bloody Sunday inquiry*, which is currently investigating the death of civilians at the hands of British soldiers in Derry, Northern Ireland.

- *the inquiry into the death of Victoria Climbié*, which investigated the role of social services, hospitals and the police in the events that led to the death of a child.

- *the Scott inquiry*, otherwise known as the *Arms to Iraq inquiry*, which investigated the role of the government in the illegal supply of arms to Iraq

- *the Southall and Paddington rail crash inquiries*.

> A typical type of public inquiry is the **planning inquiry**, which usually occurs before there is a major building development that may attract some opposition from the local community. A recent example was the inquiry into the fifth terminal at Heathrow Airport.

Benefits of public inquiries

These include:

- the discovery of important information that has not been revealed by previous investigations – the Lawrence inquiry discovered many facts that previous police internal investigations and an investigation by the POLICE COMPLAINTS AUTHORITY failed to uncover.

- recommendations designed to avoid a repetition of the incident or disaster that led to the setting up of the inquiry.

- an opportunity for the relatives of the victims to participate and, in some cases, to be able to complete the grieving process – relatives of victims often campaign for years trying to obtain an acknowledgement of responsibility for the death of their loved ones, and a public inquiry can facilitate this

- a rare occasion in our diffuse democracy for those who wield power and authority to be made accountable to the public.

LEGAL STATUTES

Public inquires may be set up under a number of different statutes. The statute that is used will influence the scope of the inquiry and its powers. A **judicial inquiry** set up under the *Tribunals of Inquiry (Evidence) Act 1921* is the most powerful form of inquiry, with the judge having more powers than usual to order witnesses to attend and obtain evidence. More commonly, however, inquiries are set up under the statutes governing the public body whose actions are to be considered. For example, the Lawrence inquiry was set up under the *Police Act 1996*.

The format

A typical format is to:

- investigate the circumstances that led to the death or disaster
- take evidence from interested groups or experts as to the existence of other similar events or problems
- take suggestions as to how they could be avoided in the future.

Such inquiries will normally last several months and in some cases several years (eg, the Bloody Sunday inquiry).

> There is no statutory duty on the government to hold a public inquiry for any particular purpose. Where an individual has died, and there has been some form of state involvement or responsibility, Article 2 of the *European Convention on Human Rights* obliges the state to hold an **independent public investigation**. This obligation may be met by the setting up of a public inquiry, or alternatively by the holding of an inquest. (see CHAPTER 18: INQUESTS and CHAPTER 16: HUMAN RIGHTS ACT).

The process

If there are thought to be strong grounds for holding a public inquiry, then there are various stages in the process:

- A request should be made to the government minister with responsibility for the particular subject matter – for example, in the Lawrence case it was the Home Secretary's responsibility.

- If, as is often the case, the minister refuses to hold a public inquiry, then legal advice should be sought.

- There may be grounds for bringing a claim for **judicial review** of the minister's decision in the High Court.

> It should be noted that, in most cases, it will be very difficult to succeed in campaigning for a public inquiry since such decisions invariably involve political considerations, which the courts try to avoid.

LEGAL REPRESENTATION

Arguing for a public inquiry can be a daunting task for many lawyers and legal firms, and demands a huge commitment of time, effort and resources. Plainly some are better equipped than others to undertake such a project, so it is important that the individual or group concerned finds out whether the lawyer has previous experience and whether there is a willingness to ensure a dedicated number of personnel for preparation and research.

FUNDING

Funding will depend on the statute under which the inquiry is established. It is likely to come from either the TREASURY, the LORD CHANCELLOR'S DEPARTMENT (now the DEPARTMENT FOR CONSTITUTIONAL AFFAIRS), the police authority or the government department concerned.

One of the earliest stages will involve the chair of the inquiry making a public statement about its terms of reference, its ambit, and its intended schedule. At this point it will be necessary for you to establish that you are an interested party, that you wish for representation and that you require funding at public expense. These will be matters for the chair to decide.

Procedure

> Once under way the procedure is unusual. It is not a trial. No one is in the dock in that sense. It is not adversarial, more inquisitorial, with the tribunal seeking to establish the truth.

In extreme cases (the Bristol Heart inquiry, for example) all questions are channelled through counsel representing the inquiry itself. In others, all parties have an opportunity to ask questions (provided they are relevant and not repetitious) and to make opening and closing submissions.

Should you be a witness who is not a party – in other words, someone with relevant information – you may also need representation for parts of the inquiry where your information is discussed. The reason for this is the possibility that some act or omission by you could be criticised. You will be given advance notice of this in a **salmon letter** which will detail the allegations and provide you with the necessary documentation.

Public inquiries are not commonly held in other parts of the world. For example, no such thing occurs in the USA, and in South Africa and Latin America the format is more likely to be in the shape of a **truth commission**.

In a society where people feel increasingly alienated and disempowered, the public inquiry is still one of the most effective deterrents against the arbitrary and oppressive exercise of power. It is hardly surprising, therefore, that the very existence of public inquiries excites hostility from the vested interests exposed by their work.

Organisations   i

▶ **ADVICE UK (formerly THE FEDERATION OF INFORMATION AND ADVICE CENTRES)**

12th Floor
New London Bridge House
25 London Bridge Street
London SE1 9ST

Tel: 020 7407 4070
www.fiac.org.uk

▶ **BRITISH AND IRISH OMBUDSMAN ASSOCIATION (BIOA)**

www.bioa.org.uk

Ombudsmen are an independent and impartial means of resolving certain disputes outside the courts. They cover various public and private bodies and look into matters *after* a complaint has been made to the relevant body. This site lists the ombudsmen and other complaint-handling bodies.

► **DEPARTMENT FOR CONSTITUTIONAL AFFAIRS**

Selborne House
54–60 Victoria Street
London SW1E 6QW

Tel: 020 7210 8500
general.queries@dca.gsi.gov.uk
www.dca.gov.uk

► **HOME OFFICE**

Customer Information Service
7th floor, 50 Queen Anne's Gate
London SW1H 9AT

General enquiries (9.00am–5.00pm):
0870 0001585
www.homeoffice.gov.uk

► **JUSTICE**

59 Carter Lane
London EC4V 5AQ

Tel: 020 7329 5100
Fax: 020 7329 5055

admin@justice.org.uk
www.justice.org.uk

► **LAW CENTRES FEDERATION**

Duchess House
18–19 Warren Street
London W1T 5LR

Tel: 020 7387 8570
Fax: 020 7387 8368
info@lawcentres.org.uk
www.lawcentres.org.uk

► **LEGAL SERVICES COMMISSION**

85 Gray's Inn Road
London WC1X 8TX

Tel: 020 7759 0000
www.legalservices.gov.uk
www.justask.org.uk

Regional telephone helplines on various
legal subjects.

► **LIBERTY**

21 Tabard Street
London SE1 4LA

Tel: 020 7403 3888
Fax: 020 7407 5354
info@liberty-human-rights.org.uk
www.liberty-human-rights.org.uk

► **NATIONAL ASSOCIATION OF CITIZENS ADVICE BUREAUX (NACAB)**

Myddelton House
115–123 Pentonville Road
London N1 9LZ

Tel: 020 7833 2181
www.nacab.org.uk

Adviceguide: the National Association
of Citizens Advice Bureaux offers
fact sheets covering issues such as
employment, housing and taxation

www.adviceguide.org.uk

► **NATIONAL CIVIL RIGHTS MOVEMENT (NCRM)**

14 Featherstone Road
Southall
Middlesex UB2 5AA

Tel: 020 8574 0818 or 020 8843 2333
Fax: 020 8813 9734
info@ncrm.org.uk
www.ncrm.org.uk

► **POLICE COMPLAINTS AUTHORITY**

10 Great George Street
London SW1P 3AE

Tel: 020 7273 6450
info@pca.gov.uk
www.pca.gov.uk

26 **Public order**

If a generally law-abiding citizen is ever going to see behind the scenes at the local police station then it's most likely to be because they've been arrested for an offence against public order. Public order legislation covers a wide range of situations from, for example, a row in the street between neighbours about herbaceous border property rights to violent confrontations between the police and protestors; and many people fall foul of it without even knowing that they may be doing something wrong.

WHAT ARE THE OFFENCES?

The offences that people are most commonly arrested for and charged with are contained in the *Public Order Act 1986* and are set out in five sections:

Riot

Riot is a term that is often used by ordinary people to describe things having got out of control. Its technical meaning is that *at least 12 people are gathered together and use or threaten unlawful violence such that a person of reasonable firmness present at the scene would fear for their safety*. All 12 people don't have to be using or threatening violence at the same time.

Prosecutions for riot have been quite rare since the days of the miners' strike back in the 1980s, even if there have been 12 or more people together using or threatening violence. They appear to be reserved for politically motivated gatherings, such as the poll tax demonstrations or the recent Bradford disturbances.

If a person does face trial for the offence then it can only take place in the crown court and cannot be dealt with by magistrates. The sentence for riot is anything up to ten years in prison and anybody being convicted of it, or pleading guilty to it, can expect to get a custodial sentence.

Violent disorder

Violent disorder is basically the same offence as riot, except that only three people need to use or threaten violence. It is very commonly used as a charge these days when things turn nasty at political demonstrations. The offence can be tried in either the magistrates' or crown court and the maximum sentence is five years' imprisonment in the crown court or six months in the magistrates' court. Most people being found guilty or pleading guilty to violent disorder can expect to be sent to prison.

Affray

Affray is basically the same again as riot and violent disorder, except that it is only necessary for one person to threaten violence against another in circumstances where a person of reasonable firmness present at the scene would fear for their safety. That hypothetical person of reasonable firmness does not *actually* have to be at the scene. It is enough that if such a person were there then they would fear for their safety.

The maximum sentence is three years' imprisonment in the crown court or six months' in the magistrates' court. A custodial sentence is not as likely for a conviction for affray as it is for violent disorder and riot, but is nevertheless likely.

Fear of violence

A person is guilty of an offence if they:

- use threatening, abusive or insulting words or behaviour towards another person
- display a sign or similar to the same effect
- intend to cause another person to believe that immediate violence will be used against them or another
- provoke unlawful violence by that other person or another if the other person is likely to believe that such violence would be used or provoked.

> There is no offence of fear or provocation of violence committed if all parties are in a dwelling.

The offence can only be tried in the magistrates' court and the maximum sentence is six months in prison. A prison sentence is not unknown for such offences but is by no means inevitable. Indeed, the range of sentences for adults for such an offence can include:

- **conditional discharge** (where no penalty is imposed provided no further offence is committed within the specified period, such as one year)
- a **fine**
- **community rehabilitation order** (what used to be called a probation order)
- **community punishment order** (in the past called community service)
- **suspended sentence** of imprisonment (a person receives a custodial sentence but is not sent to prison unless they commit another offence within a specified time period, such as a year)
- immediate **sentence of imprisonment**.

Harassment

A person is guilty of an offence if they use threatening, abusive or insulting words or behaviour (or display a sign or similar to the same effect) intending to cause another person harassment, alarm or distress and in fact causes that person such harassment, alarm or distress. The offence can only be tried in the magistrates' court and the maximum penalty is a fine.

Racial aggravation

While some offences can only be tried in the magistrates' court, if they are racially aggravated then different consequences can occur. Those differences were created by *Section 31* of the *Crime and Disorder Act 1998*.

FEAR OR PROVOCATION OF VIOLENCE

If the offence was either motivated by racial hostility, or at the time of the commission of the offence racial hostility was displayed, then the offence can be tried in the crown court and a sentence of up to two years' imprisonment can be imposed.

HARASSMENT, ALARM OR DISTRESS

For a racially aggravated form of such an offence a higher fine can be imposed, but the offence can still only be tried in the magistrates' court.

Minor offences

Usually used by the police when apprehending or charging people following political demonstrations, these include:

- **breach of the peace**
- **obstructing the police.**

> It is important for groups planning rallies, pickets, marches, protests or demonstrations to be aware of these offences and to be prepared in the event of arrest. It is useful for stewards or individuals to keep the name and telephone number of a sympathetic solicitor or advice group to hand.

Legal representation

If you are prosecuted for affray or anything more serious then, provided you do not earn more than a certain amount, you will probably receive **legal aid** and be able to get the services of a solicitor and barrister. Always ask if they have dealt with these kind of cases before, and how often (see CHAPTER 1: FINDING AND MEETING YOUR LAWYER).

With the lesser offences, it is less likely that you will receive legal aid, but you have nothing to lose by going to a solicitor to see if you are eligible. Also, even if you can't get legal aid, not all lawyers are only in business for the money (surprising as that may seem) and some will be prepared to act for you without payment – particularly if you have been arrested during political activity. If the solicitor you first go to is not prepared to do so, then ask them if they think there are any lawyers who might be able to help you without asking for a fee.

Organisations   i

▶ **ADVICE UK (formerly THE FEDERATION OF INFORMATION AND ADVICE CENTRES)**
12th Floor
New London Bridge House
25 London Bridge Street
London SE1 9ST
Tel: 020 7407 4070
www.fiac.org.uk

▶ **BAR PRO BONO UNIT AND BAR IN THE COMMUNITY**
7 Gray's Inn Square
Gray's Inn
London WC1R 5AZ
Bar Pro Bono Unit: 020 7831 9711
Bar in the Community: 020 7841 1341
Fax: 020 7831 9733
enquiries@barprobono.org.uk
www.barprobono.org.uk

▶ **JUSTICE**
59 Carter Lane
London EC4V 5AQ
Tel: 020 7329 5100
Fax: 020 7329 5055
admin@justice.org.uk
www.justice.org.uk

▶ **LAW CENTRES FEDERATION**
Duchess House
18–19 Warren Street
London W1T 5LR
Tel: 020 7387 8570
Fax: 020 7387 8368
info@lawcentres.org.uk
www.lawcentres.org.uk

▶ **LEGAL SERVICES COMMISSION**
85 Gray's Inn Road
London WC1X 8TX
Tel: 020 7759 0000
www.legalservices.gov.uk
www.justask.org.uk
Regional telephone helplines on various legal subjects.

▶ **LIBERTY**

21 Tabard Street
London SE1 4LA

Tel: 020 7403 3888
Fax: 020 7407 5354
info@liberty-human-rights.org.uk
www.liberty-human-rights.org.uk

▶ **NATIONAL ASSOCIATION OF CITIZENS ADVICE BUREAUX (NACAB)**

Myddelton House
115–123 Pentonville Road
London N1 9LZ

Tel: 020 7833 2181
www.nacab.org.uk

Adviceguide: the National Association of Citizens Advice Bureaux offers fact sheets covering issues such as employment, housing and taxation

www.adviceguide.org.uk

▶ **NATIONAL CIVIL RIGHTS MOVEMENT (NCRM)**

14 Featherstone Road
Southall
Middlesex UB2 5AA

Tel: 020 8574 0818 or 020 8843 2333
Fax: 020 8813 9734
info@ncrm.org
www.ncrm.org.uk

▶ **POLICE COMPLAINTS AUTHORITY**

10 Great George Street
London SW1P 3AE

Tel: 020 7273 6450
info@pca.gov.uk
www.pca.gov.uk

▶ **STATEWATCH**

PO Box 1516
London N16 0EW

Tel: 020 8802 1882
Fax: 020 8880 1727
info@statewatch.org
www.statewatch.org

Research papers/regular bulletins on policing, immigration, prisons, Europe, etc.

▶ **THE TREASURY**

www.hm-treasury.gov.uk

▶ **TRADES UNION CONGRESS (TUC)**

Congress House
Great Russell Street
London WC1B 3LS

Tel: 020 7636 4030
info@tuc.org.uk
www.tuc.org.uk

27 **Welfare benefits**

Most people will, at some stage in their life, receive one of the many forms of state benefit. This may be child benefit, paid to the main carer of a child, or a state pension, paid out to people when they have retired. However, the range of benefits available and the rules set out to decide whether a person is entitled to receive them are complicated and subject to frequent changes.

The aim of this chapter is to give an introduction to the sorts of benefits that are paid, with examples of the situations in which you may be able to claim them, and to tell you where you should go to find out more or to make a claim.

This chapter does not give advice on each and every benefit available, so if you think that you may be entitled to a benefit, you should contact one of the organisations listed at the end of the chapter for some independent advice.

Applying for benefits

Benefits are dealt with by the state or by government departments, the main one being the DEPARTMENT FOR WORK AND PENSIONS. This department deals with the overall administration and policy of all social security benefits, except housing benefit and council tax benefit. These two benefits are administered locally and will be dealt with by your local council.

Tax credits are dealt with by the TAX CREDIT OFFICE of the INLAND REVENUE.

To find your local benefits office, try looking in any of the following:

- local telephone directory
- local library
- town hall or other council office (you may have a neighbourhood office which deals with benefits)
- local Citizens Advice Bureau (CAB).

Remember, if you want independent advice about what you may be entitled to and why, you should go to an advice centre that is independent of the council or the DEPARTMENT FOR WORK AND PENSIONS.

What are benefits?

Benefits in the UK are paid to people to:

- replace, supplement or assist with a lost income or a low income
- support or help someone in a particularly difficult situation, such as bringing up a child alone or looking after an elderly relative
- support someone who cannot work because they have a disability.

Some of the most common benefits are:

- income support
- family tax credits
- housing benefits

all of which give financial support to those on a low income or with no income.

Entitlement

Whether or not you are entitled to a benefit depends on both your own personal circumstances and your financial circumstances.

Some examples:

STATUTORY MATERNITY PAY

This is a benefit which is paid as income replacement to women who stop work because they are pregnant or because they have recently had a baby. The main condition is that the woman must have worked for her employer for a certain number of weeks and paid National Insurance contributions before she can receive the benefit.

JOBSEEKER'S ALLOWANCE

This can be paid to someone who is:

- not working full-time themselves, and whose partner is not working full-time either
- capable of work
- not in relevant full-time education
- available for, and actively seeking, work
- below pensionable age
- in the UK
- not receiving income support.

The payment of benefits depends on different criteria, which vary from benefit to benefit.

Types of benefit

Benefits can be divided into the following:

- means-tested benefits
- non-means-tested benefits, which can be either
  - □ contributory
  - □ or non-contributory
- tax credits.

MEANS-TESTED BENEFITS

The main means-tested benefits are:

- income support
- income-based jobseeker's allowance
- housing benefit
- council tax benefit
- health benefits
- some housing renovation grants.

These are benefits which depend on the amount of income, or savings, or other means that you have. Before a benefit is paid to you, you will have to provide details of any income you or your partner receive, from any source, including paid work, savings, income from savings or shares, or from other benefits.

For most benefits, any savings up to £8000 will be discounted, with extra amounts disregarded if you have children.

> If you do not tell the department about a source of income this can in some circumstances amount to **fraud** and can lead to prosecution, so if you are going to make a claim you must make sure that you are very clear about what you need to tell the benefits agency.

Many benefits take into account both your means as the person claiming and the means of your partner. If you are married, then your husband or wife will be your partner, if you are still living together. If you are not married, but living with someone, then they are likely to be considered to be your partner for benefits purposes. If you are in any doubt about this, take independent advice before you talk to the benefits agency.

NON-MEANS-TESTED BENEFITS

Some benefits are payable because you have lost an income, perhaps because you are old, or sick or pregnant. These benefits replace your income.

Other benefits that do not rely on your means are those which are paid to people who have a particular need, for childcare or a disability. You can claim one of these benefits if you can show that you are in the group it is aimed at (eg, that you are pregnant) and that you have paid the necessary National Insurance contributions.

This group of benefits does not depend upon the amount of money that you have, but on whether you have paid National Insurance contributions in the past, or, for non-means-tested non-contributory benefits, whether you are in the category of people who qualify.

NON-MEANS-TESTED CONTRIBUTORY BENEFITS

These are benefits which depend upon you having paid National Insurance contributions for a certain length of time. You do not also have to demonstrate that you are on a low income, because these benefits are not means-tested. The main contributory non-means-tested benefits are:

- contribution-based jobseeker's allowance

- incapacity benefit

- maternity allowance

NON-MEANS-TESTED NON-CONTRIBUTORY BENEFITS

An example of this type of benefit is child benefit. This is paid to the main carer of *every* child under the age of 16, or every child between 16 and 19 who is receiving full-time non-advanced education.

TAX CREDITS

Tax credits are paid to people who are in full-time work as an income top-up. These benefits are means-tested, and are thus paid to those who work but receive low pay. The main benefits are:

- working family tax credits

- disabled person tax credits (see CHAPTER 9: DISABILITY).

Information about benefits

There are lots of different leaflets available, often in post offices, libraries and other public places. You can try ringing or visiting your local council, which may have its own advisers. If there is a Citizens Advice Bureau in your local town, you can ask to see an adviser, or pick up some information leaflets from them.

> The **CHILD POVERTY ACTION GROUP** is a charity which produces a guide to benefits, which explains each benefit, what the conditions are, and how to claim it. The *Welfare Benefits Handbook* is often available in public libraries and is a good starting point for research.

Finding the right Welfare Rights Lawyer

The Citizens Advice Bureau (CAB) is a good place to start when you need advice. If the CAB cannot help you, they should be able to suggest another organisation which can, and if you need a solicitor many CABs will have lists of local solicitors who do welfare rights work.

Find a solicitor with a franchise to do welfare rights work by contacting the **LEGAL SERVICES COMMISSION**. High street solicitors' firms that do legal aid work should also be able to spot welfare rights problems associated with the case and make referrals. However, this does not mean that all legal aid solicitors specialise in welfare rights.

An alternative source of advice and information would be a charity, a trade union or voluntary organisation. Many charities have information about welfare rights for their particular client groups. For example, **HELP THE AGED** has a free telephone helpline for elderly people and their carers, specifically for advice on welfare rights.

Organisations   [i]

▶ **ADVICE UK (formerly THE FEDERATION OF INFORMATION AND ADVICE CENTRES)**
12th Floor
New London Bridge House
25 London Bridge Street
London SE1 9ST
Tel: 020 7407 4070
www.fiac.org.uk

▶ **AGE CONCERN ENGLAND**
Astral House
1268 London Road
London SW16 4ER
Tel: 0800 009966
(seven days a week, 7.00am–7.00pm)
www.ageconcern.org.uk

▶ **CHILD POVERTY ACTION GROUP**
94 White Lion Street
London N1 9PF
Tel: 020 7837 7979
Fax: 020 7837 6414
staff@cpag.demon.co.uk
www.cpag.org.uk

▶ **CHILD SUPPORT AGENCY**
P.O. Box 55
Brierly Hill
West Midlands DY5 1YL
Tel: 08457 133 133
Minicom: 08457 138 924
csa-nel@dwp.gsi.gov.uk
www.csa.gov.uk

▶ **DEPARTMENT FOR WORK AND PENSIONS (DWP)**
Adelphi
1–11 John Adam Street
London WC2N 6HT
Tel: 020 7962 8000
www.dwp.gov.uk

▶ **HELP THE AGED**
207–221 Pentonville Road
London N1 9UZ
Tel: 020 7278 1114
Senior line:
0808 800 6565 *(England and Wales);*
0808 808 7575 *(Northern Ireland)*
Textphone: 0808 269626
Fax: 020 7278 1116
info@helptheaged.org.uk
www.helptheaged.org.uk

▶ **INLAND REVENUE**
www.inlandrevenue.gov.uk

▶ **LAW CENTRES FEDERATION**
Duchess House
18–19 Warren Street
London W1T 5LR
Tel: 020 7387 8570
Fax: 020 7387 8368
info@lawcentres.org.uk
www.lawcentres.org.uk

▶ **LEGAL ACTION GROUP**
242 Pentonville Road
London N1 9UN
Tel: 020 7833 2931
Fax: 020 7837 6094
lag@lag.org.uk
www.lag.org.uk

▶ **LEGAL SERVICES COMMISSION**
85 Gray's Inn Road
London WC1X 8TX
Tel: 020 7759 0000
www.legalservices.gov.uk
www.justask.org.uk
Regional telephone helplines on various legal subjects.

▶ **MATERNITY ALLIANCE**
3rd Floor West
2–6 Northburgh Street
London EC1V 0AY
Tel: 020 7588 8583
Information line: 020 7490 7638
Fax: 020 7014 1350
info@maternityalliance.org.uk
www.maternityalliance.org.uk

▶ **NATIONAL ASSOCIATION OF CITIZENS ADVICE BUREAUX (NACAB)**

Myddelton House
115–123 Pentonville Road
London N1 9LZ

Tel: 020 7833 2181
www.nacab.org.uk

Adviceguide: the National Association of Citizens Advice Bureaux offers fact sheets covering issues such as employment, housing and taxation

www.adviceguide.org.uk

▶ **NATIONAL COUNCIL FOR VOLUNTARY ORGANISATIONS (NCVO)**

Regent's Wharf
8 All Saints Street
London N1 9RL

Tel: 020 7713 6161
Helpdesk: 0800 2 798 798
ncvo@ncvo-vol.org.uk
www.ncvo-vol.org.uk

▶ **SOLICITORS FOR THE ELDERLY**

PO Box 9
Peterborough
Cambridgeshire PE4 7WN

Tel/Fax: 01733 326769
info@solicitorsfortheelderly.com
www.solicitorsfortheelderly.com

Further reading

Elderly Client Adviser Magazine

Ark Group Ltd

2nd Floor, 86/88 Upper Richmond Road
Putney
London SW15 2SH

Tel: 020 8785 2700
Fax: 020 8785 9373

Magazine for professionals advising on the area of elderly client law and services.

The Welfare Benefits Handbook
Published by CPAG; ISBN: 1901698513

The contributors

AUTHOR

Michael Mansfield QC was born in 1941 and educated at Highgate School and Keele University. Called to the bar in 1967, he established his own set of chambers, *Tooks Court*, in 1984 and became Queen's Counsel in 1989. Michael has represented defendants in criminal trials, appeals and inquiries in some of the most controversial legal cases the country has seen, particularly where issues of civil liberty have arisen. Amongst the most recent are: Barry George, accused of killing TV presenter Jill Dando; the family of Stephen Lawrence, both in the private prosecution for murder and the public inquiry; and the families of victims at the ongoing Bloody Sunday inquiry in Derry and London. He also chaired an inquiry into the 'Shoot to Kill' policy in the North of Ireland at Cullyhanna in 1991.

Michael has represented many families at inquests, including the *Marchioness* disaster, the Deptford/New Cross fire; the Lockerbie, Omagh, Dublin and Monaghan bombings; and, soon, Mohammed Al Fayed in his pursuit of the truth surrounding the death of his son, Dodi, and Princess Diana in Paris in 1997.

Michael's past clients include: the Orgreave miners who were unjustly accused of riot during the miners' strike in 1984; the Birmingham Six, who were released in 1991, nearly sixteen years after being wrongly convicted; those in the ABC Official Secrets case and the Operation Julie drugs trial; James Hanratty, hanged in 1962 for murder; the 'spy' Michael Bettany; Frank Critchlow and the Mangrove; the Bradford Twelve and the Newham Seven against the National Front; robbers in the Knightsbridge heist; Colin Wallace; the 'Camberwell', 'Torso', 'Big H' and M25 murder trials; Judith Ward; Iraqi dissidents fleeing Saddam Hussein; Turkish and Kurdish exiles; Palestinians charged with the Israeli embassy bombing in London; Angela Cannings, the so-called cot death mother; and, soon, Ruth Ellis, the last woman to be hanged in Britain.

Michael is married to Yvette Vanson and has six children – Jonathan, Anna, Louise, Leo, Kieron and Freddy – and three grandchildren (so far!): Larissa, Elyse and Myles.

Tooks Court Chambers brings together over seventy barristers under the leadership of Michael Mansfield QC, who share two fundamental aims: social justice for the marginalised and the highest quality of representation for all failed by the justice process. The chambers has a reputation for high profile civil liberties work and specialises in actions against the police, crime, discrimination, employment, family, immigration and public law. clerks@tooks.law.co.uk

EDITOR

Yvette Vanson was for twenty years an independent producer/director of contentious award-winning documentaries: described as 'television of a high order, well crafted and aimed unerringly to engage both intellect and emotions' (*Financial Times*). Including: *The Murder of Stephen Lawrence*, Bafta winner 2000; *Kentucky Fried Medicine*; *The Battle for Orgreave*; *Presumed Guilty*, with Michael Mansfield; *Two Boys from Bangkok*; *The Birmingham Wives*; *Making Advances*, RTS Best Adult Education Series on sexual harassment at work. Also developed and managed the *East Sussex Social Services Media Unit*, making training videos for social services staff nationally and internationally. In addition, produced many training and promotional videos for major charities and NGOs, covering issues as diverse as disability, rural transport, children in care, senile dementia and trade union rights. Produced the first DHSS film on the plight of carers. An actress for several years, in theatre and on TV, Yvette returned to study as a mature student and gained a BA Hons 1st class in Social Science before becoming a TV producer. She has been married to Michael Mansfield for nineteen years; they have a son, Freddy.

Lucy Barker is the CEO of Barker Brooks, which she set up in 1999. Barker Brooks has published some of the most successful legal and business publications, including *The STEP Journal*, *Legal & Medical* and *The Insider*. It also organises major conferences, events and award ceremonies, aimed at the professional market, and recently launched Etc!, a magazine aimed at 16–18 year-old school-leavers with a readership of over 150,000. Barker Brooks is now developing new titles and products for the student market. Lucy Barker worked with Michael Mansfield and Yvette Vanson on developing *The Home Lawyer*.

CONTRIBUTORS

Navtej Singh Ahluwalia (LLM, International Human Rights Law) is a barrister practising from Tooks Court Chambers in immigration, asylum and public law. Former assistant director Advice on Individual Rights in Europe (AIRE Centre), a specialist centre providing legal advice on EU and ECHR law, and representation before the European Court of Human Rights. Former head of international legal department, Sikh Human Rights Group.

Jonathan Manning and **Annette Cafferkey** are barristers specialising in housing and local government law and are members of **Arden Chambers**. It was founded in April 1993 in order to provide a specialist centre for the practice of housing and local government law, corresponding with the authoritative publications edited or authored by Andrew Arden QC and now also by various other members of chambers. Today, the chambers specialises in all aspects of housing, local government, property and planning law. It provides a comprehensive advisory and advocacy service on behalf of individuals and public, social and private bodies, including: local and other public authorities, registered social landlords, trusts, owner-occupiers, leaseholders, tenants and the homeless. It handles cases in all courts and tribunals, as well as arbitrations and inquiries. www.ardenchambers.com

Nick Armstrong is a barrister practising from Tooks Court Chambers. Formerly a solicitor in the public law unit at Irwin Mitchell and, before that, holder of a postdoctoral research fellowship at the Nottingham Law School. PhD (1995) in civil justice. Frequent lecturer and writer on public law, civil justice and the legal profession, co-editor of *Jordans' Civil Court Service Newsletter*, assistant editor of *Jordans' Human Rights*, visiting lecturer in public law at the College of Law, London, advocacy trainer for the Nottingham Law School.

Susan Barrett (BA Hons, English, Bristol) worked for over a decade as a television researcher and director on a variety of magazine programmes (tackling consumer issues and the rights of the elderly, amongst others), documentaries and children's programming for the BBC, ITV, Channel 4 and Film 4. She continues to work on a freelance basis as a feature film script reader/editor and writer for television. Susan has recently completed her first novel.

Sandhya Drew is a barrister specialising in equality and human rights law based at Tooks Court Chambers. She has advised various NGOs including Friends of the Earth and Save the Children. She assisted David Morris in the preparation of the submissions made in the McLibel case on damage to the environment. She has worked on environmental cases in India. She lives in Oxford and is a member of the Green Party. Chief thanks to Don O'Neal and Craig Simmons for their assistance.

Anna Harding is a barrister in the **Mind Legal Unit.** Mind is a charity concerned with the legal and civil rights of mental health service users. It provides general information and advice on mental health matters via the information line and its many publications. It has a small specialist legal team, which responds to queries from advocates, users, carers and other legal professionals. It does not generally take on cases, but provides initial advice and information in the fields of mental health, community care and disability discrimination. The team also works closely with many lawyers who specialise in mental health law. It provides a database of lawyers who work in mental health law, and those who specialise in different areas but who are willing to take cases with a mental health element. Details of these lawyers can be made available to people who approach the unit for advice. Most requests for advice arrive via the legal advice line, which is open on Monday, Wednesday and Friday afternoons between 2.00pm and 4.30pm. This is accessible via the main switchboard number. The unit also responds to written and email queries. Mind relies on donations to carry out its work. www.mind.org.uk

Martin Huseyin (BA Hons, Sussex; Dip Law, Westminster). Called to the bar (Inner Temple) 1988. Practising in criminal law, public law and police and prison-related litigation from Tooks Court Chambers. Undertakes *pro bono* work for families at inquests and on criminal miscarriage of justice cases. Member of the Criminal Bar Association, Lawyers for Liberty and Haldane Society of Socialist Lawyers.

Birinder Kang (MPhil, Cantab) specialises in children's cases, both public and private law (including child abduction) and domestic violence. She practises at all levels, including the High Court, and has a particular interest in the areas of race and human rights, on which she has provided training seminars and addressed national conferences.

Tim Moloney was called to the bar in 1993 and is a member of Tooks Court Chambers specialising in criminal law. He has been and continues to be instructed in a number of trials concerning public order issues.

Andrew Norris is a barrister at Hogarth Chambers, Lincoln's Inn, and specialises in intellectual property, media and entertainment law. He deals with disputes involving confidential information, patents, copyrights, designs, brands and the rights of performers and businesses in the music and entertainment industry. He graduated from the University of St Andrews with an honours degree in biological sciences before being called to the bar in 1995.

Catherine Rayner was called to the bar in 1989, after several years as a lecturer and researcher in Law. She practises employment law at Tooks Court Chambers, where she specialises in all aspects of discrimination work, mainly for applicants supported by trade unions. Catherine worked for many years in law and policy in a variety of public and voluntary sector organisations including a London law centre and the National Council for Voluntary Organisations. She continues to combine practice with training and writing for a variety of audiences.

Patrick Roche (MA, Modern History, Oxford) qualified as a barrister in 1977. He is deputy head of chambers at Tooks Court Chambers. He has a wide-ranging practice specialising in crime, where his experience includes leading and appellate work, public law, especially in the areas of actions against the police, prisoners' rights and inquests, and family work. Patrick has lectured on the impact of the Human Rights Act and is a member of the Bar Human Rights Committee.

RSPCA: Sally Ann Case is a qualified barrister and is currently employed by the Royal Society for the Prevention of Cruelty to Animals as their legal department's commercial campaign lawyer. Called in 1996, she has been employed by the RSPCA since 2000.

Martin Soorjoo is a barrister at Tooks Court Chambers. Called in 1990, he specialises in human rights and administrative law, immigration and asylum, prisoners' rights, extradition and mental health. Reported cases of particular significance include those which led to a change in the way the Home Office calculates terms of imprisonment and to a duty on the state to provide an independent public inquiry in death in custody cases. He was junior counsel for the family of Stephen Lawrence during the Lawrence inquiry and other actions. In addition, he has taken cases to Europe involving breaches of Articles 3, 6 and 8 of the ECHR. Credited in *Chambers Guide to the Legal Profession* as a leading junior, 'thorough, committed and imaginative' whom 'you can rely on for original solutions' and by *The Lawyer* as 'very efficient, approachable and knowledgeable'. Former member of ILPA executive committee and course trainer for ILPA, JCWI and the Refugee Council. Regular contributor to BBC legal network series. Co-author of *Immigration Law Practitioner's 'Best Practice Guide to Asylum'*.

Hugh Southey was admitted as a solicitor in 1991 but transferred to the bar in 1996 and is a member of Tooks Court Chambers. As a solicitor he headed the immigration and crime department at Glazer Delmar. Since transferring to the bar, Hugh has specialised in public law in the fields of human rights, prison law, crime, mental health and immigration. Hugh is listed in *Chambers Guide to the Legal Profession* as a leading junior in human rights and immigration and commended for his 'dedicated approach'. In *Legal Business* he is listed as an expert in civil liberties. Hugh undertakes a considerable amount of *pro bono* work on American death penalty cases.

Peter Wilcock (LLB, LSE) is a barrister practising from Tooks Court Chambers. Called in 1988, his areas of practice are criminal defence and appeals, civil actions against police, inquests and mental health. Publications: 'Crime and Disorder Act', *LAG*, Jan 1999; 'Fitness to Plead Procedure: An Adequate Protection?', *NLJ*, 2002; 'Pendleton: The Principle', *NLJ*, 2002. Member of the Society of Labour Lawyers.

Thanks to Iftikhar Manzoor, of Irwin Mitchell solicitors.

Directory of organisations

▶ **ACTION FOR THE PROPER REGULATION OF PRIVATE HOSPITALS (APROP)**
Tel: 01932 849403

▶ **ACTION FOR VICTIMS OF MEDICAL ACCIDENTS**
44 High Street
Croydon CRO 1YB
Tel: 020 8686 8333
www.avma.co.uk

▶ **ACTION ON ELDER ABUSE**
Helpline: 0808 808 8141
aea@ace.org.uk
www.elderabuse.org

▶ **ADVICE ON INDIVIDUAL RIGHTS IN EUROPE**
The AIRE Centre
3rd Floor, 17 Red Lion Square
London WC1R 4QH
Advice line: 020 7831 3850
info@airecentre.org
www.airecentre.org

▶ **ADVICE UK (formerly THE FEDERATION OF INFORMATION AND ADVICE CENTRES)**
12th Floor
New London Bridge House
25 London Bridge Street
London SE1 9ST
Tel: 020 7407 4070
www.fiac.org.uk

▶ **ADVISORY CENTRE FOR EDUCATION (ACE) LTD**
1c Aberdeen Studios
22 Highbury Grove
London N5 2DQ
General advice line: 0808 800 5793
www.ace-ed.org.uk

▶ **ADVISORY SERVICE FOR SQUATTERS**
2 St Paul's Road
Islington
London N1 2QN
Tel: 020 7359 8814 or 0845 644 5814
advice@squat.freeserve.co.uk
www.squat.freeserve.co.uk

▶ **AGE CONCERN ENGLAND**
Astral House
1268 London Road
London SW16 4ER
Tel: 0800 009966
(seven days a week 7.00am–7.00pm)
www.ageconcern.org.uk

▶ **ALLIANCE FOR INCLUSIVE EDUCATION (formerly INTEGRATION ALLIANCE)**
Unit 2, Ground Floor
70 South Lambeth Road
London SW8 1RL
Tel: 020 7735 5277
www.allfie.org.uk

▶ **AMNESTY INTERNATIONAL**
99–119 Rosebery Avenue
London EC1R 4RE
Tel: 020 7814 6200
Fax: 020 7833 1510
information@amnesty.org.uk
www.amnesty.org.uk

▶ **ANIMAL DEFENDERS**
261 Goldhawk Road
London W12 9PE
Tel: 020 8846 9777
Fax: 020 8846 9712
info@animaldefenders.org.uk
www.animaldefenders.org.uk

▶ **APEX CHARITABLE TRUST**
St Alphage House
Wingate Annexe
2 Fore Street
London EC2Y 5DA
Tel: 020 7638 5931
Fax: 020 7638 5977
jobcheck@apextrust.com
www.apextrust.com

▶ **ARBITRATION AND
CONCILIATION SERVICE (ACAS)**
Brandon House
180 Borough High Street
London SE1 1LW
National ACAS helpline: 08457 47 47 47
www.acas.org.uk

▶ **ASSOCIATION OF
BRITISH TRAVEL AGENTS (ABTA)**
68–71 Newman Street
London W1T 3AH
Tel: 020 7637 2444
Fax: 020 7637 0713
www.abtanet.com

▶ **ASSOCIATION OF
PERSONAL INJURY LAWYERS (APIL)**
11 Castle Quay
Castle Boulevard
Nottingham NG7 1FW
Tel: 0115 958 0585
Fax: 0115 958 0885
mail@apil.com
www.apil.com

▶ **ASSOCIATION OF PRISONERS**
www.associationofprisoners.org.uk

▶ **ASYLUM AID**
28 Commercial Street
London E1 6LS
Tel: 020 7377 5123
Fax: 020 7247 7789
advice@asylumaid.org.uk
www.asylumaid.org.uk

▶ **AUTOMOBILE ASSOCIATION (AA)**
Contact Centre
Carr Ellison House
William Armstrong Drive
Newcastle upon Tyne NE4 7YA
Tel: 0870 600 0371
(24 hours a day, seven days a week)
Fax: 0191 235 5111
www.theaa.com

▶ **BAR PRO BONO UNIT AND
BAR IN THE COMMUNITY**
7 Gray's Inn Square
Gray's Inn
London WC1R 5AZ
Bar Pro Bono Unit: 020 7831 9711
Bar in the Community: 020 7841 1341
Fax: 020 7831 9733
enquiries@barprobono.org.uk
www.barprobono.org.uk

▶ **BLUE CROSS HQ**
Shilton Road
Burford
Oxfordshire OX18 4PF
Tel: 01993 825500
Fax: 01993 823083
www.thebluecross.org.uk

▶ **BRITISH DYSLEXIA ASSOCIATION**
98 London Road
Reading RG1 5AU
*Helpline (Monday to Friday 10.00am–12.45pm
and 2.00–4.45pm):* 0118 966 8271
Fax: 0118 935 1927
admin@bda-dyslexia.demon.co.uk
www.bda-dyslexia.org.uk

▶ **BRITISH EPILEPSY ASSOCIATION**
New Anstey House
Gate Way Drive
Yeadon
Leeds LS19 7XY
Free helpine: 0808 800 5050
From abroad: 0113 210 8850
helpline@epilepsy.org.uk
www.epilepsy.org.uk

▶ **BRITISH HEART FOUNDATION**
14 Fitzhardinge Street
London W1H 6DH
Tel: 020 7935 0185
Fax: 020 7486 5820
www.bhf.org.uk

▶ **BRITISH AND IRISH OMBUDSMAN
ASSOCIATION (BIOA)**
www.bioa.org.uk

▶ **BRITISH MEDICAL ASSOCIATION
(BMA)**
BMA House
Tavistock Square
London WC1H 9JP
Tel: 020 7387 4499
Fax: 020 7383 6400
info.web@bma.org.uk
www.bma.org.uk

▶ **BRITISH SAFETY COUNCIL**
70 Chancellors Road
London W6 9RS
Tel: 020 8741 1231
Fax: 020 8741 4555
www.britishsafetycouncil.org

▶ **BRITISH VETERINARY ASSOCIATION (BVA)**
7 Mansfield Street
London W1G 9NQ
Tel: 020 76366541
Fax: 020 74362970
bvahq@bva.co.uk
www.bva.co.uk

▶ **BROADCASTING STANDARDS COMMISSION**
7 The Sanctuary
London SW1P 3JS
Tel: 020 7808 1000
Fax: 020 7233 0397
bsc@bsc.org.uk
www.bsc.org.uk

▶ **CAMPAIGN AGAINST DOMESTIC VIOLENCE (CADV)**
PO Box 2371
London E1 5NQ
Tel: 020 8520 5881
Fax: 020 8988 8767
enquiries@cadv.org.uk
www.cadv.org.uk

▶ **CAMPAIGN AGAINST RACISM AND FASCISM (CARF)**
BM Box 8784
London WC1N 3XX
Tel: 020 7837 1450
info@carf.demon.co.uk
www.carf.demon.co.uk

▶ **CAMPAIGN FOR STATE EDUCATION (CASE)**
158 Durham Road
London SW20 0DG
Tel: 020 8844 8206
www.casenet.org.uk

▶ **CENTRAL ARBITRATION COMMITTEE (CAC)**
Third Floor, Discovery House
28–42 Banner Street
London EC1Y 8QE
Tel: 020 7251 9747
Fax: 020 7251 3114
enquiries@cac.gov.uk
www.cac.gov.uk

▶ **CENTRAL AUTHORITY FOR ENGLAND AND WALES**
The Child Abduction Unit
Lord Chancellor's Department
81 Chancery Lane
London WC2A 1DD
Tel: 020 7911 7045 / 7047
www.offsol.demon.co.uk

▶ **CENTRAL AUTHORITY FOR NORTHERN IRELAND**
Northern Ireland Courts Service
Windsor House
9–15 Bedford Street
Belfast BT2 7LT
Tel: 02890 328594
www.nics.gov.uk

▶ **CENTRE FOR ADOLESCENT REHABILITATION (C-FAR)**
Burdon Grange
Burdon Lane
Highampton
Devon EX21 5LX
Tel: 01409 231 665
Fax: 01409 231 593
info@c-far.org.uk
www.c-far.org.uk

▶ **CENTRE FOR DISPUTE RESOLUTION**
1 Harbour Exchange Square
London E14 9GB
Tel: 020 7536 6000
Fax: 020 7536 6001
info@cedr.co.uk
www.cedr.co.uk

▶ **CENTRE FOR STUDIES ON INCLUSIVE EDUCATION (CSIE)**
New Redland
Frenchay Campus
Coldharbour Lane
Bristol BS16 1QG
Tel: 0117 328 4007
Fax: 0117 328 4005

▶ **CENTREPOINT**
Neil House
7 Whitechapel Road
London E1 1DU
Tel: 020 7426 5300
Fax: 020 7426 5301
www.centrepoint.org.uk

▶ **CHARITIES AID FOUNDATION**
Kings Hill
West Malling
Kent ME19 4TA
Tel: 01732 520 000
Fax: 01732 520 001
enquiries@cafonline.org
www.cafonline.org

▶ **CHARTER 88**
18a Victoria Park Square
London E2 9PF
Tel: 020 888 6088
Fax: 020 8880 6089
info@charter88.org.uk
www.charter88.org.uk

▶ **CHARTERED INSTITUTE
OF ARBITRATORS**
International Arbitration Centre
12 Bloomsbury Square
London WC1A 2LP
Tel: 020 7421 7444
Fax: 020 7404 4023
info@arbitrators.org
www.arbitrators.org

▶ **CHARTERED INSTITUTE
OF PATENT ATTORNEYS**
95 Chancery Lane
London WC2A 1DT
Tel: 0207 7405 9450
mail@cipa.org.uk
www.cipa.org.uk

▶ **CHILD BRAIN INJURY TRUST**
The Radcliffe Infirmary
Woodstock Road
Oxford OX2 6HE
Tel: 01865 552467
info@cbituk.org
www.cbituk.org

▶ **CHILD POVERTY ACTION GROUP**
94 White Lion Street
London N1 9PF
Tel: 020 7837 7979
Fax: 020 7837 6414
staff@cpag.demon.co.uk
www.cpag.org.uk

▶ **CHILD SUPPORT AGENCY**
P.O. Box 55
Brierly Hill
West Midlands DY5 1YL
Tel: 08457 133 133
Minicom: 08457 138 924
csa-nel@dwp.gsi.gov.uk
www.csa.gov.uk

▶ **CHILDREN AND FAMILY COURT
ADVISORY AND SUPPORT SERVICE
(CAFCASS)**
2nd Floor, Newspaper House
8–16 Great New Street
London
EC4A 3BN
Tel: 020 7210 4400
Fax: 020 7210 4422
webenquiries@cafcass.gov.uk
www.cafcass.gov.uk

▶ **CHILDREN'S LEGAL CENTRE**
University of Essex
Wivenhoe Park
Colchester
Essex CO4 3SQ
Advice line: 01206 873820
www.essex.ac.uk

▶ **CITIZEN'S ADVICE BUREAU**
see NATIONAL ASSOCIATION OF CITIZENS
ADVICE BUREAUX (NACAB)

▶ **COMMISSION FOR
RACIAL EQUALITY (CRE)**
St Dunstan's House
201–211 Borough High Street
London SE1 1GZ
Tel: 020 7939 0000
Fax: 020 7939 0001
info@cre.gov.uk
www.cre.gov.uk

▶ **COMMUNITY LEGAL SERVICE**
www.justask.org.uk *for the online Directory
and legal information and advice.*
Tel: 0845 608 1122
(all calls charged at local rate)
minicom: 0845 609 6677

► **COMMUNITY LIAISON UNIT**

G55 Foreign and Commonwealth Office
Old Admiralty Building
London SW1A 2PA

Tel: 020 7008 0230/0135
clu@fco.gov.uk
www.fco.gov.uk

► **COMPASSION IN WORLD FARMING**

Charles House
5A Charles Street
Petersfield
Hampshire GU32 3EH

Tel: 01730 264208 / 268863
Fax: 01730 260791
compassion@ciwf.co.uk

► **COMPASSIONATE FRIENDS**

Helpline: 01179 539 639
www.compassionatefriends.org
www.tcf.org.uk

► **CONSUMERS' ASSOCIATION**

2 Marylebone Road
London NW1 4DF

Tel: 020 7770 7062/7373

► **CONTACT A FAMILY**

209–211 City Road
London EC1V 1JN

Tel: 020 7608 8700
Fax: 020 7608 8701
www.cafamily.org.uk

Links up parents of children with
learning difficulties.

► **COUNCIL FOR DISABLED CHILDREN**

8 Wakeley Street
London EC1V 7QE

Tel: 020 7843 6000
Fax: 020 7278 9512
www.ncb.org.uk

► **COURT OF PROTECTION
PUBLIC GUARDIANSHIP OFFICE**

Archway Tower
2 Junction Road
London N19 5SZ

Tel: 0845 330 2900
Fax: 020 7664 7705
custserv@guardianship.gov.uk
www.guardianship.gov.uk

► **COURT SERVICE CUSTOMER UNIT**

Southside
105 Victoria Street
London SW1 6QT

Tel: 020 7210 2269
Court Service disability helpline:
0800 358 3506
www.courtservice.gov.uk

► **CRIMINAL CASES
REVIEW COMMISSION**

Alpha Tower
Suffolk Street
Queensway
Birmingham B1 1TT

Tel: 0121 633 1800
Fax: 0121 633 1804/1823
info@ccrc.gov.uk
www.ccrc.gov.uk

► **CRIMINAL DEFENCE SERVICE**

www.legalservices.gov.uk/cds/index.htm

► **CRIMINAL INJURIES
COMPENSATION AUTHORITY (CICA)**

Tay House
300 Bath Street
Glasgow G2 4LN

Tel: 0141 331 2726
Fax: 0141 331 2287
Advice line: 0800 358 3601
www.cica.gov.uk

► **CRISIS**

64 Commercial Street
London E1 6LT

Tel: 0870 011 3335
Fax: 0870 011 3336
enquiries@crisis.org.uk
www.crisis.org.uk

► **CROWN ESTATES COMMISSIONERS**

www.crownestate.co.uk

London Office:
The Crown Estate
16 Carlton House Terrace
London SW1Y 5AH

Tel: 020 7210 4377
Fax: 020 7210 4236
pr@crownestate.co.uk

Edinburgh Office:
The Crown Estate
6 Bell's Brae
Edinburgh EH4 3BJ

Tel: 0131 260 6070
cescotland@crownestate.co.uk

▶ **CROWN PROSECUTION SERVICE (CPS)**
www.cps.gov.uk

▶ **CRUSE – BEREAVEMENT CARE**
126 Sheen Road
Richmond
Surrey TW9 1UR
Helpline: 0808 808 1677
www.crusebereavementcare.org.uk

▶ **HM CUSTOMS AND EXCISE**
National Advice Line: 0845 010 9000
+44 208 929 0152 *for international callers*
www.hmce.gov.uk

▶ **DEPARTMENT FOR CONSTITUTIONAL AFFAIRS**
Selborne House
54–60 Victoria Street
London SW1E 6QW
Tel: 020 7210 8500
general.queries@dca.gsi.gov.uk
www.dca.gov.uk

▶ **DEPARTMENT FOR EDUCATION AND SKILLS**
Tel: 0870 000 2288
Fax: 01928 794 248
info@dfes.gsi.gov.uk
www.dfes.gov.uk

▶ **DEPARTMENT OF HEALTH**
Richmond House
75 Whitehall
London SW1A 2NL
Tel: 020 7210 4850
dhmail@doh.gsi.gov.uk
www.doh.gov.uk

▶ **DEPARTMENT OF TRADE AND INDUSTRY**
DTI Enquiry Unit
1 Victoria Street
London SW1H 0ET
Tel: 020 7215 5000
dti.enquiries@dti.gsi.gov.uk
www.dti.gov.uk

▶ **DEPARTMENT FOR WORK AND PENSIONS (DWP)**
Adelphi
1–11 John Adam Street
London WC2N 6HT
Tel: 020 7962 8000
www.dwp.gov.uk

▶ **DEPRESSION ALLIANCE**
Tel: 020 7633 0557
www.depressionalliance.org

▶ **DIAL UK**
www.dialuk.org.uk

▶ **DISABILITY LAW SERVICE**
39–45 Cavell Street
London E1 2BP
Tel: 020 7791 9800
Fax: 020 7791 9802
advice@dls.org.uk

▶ **DISABILITY RIGHTS COMMISSION**
Freepost MID02164
Stratford-upon-Avon CV37 9BR
Helpline: 08457 622 633
enquiry@drc-gb.org
www.drc-gb.org

▶ **DISABILITY WALES**
Wernddu Court
Caerphilly Business Park
Van Road
Caerphilly CF83 3ED
Wales
Tel: 029 2088 7325
Fax: 029 2088 8702
www.dwac.demon.co.uk

▶ **DISCRIMINATION LAW ASSOCIATION**
PO Box 6715
Rushden
Northamptonshire NN10 9WL
Tel/Fax: 01933 412 337
info@discrimination-law.org.uk
www.discrimination-law.org.uk

▶ **DOWN'S SYNDROME EDUCATIONAL TRUST / SARAH DUFFEN CENTRE**
The Sarah Duffen Centre
Belmont Street
Southsea PO5 1NA
Tel: 023 9282 4261
Fax: 023 9282 4265
www.downsed.org

▶ **DRIVER AND VEHICLE LICENSING AGENCY (DVLA)**
Customer Enquiries (**Drivers**) Unit
DVLC
Swansea SA6 7JL
Tel: 0870 240 0009
Fax: 01792 783071
drivers.dvla@gtnet.gov.uk
www.dvla.gov.uk

▶ **DRIVER AND VEHICLE LICENSING AGENCY (DVLA)**

Customer Enquiries (**Vehicles**) Unit
DVLC
Swansea SA99 1BL

Tel: 0870 240 0010
Fax: 01792 782793
vehicles.dvla@gtnet.gov.uk
www.dvla.gov.uk

▶ **DYSLEXIA INSTITUTE**

Broom Hall
8–10 Broom Hall Road
Sheffield S10 2DR

Tel: 0114 281 5905
www.dyslexia-inst.org.uk

▶ **EARTHRIGHTS CHARITY**

Jamie Woolley
41 Rupert Road
Sheffield SR7 1RN

Tel: 01142 205575 / 020 8977 7413
www.earthrights.org.uk

▶ **EARTHRIGHTS SOLICITORS**

Little Orchard
School Lane
Molehill Green
Takeley
Essex CM22 6PJ

Tel: 01279 870391
earthrights@gn.apc.org

▶ **EMPLOYMENT APPEAL TRIBUNAL**

Audit House
58 Victoria Embankment
London EC4Y 0DS

Tel: 020 7273 1040
Enquiry line: 020 7273 1041
Fax: 020 7273 1045
www.employmentappeals.gov.uk

▶ **EMPLOYMENT SOLICITORS ONLINE**

www.employment-solicitors.co.uk

▶ **ENVIRONMENT AGENCY**

www.environment-agency.gov.uk

▶ **ENVIRONMENTAL LAW ALLIANCE WORLDWIDE (E-LAW)**

1877 Garden Avenue
Eugene OR 97403
USA

elawus@elaw.org
www.elaw.org

▶ **ENVIRONMENTAL LAW FOUNDATION**

Suite 309, 16 Baldwin's Gardens
Hatton Square
London EC1N 7RJ

Tel: 020 7404 1030
Fax: 020 7404 1032
info@elflaw.org
www.elflaw.org

▶ **EQUAL OPPORTUNITIES COMMISSION (EOC)**

Arndale House
Arndale Centre
Manchester M4 3EQ

Tel: 0845 601 5901
Fax: 0161 838 1733
info@eoc.org.uk
www.eoc.org.uk

▶ **EUROGROUP**

www.eurogroupanimalwelfare.org

▶ **EUROPEAN COUNCIL ON REFUGEES AND EXILES**

ECRE Secretariat
Clifton Centre
Unit 22, 3rd Floor, 110 Clifton Street
London EC2A 4HT

Tel: 020 7729 5152
Fax: 020 7729 5141
ecre@ecre.org

▶ **EUROPEAN PATENT OFFICE**

Erhardstrasse 27
D-80331 München
Germany

Tel: 00 49 89 23 9 90
www.epo.org

▶ **FAIR TRIALS ABROAD**

Bench House
Ham Street
Richmond
Surrey TW10 7HR

Tel: 020 8332 2800
Fax: 020 8332 2810
www.f-t-a.freeserve.co.uk

▶ **FEDERATION OF BLACK HOUSING ORGANISATIONS (FBHO)**

1 King Edwards Road
London E9 7SF

Tel: 020 8533 7053
Fax: 020 8985 9166
www.fbho.org.uk

► **FIELD**

52–53 Russell Square
London WC1B 4HP

Tel: 020 7637 7950
Fax: 020 7637 7951
field@field.org.uk

► **FINANCIAL OMBUDSMAN SERVICE (formerly BANKING OMBUDSMAN)**

South Quay Plaza
183 Marsh Wall
London E14 9SR

Helpline: 0845 080 1800
www.financial-ombudsman.org.uk

► **FOREIGN AND COMMONWEALTH OFFICE**

King Charles Street
London SW1A 2AH

Consular enquiries (not visas):
020 7008 0218
Travel advice: 0870 606 0290
Visa enquiries: 020 7008 8438
www.fco.gov.uk

► **FREE REPRESENTATION UNIT (FRU)**

Fourth Floor, Peer House
8–14 Verulam Street
London WC1X 8LZ

www.fru.org.uk

Please note that the FRU does NOT deal with members of the public directly.

► **FRIENDS OF THE EARTH**

26–28 Underwood Street
London N1 7JQ

Tel: 020 7490 1555
Fax: 020 7490 0881
www.foe.co.uk

► **FRONTLINE HOUSING ADVICE**

1st Floor
Elmfield House
5 Stockwell Mews
London SW9 9GX

Tel: 020 7501 9573

► **GENERAL COUNCIL OF THE BAR**

3 Bedford Row
London WC1R 4DB

Tel: 020 7242 0082
Records Office: 020 7242 0934
Fax: 020 7831 9217
www.barcouncil.org.uk

► **GENERAL DENTAL COUNCIL**

37 Wimpole Street
London W1G 8DQ

Tel: 020 7887 3800
Fax: 020 7224 3294
www.gdc-uk.org

► **GENERAL MEDICAL COUNCIL**

178 Great Portland Street
London W1W 5JE

Tel: 020 7580 7642
www.gmc-uk.org

► **GREATER LONDON AUTHORITY (GLA)**

City Hall
The Queen's Walk
London SE1 2AA

Tel: 020 7983 4000
www.london.gov.uk

► **GREENPEACE UK**

Canonbury Villas
London N1 2PN

Tel: 0207 865 8100
Fax: 020 7865 8200
info@uk.greenpeace.org
www.greenpeace.org

► **HEAD INJURY RE-EDUCATION (HIRE)**

Manor Farm House
Wendlebury
Bicester
Oxfordshire OX25 2PW

Tel: 01869 324 339
Fax: 01869 234 683
www.headinjuryreeducation.org.uk

► **HEADWAY**

4 King Edward Court
King Edward Street
Nottingham NG1 1EW

Tel: 0115 924 0800
Fax: 0115 958 4446
enquiries@headway.org.uk
www.headway.org.uk

► **HEALTH AND SAFETY EXECUTIVE**

Postal enquiries:
HSE Infoline
Caerphilly Business Park
Caerphilly CF83 3GG

Infoline (Monday to Friday, 8.30am to 5.00pm):
08701 545500

Fax: 02920 859260
hseinformationservices@natbrit.com
www.hse.gov.uk

► **HEALTH SERVICE OMBUDSMAN**
Millbank Tower
Millbank
London SW1P 4QP
Tel: 020 7217 4051
Fax: 020 7217 4000
ohsc.enquiries@ombudsman.gsi.gov.uk
www.ombudsman.org.uk

► **HELP AND ADVICE FOR
RELATIVES OF PRISONERS (HARP)**
*Helpline (Tuesday–Friday, 10.00am–4.00pm;
Monday and Wednesday, 7.00pm–9.30pm):*
0800 389 3003.
www.harpinfo.org.uk

► **HELP THE AGED**
207–221 Pentonville Road
London N1 9UZ
Tel: 020 7278 1114
Senior line:
0808 800 6565 *(England and Wales)*
0808 808 7575 *(Northern Ireland)*
Textphone: 0808 269626
Fax: 020 7278 1116
info@helptheaged.org.uk
www.helptheaged.org.uk

► **HER MAJESTY'S STATIONERY OFFICE
(HMSO)**
www.hmso.gov.uk

► **HOME OFFICE**
Customer Information Service
7th floor, 50 Queen Anne's Gate
London SW1H 9AT
General enquiries (9.00am–5.00pm):
0870 0001585
www.homeoffice.gov.uk

► **HOUSING CORPORATION
CORPORATE SERVICES**
Maple House
149 Tottenham Court Road
London W1T 7BN
Tel: 020 7393 2000
Fax: 020 7393 2111
enquiries@housingcorp.gsx.gov.uk
www.housingcorp.gov.uk

► **HOWARD LEAGUE FOR
PENAL REFORM**
1 Ardleigh Road
London N1 4HS
Tel: 020 7249 7373
Fax: 020 7249 7788
howardleague@ukonline.co.uk

► **IMMIGRATION ADVISORY SERVICE**
County House
190 Great Dover Street
London SE1 4YB
Tel: 020 7967 1200
Fax: 020 7378 0665
advice@iasuk.org
www.iasuk.org

► **IMMIGRATION APPEAL TRIBUNAL**
see IMMIGRATION APPELLATE AUTHORITY

► **IMMIGRATION APPELLATE
AUTHORITY**
Arnhem House
PO Box 6987
Leicester LE1 6ZX
Tel: 0845 6000 877
Fax: 0116 249 4130
webmaster@courtservice.gsi.gov.uk
www.iaa.gov.uk

► **IMMIGRATION LAW PRACTITIONERS
ASSOCIATION**
Lindsey House
40–42 Charterhouse Street
London EC1M 6JN
Tel: 020 7251 8383
Fax: 020 7251 8384
info@ilpa.org.uk
www.ilpa.org.uk

► **IMMIGRATION SERVICES
COMMISSIONER**
Fleetbank House
2–6 Salisbury Square
London EC4Y 8JX
Tel: 020 7211 1500
Fax: 020 7211 1553

► **INDEPENDENT PANEL FOR
SPECIAL EDUCATION ADVICE
(IPSEA)**
6 Carlow Mews
Woodbridge
Suffolk IP12 1DH
Tel: England and Wales: 0800 018 4016
    Scotland: 0131 454 0082
    N. Ireland: 01232 705 654
www.ipsea.org.uk

► **INLAND REVENUE**
www.inlandrevenue.gov.uk

► **INQUEST**

89–93 Fonthill Road
London N4 3JH

Tel: 020 7263 1111
Fax: 020 7561 0799
www.inquest.org.uk

► **INSTITUTE OF LEGAL EXECUTIVES**

Kempston Manor
Kempston
Bedfordshire
MK42 7AB

DX 124780-KEMPSTON 2

Tel: 01234 841000
Fax: 01234 840373
info@ilex.org.uk
www.ilex.org.uk

► **INSTITUTE OF
TRADEMARKS ATTORNEYS**

Canterbury House
2–6 Sydenham Road
Croydon
Surrey CRO 9XE

Tel: 020 8686 2052
Fax: 020 8680 5723
www.itma.org.uk

► **INTERPOL**

www.interpol.int

► **INTERIGHTS**

Lancaster House
33 Islington High Street
London N1 9LH

Tel: 020 7278 3230
Fax: 020 7278 4334
ir@interights.org
www.interights.org

► **JOINT COUNCIL FOR THE
WELFARE OF IMMIGRANTS**

115 Old Street
London EC1V 9RT

Tel: 020 7251 8708
Fax: 020 7251 8707
info@jcwi.org.uk
www.jcwi.org.uk

► **LAND REGISTRY**

See website for contact details:
www.landreg.gov.uk

► **JUSTICE**

59 Carter Lane
London EC4V 5AQ

Tel: 020 7329 5100
Fax: 020 7329 5055
admin@justice.org.uk
www.justice.org.uk

► **LAW CENTRES FEDERATION**

Duchess House
18–19 Warren Street
London W1T 5LR

Tel: 020 7387 8570
Fax: 020 7387 8368
info@lawcentres.org.uk
www.lawcentres.org.uk

► **LAW SOCIETY**

113 Chancery Lane
London WC2A 1PL

Tel: 020 7242 1222
Fax: 020 7831 0344
info.services@lawsociety.org.uk
www.lawsoc.org.uk

► **LEGAL ACTION GROUP**

242 Pentonville Road
London N1 9UN

Tel: 020 7833 2931
Fax: 020 7837 6094
lag@lag.org.uk
www.lag.org.uk

► **LEGAL SERVICES COMMISSION**

85 Gray's Inn Road
London WC1X 8TX

Tel: 020 7759 0000
www.legalservices.gov.uk
www.justask.org.uk

► **LEGAL SERVICES OMBUDSMAN**

Office of the Legal Services Ombudsman
3rd Floor
Sunlight House
Quay Street
Manchester M3 3JZ

Lo Call No: 0845 601 0794
(Charged at local rates – available nationally)
Tel: 0161 839 7262
Fax: 0161 832 5446

DX 18569 Manchester 7
lso@olso.gsi.gov.uk
www.olso.org

▶ **LIBERTY**
21 Tabard Street
London SE1 4LA
Tel: 020 7403 3888
Fax: 020 7407 5354
info@liberty-human-rights.org.uk
www.liberty-human-rights.org.uk

▶ **LOCAL GOVERNMENT OMBUDSMAN**
www.lgo.org.uk

▶ **LORD CHANCELLOR'S DEPARTMENT**
see DEPARTMENT FOR CONSTITUTIONAL
AFFAIRS

▶ **MAGISTRATES' ASSOCIATION**
28 Fitzroy Square
London W1T 6DD
Tel: 020 7387 2353
Fax: 020 7383 4020
www.magistrates-association.org.uk

▶ **MATERNITY ALLIANCE**
3rd Floor West
2–6 Northburgh Street
London EC1V 0AY
Tel: 020 7588 8583
Information line: 020 7490 7638
Fax: 020 7014 1350
info@maternityalliance.org.uk
www.maternityalliance.org.uk

▶ **MEDIATION UK**
Alexander House
Telephone Avenue
Bristol BS1 4BS
Tel: 0117 904 6661
Fax: 0117 904 3331
enquiry@mediationuk.org.uk
www.mediation.org.uk

▶ **MENCAP**
123 Golden Lane
London EC1Y 0RT
Tel: 020 7454 0454
Fax: 020 7696 5540
Free helpline: 0808 808 1111
Helpline Wales: 0808 8000 300
Helpline Northern Ireland: 0845 763 6227
Minicom: 0808808 8181
information@mencap.org.uk
www.mencap.org.uk

▶ **MENTAL HEALTH ACT COMMISSION**
Maid Marian House
56 Hounds Gate
Nottingham NG1 6BG
Tel: 0115 943 7100
Fax: 0115 943 7101
www.mhac.trent.nhs.uk

▶ **MIND**
15–19 Broadway
London E15 4BQ
Tel: 08457 660 163
contact@mind.org.uk
www.mind.org.uk

▶ **MISCARRIAGE OF JUSTICE
ORGANISATION**
52 Octmore Road
Sheldon
Birmingham B33 0XL
Tel: 0121 789 8443 / 01902 731088
Fax: 0121 789 8443
mojuk@mojuk.org.uk
www.mojuk.org.uk

▶ **MOTOR ACCIDENT SOLICITORS
SOCIETY**
54 Baldwin Street
Bristol BS1 1QW
Tel: 0117 929 2560
Fax: 0117 904 7220
office@mass.org.uk
www.mass.org.uk

▶ **NATIONAL ANIMAL WELFARE TRUST**
Tyler's Way
Watford Bypass
Watford
Hertfordshire WD2 8HQ
Tel: 020 8950 8215 / 0177
Fax: 020 8420 4454
watford@nawt.org.uk
www.nawt.org.uk

▶ **NATIONAL ASSOCIATION FOR
THE CARE AND RESETTLEMENT
OF OFFENDERS (NACRO)**
169 Clapham Road
London SW9 0PU
Tel: 020 7582 6500
www.nacro.org.uk

▶ **NATIONAL ASSOCIATION OF CITIZENS ADVICE BUREAUX (NACAB)**

Myddelton House
115–123 Pentonville Road
London N1 9LZ

Tel: 020 7833 2181
www.nacab.org.uk
www.adviceguide.org.uk

Adviceguide: the National Association of Citizens Advice Bureaux offers fact sheets covering issues such as employment, housing and taxation

www.adviceguide.org.uk

▶ **NATIONAL ASSOCIATION OF ESTATE AGENTS (NAEA)**

Arbon House
21 Jury Street
Warwick CV34 4EH

Tel: 01926 496800
Fax: 01926 400953
info@naea.co.uk
www.naea.co.uk

▶ **NATIONAL ASYLUM SUPPORT SERVICE (NASS)**

Frank Corrigan
27 Old Gloucester Street
Bloomsbury
London WC1N 3XX

info@asylumsupport.info
www.asylumsupport.info

▶ **NATIONAL AUTISTIC SOCIETY**

393 City Road
London EC1V 1NG

Tel: 020 7833 2299
Fax: 020 7833 9666
nas@nas.org.uk
www.nas.org.uk

▶ **NATIONAL CANINE DEFENCE LEAGUE (NCDL)**

17 Wakley Street
London EC1V 7RQ

Tel: 020 7837 0006
info@ncdl.org.uk
www.ncdl.org.uk

▶ **NATIONAL CIVIL RIGHTS MOVEMENT (NCRM)**

14 Featherstone Road
Southall
Middlesex UB2 5AA

Tel: 020 8574 0818 or 020 8843 2333
Fax: 020 8813 9734
info@ncrm.org
www.ncrm.org.uk

▶ **NATIONAL CONSUMER COUNCIL**

20 Grosvenor Gardens
London SW1W 0DH

Tel: 020 7730 3469
Fax: 020 7730 0191
info@ncc.org.uk
www.ncc.org.uk

▶ **NATIONAL COUNCIL FOR ONE PARENT FAMILIES**

255 Kentish Town Road
London NW5 2LX

Tel: 020 7428 5400
Lone Parent Helpline: 0800 018 5026
Fax: 020 7482 4851
info@oneparentfamilies.org.uk
www.oneparentfamilies.org.uk

▶ **NATIONAL COUNCIL FOR VOLUNTARY ORGANISATIONS (NCVO)**

Regent's Wharf
8 All Saints Street
London N1 9RL

Tel: 020 7713 6161
Helpdesk: 0800 2 798 798
ncvo@ncvo-vol.org.uk
www.ncvo-vol.org.uk

▶ **NATIONAL DISABLED PERSONS HOUSING SERVICE (HoDIS)**

17 Priory Street
York YO1 6ET

Tel: 01904 653888
Fax: 01904 653999
info@hodis.org.uk
www.hodis.org.uk

▶ **NATIONAL DOMESTIC VIOLENCE HELPLINE**

08457 023 468
Fax: 0117 924 1703

▶ **NATIONAL FEDERATION
OF SERVICES SUPPORTING
FAMILIES OF PRISONERS**

Unit 102, Riverbank House
1 Putney Bridge Approach
London SW6 3JD

Tel: 0207 384 1987
Fax: 0207 384 1855
www.prisonersfamilies.org.uk

▶ **NATIONAL HOMELESS ALLIANCE**

Homeless Link
First Floor, 10–13 Rushworth Street
London SE1 0RB

Tel: 020 7960 3010
www.homeless.org.uk

Membership organisation for those
providing services to homeless people.

▶ **NATIONAL MISSING PERSONS
HELPLINE**

0500 700 700

If you are calling from outside the UK:
++ 44 20 8392 4545

▶ **NATIONAL PROBATION SERVICE**

Home Office
Horseferry House
Dean Ryle Street
London SW1P 2AW

Tel: 020 7217 0659
Fax: 020 7217 0660
NPD.PublicEnquiry@
   homeoffice.gsi.gov.uk
www.probation.homeoffice.gov.uk

▶ **NATIONAL SOCIETY FOR THE
PREVENTION OF CRUELTY
TO CHILDREN (NSPCC)**

0800 800 500
www.nspcc.org.uk

▶ **NATIONAL YOUTH ADVOCACY
SERVICE**

99–105 Argyle Street
Birkenhead
Wirral CH41 6AD

Freephone: 0800 616 101
Tel: 0151 649 8700
Young people: help@nyas.net
General enquiries: main@nyas.net

▶ **NEWHAM ASIAN WOMEN'S PROJECT**

661 Barking Road
Plaistow
London E13 9EX

Tel (general): 020 8472 0528
Tel (advice): 020 8552 5524
info@nawp.org
www.nawp.org

▶ **NORTHERN IRELAND
PRISON SERVICE**

Prison Service Headquarters
Dundonald House
Upper Newtownards Road
Belfast BT4 3SU

Tel: 028 9052 5065
info@niprisonservice.gov.uk
www.niprisonservice.gov.uk

▶ **NURSING AND MIDWIFERY
COUNCIL (NMC)**

23 Portland Place
London W1B 1PZ

Tel: 020 7637 7181
www.nmc-uk.org

▶ **OFFICE OF THE
DEPUTY PRIME MINISTER (ODPM)**

Tel: 0207 944 4400
www.odpm.gov.uk

▶ **OFFICE OF FAIR TRADING**

Fleetbank House
2–6 Salisbury Square
London EC4Y 8JX

www.oft.gov.uk

For general enquiries and guidance
on who to contact for consumer
complaints:

Public Liaison Unit: 08457 22 44 99
enquiries@oft.gsi.gov.uk

▶ **OFFICE FOR HARMONIZATION
IN THE INTERNAL MARKET (OHIM)**

Avenida de Europa 4
E-03080 Alicante
Spain

Tel: ++ 34 965 139 100
www.oami.eu.int

► **OFFICE FOR THE SUPERVISION OF SOLICITORS**

Victoria Court
8 Dormer Place
Royal Leamington Spa
Warwickshire CV32 5AE

Public advice line: 0845 608 6565
enquiries@lawsociety.org.uk
www.oss.lawsociety.org.uk

► **PARENTS AND ABDUCTED CHILDREN TOGETHER (PACT)**

PO Box 31389
London SW11 4WY
www.pact-online.org

► **PARENTS FOR INCLUSION**

Unit 2, 70 South Lambeth Road
London SW8 1RL

Tel: 020 7735 7735
Helpline: 020 7582 5008 (Tues, Wed, Thurs 10–12pm and 1–3pm)
www.parentsforinclusion.org

► **PATENT OFFICE**

Concept House
Cardiff Road
Newport
South Wales NP10 8QQ

Tel: 08459 500 505
enquiries@patent.gov.uk
www.patent.gov.uk

► **PENSIONS OMBUDSMAN**

11 Belgrave Road
London SW1V 1RB

Tel: 020 7834 9144
enquiries@pensions-ombudsman.org.uk
www.pensions-ombudsman.org.uk

► **PETA EUROPE LTD**

PO Box 36668
London SE1 1WA

Tel: 020 7357 9229
Fax: 020 7357 0901
info@petauk.org
www.petauk.org

► **POLICE COMPLAINTS AUTHORITY**

10 Great George Street
London SW1P 3AE

Tel: 020 7273 6450
info@pca.gov.uk
www.pca.gov.uk

► **PRESS COMPLAINTS COMMISSION (PCC)**

1 Salisbury Square
London EC4Y 8JB

Tel: 020 7353 3732
pcc@pcc.org.uk
www.pcc.org.uk

► **PREVENTION OF PROFESSIONAL ABUSE NETWORK (POPAN)**

Wyvil Court
Wyvil Road
London SW8 2T6

Tel: 020 7622 6334
info@popan.org.uk
www.popan.org.uk

► **PRINCIPAL REGISTRY OF THE FAMILY DIVISION**

First Avenue House
42–49 High Holborn
London WC1V 6NP

Tel: 020 7947 6980
www.courtservice.gov.uk

► **PRISON ADVICE AND CARE TRUST (PACT)**

Lincoln House
1–3 Brixton Road
London SW9 6DE

Tel: 020 7582 1313
www.imprisonment.org.uk

► **PRISON REFORM TRUST**

15 Northburgh Street
London EC1V 0JR

Tel: 020 7251 5070
Fax: 020 7251 5076
prt@prisonreformtrust.org.uk
www.prisonreformtrust.org.uk

► **HM PRISON SERVICE**

www.hmprisonservice.gov.uk

► **PRISONERS ABROAD**

89–93 Fonthill Road
Finsbury Park
London N4 3JH

Tel: 020 7561 6820
Fax: 020 7561 6821
info@prisonersabroad.org.uk
www.prisonersabroad.org.uk

▶ **PRISONERS' ADVICE SERVICE**

Unit 210, Hatton Square
16–16a Baldwins Gardens
London EC1N 7RJ

Tel: 020 7405 8090
Fax: 020 7405 8045
admin@prisoneradvice.demon.co.uk

▶ **PRISONERS' FAMILIES AND FRIENDS SERVICE**

20 Trinity Street
London SE1 1DB

Tel: 0800 808 3444
Fax: 0207 357 9722
pffs@btclick.com

▶ **PRISONS AND PROBATION OMBUDSMAN**

Ashley House
2 Monck Street
London SW1P 2BQ

Tel: 020 7035 2876 or 0845 010 7938
Fax: 020 7035 2860
mail@ppo.gsi.gov.uk
www.ppo.gov.uk

▶ **RAC MOTORING SERVICES**

Great Park Road
Bradley Stoke
Bristol BS32 4QN

Legal help and information (Monday–Friday 8.00am–8.00pm, Saturday 9.00am–5.00pm):
08705 533 533

Fax: 01454 208 222
www.rac.co.uk

▶ **RADAR**

12 City Forum
250 City Road
London EC1V 8AF

Tel: 020 7250 3222
Fax: 020 7250 0212
Minicom: 020 7250 4119
radar@radar.org.uk
www.radar.org.uk

▶ **RAPE CRISIS FEDERATION WALES AND ENGLAND**

Unit 7, Provident Works
Newdigate Street
Nottingham NG7 4FD

Tel: 0115 900 3560
Fax: 0115 900 3562
info@rapecrisis.co.uk
www.rapecrisis.co.uk

▶ **REFUGE**

Helpline (open seven days a week, 24 hours a day): 0870 599 5443

▶ **REFUGEE LEGAL CENTRE**

Nelson House
153–157 Commercial Road
London E1 2DA

Tel: 020 7780 3200
General enquiries:
RLC@refugee-legal-centre.org.uk
www.refugee-legal-centre.org.uk

▶ **RELEASE**

388 Old Street
London EC1V 9LT

Tel: 020 7749 4054
info@release.org.uk
www.release.org.uk

▶ **RETHINK (formerly THE NATIONAL SCHIZOPHRENIA FEDERATION)**

30 Tabernacle Street
London EC2A 4DD

Tel: 020 7330 9100/01
Fax: 020 7330 9102

National advice line (Monday–Friday, 10.00am–3.00pm): 020 8974 6814

advice@rethink.org
www.rethink.org

▶ **REUNITE INTERNATIONAL**

P.O. Box 7124
Leicester
LE1 7XX

Advice line: 0116 2256 234
reunite@dircon.co.uk
www.reunite.org

▶ **ROYAL NATIONAL INSTITUTE FOR THE BLIND (RNIB)**

Helpline: 0845 766 9999 *(UK callers)*

Textphone:
add 18001 before the above number
www.rnib.org.uk

▶ **ROYAL NATIONAL INSTITUTE FOR THE DEAF (RNID)**

19–23 Featherstone Street
London EC1Y 8SL

Tel: 0808 808 0123
Fax: 020 7296 8199
Textphone: 0808 808 9000
information@rnid.org.uk
www.rnid.org.uk

▶ **ROYAL SOCIETY FOR THE PROTECTION OF BIRDS (RSPB)**
UK Headquarters
The Lodge
Sandy
Bedfordshire SG19 2DL
Tel: 01767 680551
www.rspb.org.uk

▶ **RSPCA**
To report an act of cruelty, neglect or concern for the welfare of an animal, call the RSPCA's 24-hour national cruelty and advice line:
0870 55 55 999

▶ **THE SALVATION ARMY**
The Salvation Army HQ
101 Newington Causeway
London SE1 6BN
Tel: 020 7367 4500
Helpline: 0845 634 0101
thq@salvationarmy.org.uk
www.salvationarmy.org.uk

▶ **THE SAMARITANS**
Helpline: 08457 90 90 90
jo@samaritans.org
www.samaritans.org.uk

▶ **SCOPE**
Helpline: 0808 800 3333
cphelpline@scope.org.uk
www.scope.org.uk

▶ **SEARCH UK**
www.missingkids.co.uk

▶ **SHELTER**
88 Old Street
London EC1V 9HU
Tel: 020 7505 4699
Free helpline for housing help and advice:
0808 800 4444
info@shelter.org.uk
www.shelter.org.uk

▶ **SOLICITORS FOR THE ELDERLY**
PO Box 9
Peterborough
Cambridgeshire PE4 7WN
Tel/Fax: 01733 326769
info@solicitorsfortheelderly.com
www.solicitorsfortheelderly.com

▶ **SOLICITORS' FAMILY LAW ASSOCIATION**
PO Box 302
Orpington
Kent BR6 8QX
Tel: 01689 850227
Fax: 01689 855833
sfla@btinternet.com
www.sfla.co.uk

▶ **SOLICITOR'S PRO BONO GROUP MEDIATION SERVICE**
Tel: 0870 777 5601 (extension 25)
mediate@probonogroup.org.uk
www.probonogroup.org.uk

▶ **SOUTHALL BLACK SISTERS**
52 Norwood Road
Southall
Middlesex UB2 4DW
Tel: 020 8571 9595

▶ **SPECIAL EDUCATIONAL NEEDS AND DISABILITY TRIBUNAL (SENDIST)**
7th Floor, Windsor House
50 Victoria Street
London SW1H 0NW
Tel: 020 7925 6926
tribunalenquiries@sendist.gsi.gov.uk
www.sendist.gov.uk

▶ **SPINAL INJURIES ASSOCIATION**
76 St James Lane
London N10 3DF
Tel: 0800 980 0501
www.spinal.co.uk

▶ **STATEWATCH**
PO Box 1516
London N16 OEW
Tel: 020 8802 1882
Fax: 020 8880 1727
info@statewatch.org
www.statewatch.org

▶ **STILLBIRTH AND NEONATAL DEATH (SANDS)**
28 Portland Place
London W1B 1LY
Helpline: 020 7436 5881
support@uk-sands.org
www.uk-sands.org

▶ **SUPPORT AFTER MURDER AND MANSLAUGHTER (SAMM)**
Cranmer House
39 Brixton Road
London SW9 6DZ

Tel: 020 7735 3838
Helpline: 0845 3030 900
enquiries@samm.org.uk
www.samm.org.uk

▶ **THE TREASURY**
www.hm-treasury.gov.uk

▶ **TRADING STANDARDS**
www.tradingstandards.gov.uk

▶ **TRAUMA AFTERCARE TRUST (TACT)**
Buttfields
The Farthings
Withington
Gloucestershire GL54 5DF

Helpline: 01242 89 03 06
tact@tacthq.demon.co.uk
www.tacthq.demon.co.uk

▶ **TRADES UNION CONGRESS (TUC)**
Congress House
Great Russell Street
London WC1B 3LS

Tel: 020 7636 4030
info@tuc.org.uk
www.tuc.org.uk

▶ **UNITED KINGDOM PASSPORT SERVICE**
Tel: 0870 521 0410
www.ukps.gov.uk

▶ **UNLOCK (NATIONAL ASSOCIATION OF EX-OFFENDERS)**
35a High Street
Snodland
Kent ME6 5AG

Tel: 01634 247350
Fax: 01634 24735
info@unlockprison.org.uk
www.unlockprison.org.uk

▶ **VICTIM SUPPORT**
National Office
Cranmer House
39 Brixton Road
London SW9 6DZ

Tel: 020 7735 9166
Fax: 020 7582 5712
contact@victimsupport.org.uk
www.victimsupport.org.uk

▶ **VIVA!**
Vegetarians International Voice
   for Animals
8 York Court
Wilder Street
Bristol BS2 8QH

Tel: 0117 944 1000
Fax: 0845 456 8230
info@viva.org.uk
www.viva.org.uk

▶ **WOMEN'S AID FEDERATION**
PO Box 391
Bristol BS99 7WS

*National Domestic Violence helpline
(24 hour):* 08457 023468
Fax: 0117 924 1703
info@womensaid.org.uk
www.womensaid.org.uk

▶ **WOMEN IN PRISON**
3b Aberdeen Studios
22 Highbury Grove
London N5 2EA

Tel: 020 7226 5879
Fax: 020 7354 8005
info@womeninprison.org.uk
www.womeninprison.org.uk

▶ **WORKITOUT**
63 Lincoln's Inn Fields
London WC2A 3LW

Tel: 020 7692 5502
www.workitout.co.uk

▶ **WORLD WILDLIFE FUND (WWF)**
WWF–UK
Panda House
Weyside Park
Godalming
Surrey GU7 1XR

Tel: 01483 426444
Fax: 01483 426409
www.wwf.org.uk/core/index.asp

Index

A

abandonment 187
Abandonment of Animals Act 1960 53
abatement notices 191
abduction to a non-convention country 257
access to court 219
acts tending to pervert the course of justice 83
actuarial tables 40
additional orders 165
adjudicators, independent 307
administrative court 25
Admiralty court 25
admissions appeals panels 109
Adoption Act 1976 164
Adoption and Children Act 2002 151, 152, 161, 162
adoption order 160, 161, 162
advance disclosure 237
adverse possession 186
advocacy services 291
ancillary relief 146
anti-social behaviour order 191
appeal, grounds for 81, 231
appeal court 22
appeals from crown court cases 81
application, originating 128
applications by children 154
Arms to Iraq inquiry 314
assignment 172, 182
assured shorthold tenancy 178, 179, 180, 189
assured tenancies 179
assured tenants 179, 181, 184
Asylum and Immigration Act 1996 230
Asylum and Immigration Appeals Act 1993 230
attendance allowance 94

B

bail 76
Bail Act 218
balance of harm test 165
beneficial interest 169
Births and Deaths Registration Act 1953 151
Bloody Sunday inquiry 314
board of visitors 309
breach of contract 113
breach of covenant 172
breach of duty 38
breach of duty as cause of injury 38
breach of the peace 322
brief 20, 74

C

capability 120
care order 159
causation as loss 38
causing danger to road users 295
CE mark 62
chambers 20
Chancery division 26
charge over the property 174
charge sheet 72
Child Abduction Act 1985 253
Child Abduction and Custody Act 1985 255
child assessment order 158, 160
child maintenance 146
Child Support Acts 1991 plus 1995 147
Child Support Appeal Tribunal 24
Child Support, Pensions and Social Security Act 2000 147
child witness officer 32
children
    child abduction 252
    child witness 32
    disappearance of a child 156
    leave 164
    relevant child 164
Children Act 1989 149, 150, 151, 155, 164

Children's Act 1989, Section 8 Orders 152, 153, 156
    Section 8 application 154, 155
children's guardian 160
circuit judge 21
civil action against the police 218
civil claim for damages 45
civil juries 48
civil legal aid 11
civil liability 236
civil prisoners 303
civil procedure rules 47
civil wrongs 46, 46
claimant 23
claims for damages 113
Climbié inquiry (death of Victoria Climbié) 314
closing order 196
code of practice 72
codes of guidance 277
cohabitee 148
commercial court 25
committal 157
committal of the abducting parent 157
committal for sentence 77
committal hearing 78
commonhold system 173
community mediation 31
community punishment order 321
community rehabilitation order 77, 321
companies court 26
compatibility statement 211
complaints
    barristers 21
    libel 277
    travel agents/tour operators 65
compulsory medical treatment 283
compulsory purchase 170
conciliation appointment 155
conditional discharge 321
conditional fee agreements 11, 134
conditional fee basis 193
confiscation 81
consent to treatment 284
constructive dismissal 131
contact order 153
contract disputes 113
contracts 241
Control of Dogs Order 1992 51
control order 199
Convention Relating to the Status of Refugees 1951 230

Convention Relating to the Status of Stateless Persons 230
conveyance of land 172
conveyancing 170, 174
convicted prisoners
    access to lawyers 303
    categorisation 303
    correspondence 303
    medical treatment 303
    transfers 305
    visits 303
cooling-off period 63
copyrights 242
coroner 25
coroner's court 14, 25
    adjournment 238
coroner's officer 238
Council directive 64/221/EEC 230
Council regulation (EEC) 1612/68 230
counsel 20
Countryside and Rights of Way Act 2000 52
county court district judge 21
court of appeal 26
    criminal division 81
court duty solicitor 73
courts (civil wrongs) 46
covenants (promises) 171
credit agreements and other contracts 63
credit cards 61
Crime and Disorder Act 1998 322
    fear or provocation of violence 322
    harassment alarm or distress 322
crimes abroad 258
    assault 259
    compensation 260
    murder 260
    rape 260
    theft 259
    transfer to the UK 264
    violent/sex offences 264
criminal appeals office 81
criminal cases review commission (CCRC) 82
criminal injuries compensation 83
Criminal Injuries Compensation Scheme 39
Criminal Justice and Court Services Act 2001 31
criminal liability 236
crown court 25, 79
crown witnesses 220

D

Dangerous Dogs Act 1991 51, 52
dangerous driving 295
Dangerous Wild Animals Act 1976 51
database rights 242, 248
declaration of incompatibility 211
Decree Absolute 144
decree of nullity 146
Defamation Act 1952 275
Defamation Act 1996 276
defective premises 194
defendant 23, 72
deferred action notice 196
demolition order 196
design rights 242, 247
direct access 20
direct discrimination 100
directions appointment 155
Disability Discrimination Act 87
disability living allowance (DLA) 93
  care benefit 93
  mobility benefit 93
disability at work
  justification 89
  reasonable adjustments 89
  what does the Act say? 88
  what is covered? 91
  which providers are covered? 90
  who is covered? 88
disabled persons tax credit 94
disablement benefit 92
disappearance of a child 156
discharge of the jury 29
disciplinary procedure 127
discrimination, indirect 100
discrimination on trade union
    grounds 106
disqualification
  discretionary 297
  mandatory 297, 298
disrepair 193
divorce
  grounds 143
  petition for 144
Dog (Fouling of Land) Act 1996 51
driving
  when disqualified 295
  without insurance 296
  without a licence 296
Dublin Convention 230
duty, breach of 38
duty of care 38, 288
duty solicitor scheme 9, 10, 70

E

EC Association Agreements 230
education order 158
either-way offences 295
emergency protection order 158
employment
  bullying and harassment 131
  changes to job description 131
  deductions from pay 130
  health and safety 132
  illegal to continue to employ 120
  long hours at work 132
  pay in lieu of notice 123
  right to ask questions 122
  right to be accompanied to the
      hearing 122
  right to be shown the evidence 122
  right to a written statement of
      terms 117
Employment Appeals Tribunal 24
Employment Rights Act 1996 123
employment tribunals 14, 101, 102, 106,
    121, 124, 127, 131
  costs 129
  formality 129
  how to claim 127
  settlement of cases and ACAS 130
  time limits 128
employment/dismissal
  qualifying period 124
  reasonableness 124
  right to a written statement of the
      reason for dismissal 123
  right to notice and pay 122
enforcement 23
enfranchisement 173
  collective 173
entitled applicant 164
*Environmental Information Regulations
    1992/3240* 138
Environmental Protection Act 1990 51
equitable interest 169, 170
*European Convention (EC) Association
    Agreement* 229
European Convention (EC) Treaty 229
European Convention on Human Rights
    xviii, 26, 209, 212, 229, 230, 306,
    315
*European Convention on Human Rights,
    Article 8* 138
European court of human rights 26
European court of justice 26
European Directives 39

ex parte application 158, 166
exclusion 110

F

Factories Act 1961 39
failing to stop after an accident 295
failure to provide a breath specimen
   (when requested) 296
Family Division 26
family help 12
Family Law Act 1986 156
Family Law Act 1996 143, 145, 163
fast track 23
Fatal Accidents Act 1976 39
fines 321
fit for human habitation 195
fixed-term tenancy 175, 176
food (consumer law) 63
Foreign and Commonwealth Office
   (FCO) 253
franchise certificate xix
freedom of conscience 221
freehold 169
   interest 170
freeing order 161
full representation 13

G

general family help 13
goods, new 60
grants 196
green form advice (initial help) 129
grievance procedure 121
gross misconduct 123
guardian 151

H

habitual residence 256
Hague Convention on Child Abduction 253
*Hague Convention on International Child
   Abduction* 254
Health and Safety at Work Act 1974 39
help at court 12
high court 22, 25
high court judge 22
high risk offenders 298
higher court advocates 74
Highway Code 294
holiday timeshares 63
Home Secretary 266

homelessness
   advice and assistance 202
   challenging decisions 204
   duties to the 204
   eligible for assistance 203
   enquiries 204
   full housing duty 202
   intentional homelessness 203
   interim accommodation 202
   local connection 204
   priority need 203
House of Lords 26
houses in multiple occupation (HMOs)
   195, 197–200
   control orders 199
   management regulations 199
   overcrowding controls 198
   registration schemes 198
   regulation and management 198
   works notices 199
housing association 178
human rights 177
Human Rights Act 224, 227, 238, 287, 290,
   301, 306
Human Rights Act 1998 xviii 26, 138, 139,
   209, 210, 230

I

identification parade 70
immediate imprisonment 321
Immigration Act 1971 230
Immigration Act 1978 230
immigration adjudicators 13
Immigration and Asylum Act 1999 216, 230
immigration appeal tribunal 13, 231
Immigration Rules (HC 395) 230
indictable offences 79
industrial injuries benefits 92
injunction to restrain 191
intellectual property rights 241, 242
internal complaints 127
   procedure 102
investigative help 13

J

jobseeker's allowance 327
joint tenancy 175
judicial inquiry 315
judicial review 110, 201, 212, 231, 290,
   303, 307, 316
jurisdiction 127

jurors
offences against 29
payment of 27
selection of 27
jury service 27
when you do not have to serve 27
jury trial, electing 78
just and equitable 101
just satisfaction 212
Justices of the Peace (JPs) 21

L

land, interests in 169
land registry 174
law lords 22
lawful removal 157
Lawrence inquiry (death of Stephen
Lawrence) 313
lawyers: how do I find a lawyer to
help? 95
laying an information 75
lease 171
buying and selling 171
forfeiting the 172
granting a 171
leasehold 169, 171
leasehold valuation tribunal 190
leave to appeal 81
leave to apply 154
legal aid xix, 41, 114, 129, 239, 294, 323
legal aid franchise 133
legal aid scheme 84
legal help 12, 114
liability 37
libel/slander, law of 138
licence notice 185
licences 185
excluded 181, 185
secure 185
licensed conveyancer 170
licensee 184
litigant in person (LIP) 21
litigation (legal action) 20, 112
litigation friend 286
litigation support 12
lodgers 184
Lord Chancellor 21, 22
Lord Chief Justice 22
lump sum 148

M

McKenzie friend 307
magistrate 21
magistrates' court 13, 25, 77
magistrates' court district judge 21
manslaughter 295
marriage: irretrievably broken down 143
Marriage Act 145
maternity pay, statutory 119, 327
Matrimonial Causes Act 145, 146
means-tested benefit 328
Medical Appeal Tribunal 24
mental disorder 282
mental health
admission process 283
the criminal justice system 283
legal help on behalf of other people 286
management of the affairs of a person
without capacity 288
Mental Health Act 1983 279, 281, 282,
286, 287, 289, 290
Section 2 283
Section 3 283
Mental Health Act Code of Practice 286
misconduct 120
of jurors 29
mitigating circumstances 298
mitigation 80
mortgages 174
motoring
absolute discharge 297
conditional discharge 297
fines 297
licence endorsement 297
mutual exchange 183

N

*Nationality, Immigration and Asylum
Act 2002* 230
natural growth 197
negligence 288
neighbours
condition of neighbouring
property 191
noisy 191
no security of tenure 185
no win, no fee 41, 48, 49, 104, 238
non-contentious 19
non-entitled applicant 164
non-means-tested benefits 328

non-means-tested contributory benefits 329

non-means-tested non-contributory benefits 329

non-molestation order 163–6

notice of disrepair 192

notice to quit 176, 187

nuisance
law of 137
statutory 194

O

objectively justifiable 89

obstructing the police 322

obtaining an order 166

occupation order 164, 165, 166

order for contact 162

ordinary residence 256

overcrowding 196

P

parents
married 150
parental contact with a child in care 160
parental responsibility 150
termination of parental responsibility 151
unmarried 150

parties of sides 237

partnership projects 11

passing-off, law of 242, 245

patent attorneys 243

patents court 26

pathology report 236

pension-sharing order 148

pensions, earmarking 148

performance or purported performance 46

periodic payments orders 147

personal injury 104
awards 104
cases 113

phone calls (rights of suspects held by the police) 71

placement orders 161

planning inquiry 314

plea-bargaining 80

Police Act 1996 315

Police and Criminal Evidence Act 72, 218

police detainees 72

port alert 253

possession, grounds for 177

possession order 174, 178

possessions 225

power of arrest 165

power of attorney 288

pre-sentence report 80

premium 171

preventative order 253

preventing unlawful removal 157

Prison Act 1952 301

Prison Rules 1999 301, 307

private prosecutions 75

Privy Council 26

pro bono xix, 239

prohibited steps order 153

property adjustment orders 148

proprietor 186

prosecuting solicitor 74

Protection of Animals Act 1911 53

Protocol Relating to the Status of Refugees 1967 230

public authority 211

public defenders 10

public enquiries 14

public funding (legal aid) 48

public inquiries
funding 316
legal representation 316

public investigation, independent 315

Public Order Act 1986 319

purchase notice 196

Q

Quality Mark xx

quantum 37, 39

Queen's Bench division 25

Queen's Counsel (QC) xviii, 11, 20

R

racial harassment 99

racial hatred 277

reasonable adjustments 89

recorder 22

reduced earnings allowance 93

redundancy 120
consultation 126
payments 127
selection for 126

redundancy, genuine 125

registered patents 242

registered social landlord 178, 194
registered trade marks 242
registrar of criminal appeal 81
relationship/co-ownership
    breakdown 187
relief from forfeiture 172
remedies for disrepair 193
rent
    fair 189
    marked 188
Rent Act tenancy 179, 180, 182
Rent Act tenant 179, 181, 184, 189, 197
repair 193
    implied repairing obligation 192
    repairing obligations 192
repair notice 195
residence order 152, 157, 253
respondent 143, 155, 163
retirement allowance 93
revoked (set aside) 151
right to buy 194
right to fair trial 218
Royal Courts of Justice 25

S

safety (consumer law) 62
sale or second-hand goods 60
sale/eviction 170
salmon letter 317
satisfactory quality 58
Scott inquiry 314
searches and enquiries 174
secretary of state 309
secure tenants 179, 181, 197
security 77
security of tenure 174–80, 183, 184
sentencing in the crown court 80
sentencing in the magistrates' court 77
separation, judicial 144
separation orders 144
sequestration 157
serious arrestable offence 71
service charge 190
severe disablement allowance 94
*Sex Discrimination and Race Relations
    Act* 224
sexual harassment 99
shoddy workmanship 60
sickness record 120
sight unseen 62
signposting xix
single judge 81

small claims court 23
solicitor: before you see a solicitor 41
*Southall and Paddington rail crash
    inquiries* 314
special damage 275
special education needs 110, 111
    appeals 112
    assessment 111
    funding 114
    statement of 111
    statementing 111
    time limits 114
special guardianship orders 162
*Special Immigration Appeals Commission
    Act 1997* 230
special measures 83
specialist lawyers 239
specific issue order 153
speeding (motoring) 295
spot check 293
statutory assessment 111
statutory charge 15
statutory inquiry 313
step-parents, extended rights for 151
stranded (abroad) 66
sub-letting 171, 183
succession 182
summary offences 78, 296
summary procedure 276
summons, originating 257
supervision order 159
surety 77
surrender 187
survivorship 182
suspended sentence 321
swearing an information 75

T

taking a vehicle without consent 295
tax credits 329
tenancies 171, 185
    excluded 181, 186
    introductory 177
    periodic 175, 176, 192
    periodic assured 189
    probationary 177
    secure 176
    statutory periodic 188
    surrender 187
time limits
    accidents and injuries 40
    on detention 71

timeshares 63
tort (law) of negligence 38, 39
trade unions
    discrimination on trade union
        grounds 106
    the right to join 105
trademark attorneys 244
traffic light offences 295
transfer of an undertaking 125
treasure trove 235
Treaty on European Union 230
trespass/trespasser 184, 186
triable-either-way offences 78
tribunals 24
    independent 111
Tribunals of Inquiry (Evidence) Act 1921 315
truth commission 317

U

unfair dismissal 101, 123
*UNHCR Handbook on Procedures and
    Criteria Relating to the Status of
    Refugees* 230
unsafe conviction 82
unsatisfactory quality 60

V

victim support 32, 83
visiting order 304

W

ward of court 157, 253
wardship 157
welfare checklist 155
Wild Mammals (Protection) Act 1996 53
Wildlife and Countryside Act 1981 53
witness intimidation 83
witness support 32, 83
working families tax credit 94
working time regulations 133
wrongful dismissal 123

Y

Young Offenders' Institution 79
youth court 79
Youth Offender Panel 79